CHILDREN
AND THE
THEOLOGIANS

Clearing the Way for Grace

JEROME W. BERRYMAN

CHILDREN
AND THE
THEOLOGIANS

Clearing the Way for Grace

JEROME W. BERRYMAN

Morehouse Publishing
NEW YORK · HARRISBURG · DENVER

Unless otherwise noted, the Scripture quotations contained herein are from the New Revised Standard Version Bible, copyright © 1989 by the Division of Christian Education of the National Council of Churches of Christ in the U.S.A. Used by permission. All rights reserved.

Morehouse Publishing, 4775 Linglestown Road, Harrisburg, PA 17112

Morehouse Publishing, 445 Fifth Avenue, New York, NY 10016

Morehouse Publishing is an imprint of Church Publishing Incorporated.

Cover art: "Richard Hooker and the Snow Ball Fight," John Harris (contemporary). Contributed in Aid of the Exeter Cathedral Choristers

Cover design: Brenda Klinger

Library of Congress Cataloging-in-Publication Data

Berryman, Jerome W.
Children and the theologians : clearing the way for grace / Jerome Berryman.
p. cm.
Includes bibliographical references and index.
ISBN 978-0-8192-2347-0 (cloth)

1. Children—Religious aspects—Christianity—History of doctrines. 2. Theologians. I. Title.
BT705.B47 2009
268'.432--dc22
2009023968

Printed in the United States of America

09   10   11   12   13   14   10   9   8   7   6   5   4   3   2   1

Contents

Preface...vii

Acknowledgments...ix

CHAPTER 1 From Presence To Texts:
Children in the Jesus Traditions...1

CHAPTER 2 From Texts To Theology: 50–500 29

CHAPTER 3 Latin Theology and the Schools: 500–1500............................61

CHAPTER 4 A Reformation of the Experience Base
for Knowing Children: 1500–1600..87

CHAPTER 5 Reforming the Reformation and
the New Science: 1600–1800..113

CHAPTER 6 Modern Theology: 1800–2000..143

CHAPTER 7 Today's Conversation: 2000–present....................................167

CHAPTER 8 The *De Facto* Doctrine of Children:
Ambivalence, Ambiguity, Indifference, and Grace..................197

CHAPTER 9 Children as a Means of Grace:
A Proposal for a Formal Doctrine of Children........................227

References..257

Index 266

Preface

Rowan Williams wrote in *Why Study the Past? The Quest for the Historical Church* that both the traditionalists and the progressives get it wrong when they reflect on the past. The traditionalists "don't expect to be surprised by the past; progressives miss the point because they don't expect to be interested or questioned by it. And in a cultural setting where a sensible understanding of history is not much encouraged, it isn't surprising if religious people can be as much at sea as anyone else in coming to terms with "the past" (Williams 2005, 3). This book is an attempt to come terms with the church's past views of children to see if there is a more appropriate way to think about them today. Perhaps, we have missed something during the last 2,000 years.

The method chosen to explore how the church has thought about children is to carefully construct vignettes of important theologians across the centuries to build up cases to see what general themes emerge. Each case is about half theological conclusions and half the experience on which they are based. Before the seventeenth century authoritative texts carried the most weight in the search for truth. Today, however, we place the primary emphasis on experience. This is why both concerns were included in each vignette.

The themes that emerged from this study—ambivalence, ambiguity, indifference, and grace—came into view slowly from wide reading across many decades. They seem to be not only historically valid but also true from other points of view, as will be examined in this book's last two chapters. Historical truth, however, is always at risk when individuals are presented so briefly and the historical period surveyed is so long. Since "good theology does not come from bad history" (Williams 2005, 2), every effort has been made to make this good history so good theology can be arrived at as the book concludes.

The book moves chronologically from the first century to the present time. As the vignettes of the theologians accumulate, the *de facto* doctrine of children takes shape. These vignettes might also be thought of as the game pieces by which a game can be played as the book concludes to better understand the *de facto* doctrine and move toward a more adequate formal one.

The religious tradition that Jesus grew up in considered children to be a blessing and the bearers of Torah to future generations, as well as in need of dedicated teaching and careful discipline. The gospels show Jesus thinking in this context about children as bearers of the Kingdom and of God's presence, but this is mixed in the texts with suggestions of indifference and a low view of children and families. This confusion combined with other factors shaped the informal doctrine of children by which the church operates today. This is why it is important to be open to the surprises that the story of the informal doctrine hold in store for us and to not only question it but also to be questioned by it.

Acknowledgments

The making of books always involves more people than the author on the cover. For me this has meant Thea more than anyone. As always, I want to thank her first for what she has contributed to my life and my life's work. We have enjoyed learning, thinking and teaching together with children for nearly fifty years. We married in 1961 while I was still a student at Princeton Theological Seminary and she was a student at Westminster Choir College in Princeton. She became a master teacher of Montessori music and we loved creating Godly Play™ together because we loved each other and the children who taught us how to be better teachers. Meeting her turned my sepia days into color and song. The beautiful Thea died as this book was coming to a close. The gratitude for her life, despite the pain of her loss, fills these pages with joy, as it does my own life.

David Jensen believed in this book when it was unbelievable and so woefully awkward that it looked like it would never walk off on its own. He helped get the manuscript up that first steep hill by the act of reading, underlining, and commenting on it. When he asked me to write an article for *Religious Studies Review* (Berryman 2007), which included five of the six authors reviewed in chapter 7, it took its final shape and the downhill run began.

Jeffrey Hensley gave the early manuscript a careful and critical reading, which helped it mature. Martin Marty and Marcia Bunge read yet a later stage of the manuscript and made insightful, critical, and warmly supportive comments. They gave me the confidence to go on to the end, because they thought the manuscript was worth taking the time to read and reflect on.

When the manuscript was finally sent to Church Publishing, Inc. it came under the care of Davis Perkins, the publisher. His support during the last stage of the writing by his sure editorial hand and theological wisdom contributed greatly to the book's final, polished state.

Of course, none of these people are to blame for the mistakes or opinions in this work. They are my own.

A special note of thanks goes to the people who make Arco d'Oro such a warm and beautiful Italian restaurant in Houston. Thea and I spent many quiet moments there together. We also celebrated family and friends around its tables, and many times I sat there alone quietly writing and thinking.

Finally, I want to warmly recognize the many students at the theological seminaries, where I taught as an adjunct faculty member during the last few decades while this material was being developed. Their patience, enthusiasm, and curiosity—as I explored these themes with them—and their critiques in body language as well as words are still vivid and deeply appreciated.

Thank you, all.

Jerome W. Berryman
Easter, 2009
Center for the Theology of Childhood
Houston, Texas

CHAPTER

1

FROM PRESENCE TO TEXTS:
Children in the Jesus Traditions

This painting challenges the mostly unconscious influence of Leonardo da Vinci's *Last Supper*, which in terms of this book presents a low or at least indifferent view of children. It was painted by Bohdan Piasecki, a leading contemporary artist in Poland, who lives near Warsaw.

Leonardo's great mural was painted on the dry plaster of the refectory wall of the Dominican monastery (or convent) at Santa Maria delle Grazie in Milan about 1495–1498. The celibate men (or women) reflected on the men of Leonardo's *Last Supper* as they ate their meals. This masterpiece is full of dramatic emotion and action, remarkable characterization, and a precise, single-point perspective that focuses on Christ. Only about 20 percent of the original painted surface survives, so it "hovers like a ghost on

◀ *Last Supper*, Bohdan Piasecki (1998)
Irish School of Ecumenics, Milltown Park, Ireland
(Copyright © B.A.S.I.C. [Brothers and Sisters in Chirst], Dublin, Ireland)

▼ *Last Supper*, Leonardo da Vinci (1498)
Santa Maria delle Grazie, Milan, Italy
(Scala/Ministero per i Beni e le Attività culturali / Art Resource, NY
S. Maria delle Grazie, Milan, Italy)

the wall" (Nicholl 2004, 302). Still, the absence of children and families should not go unquestioned.

Piasecki's painting also has Christ at the center but, as with other Jewish teachers and interpreters of scripture in the first century, he is surrounded with men, women, and children. The people are from Jesus' socio-economic group and century rather than what a contemporary to Leonardo called "Milanese courtiers and important citizens" (quoted in Nicholl 2004, 296). In Piasecki's painting it is evening because this may have been the Passover meal although that is not certain. The people are eating unleavened bread, roast lamb, and bitter herbs as if it were and children are present with their families because they are valued, whether the disciples themselves are married or not. Besides, if this is the Passover children must be present because they will be asked traditional questions such as, "Why is this night different from all other nights?" as they still are today.

"**D**id you hear that?"

A child pulled at my long, white alb as I hurried along the cloister, crowded with people between services on a Sunday morning at the Cathedral.

"What?" I slowed down.

"What they said in church . . . "

I came to a full stop in the midst of the swirling adults and dropped to my knees to look the eight-year-old boy in the eye. Infinity formed around us.

"What *did* they say?"

"They wanted us to do THREE parables! How can you do THREE parables all at once? There wasn't time. We didn't even have any materials!" (The child was not quite right. In Lectionary A for the Sunday closest to July 27 Episcopalians read four parables bundled into Matthew 13:31–33 and 44–49a, but the observation was still impressive!)

"I know. Sometimes grown-ups don't understand."

I took the boy's hands in mine for a moment, said goodbye, and then stood up. The time, place, and pressing adult tasks returned to consciousness and I hurried on my way to the education hour.

There was a lot packed into that brief theological encounter between a child and his priest. Most of it was nonverbal and depended on having worked with parables together in the same way with mutual respect many times. That is part of why so few words were necessary. The child felt perfectly at home talking about exegetical matters with me on a busy Sunday morning and he was right to firmly expect me to respond with intelligence, a sense of playfulness, and my full attention.

Stringing three (or four) parables together on an abstract theme of growth (or any other theme) did not make complete sense. The child was right. No single parable was allowed its unique voice and the bundling implied that a single, uniform interpretation (whatever it might be) could satisfy these unique, provocative, and artful clusters of Jesus' words. It really is better to take as much time as is needed to enter the world of each parable and wonder about it, like he had learned to do in the church school, following the method of Godly Play™.

The method by which the child learned how to identify parables and make existential meaning with them is relevant but it is not the point here. The point is that sometimes adults greatly underestimate children's experience of God and the kind of theological thought they are capable of when they have appropriate materials and informed adults to work with them. Most Christian theologians have underestimated children in this regard, so it is important to know and understand the history of what they have said about children to correct this mistake, as well as to learn from them.

We need to know what our theologians have said about children, because their words still shape our views about children in the church today. Besides, this is an exciting story, worth telling in itself. Most of all, however, we need to be aware of our inheritance from the past to move forward in the future toward being better able to cooperate with the grace of children, who have sustained the church—despite its past ambivalence, ambiguity, and indifference about them—from generation to generation.

This opening chapter will proceed "at a slant," as the poet Emily Dickinson might have said. The angle we will approach children and the theologians from invokes the image of Hermann Hesse burning leaves. Why?

Hesse did his theology in fiction and he did it impressively enough to receive the Nobel Prize for Literature in 1946, primarily for his six novels that examined all sides of spiritual development from childhood beyond adulthood. Two important influences on this book have come from Hesse. One is his "developmental history of the soul," and the other is the elegant game his last novel described. In this chapter we will first say a bit more about Hesse and then consider Jesus and the children. Finally, the four themes about children that have emerged from the gospels and the history of theology will be introduced.

The history of children and the theologians will then be told beginning with St. Paul as the first Christian theologian and it will proceed to the discussion about children among theologians today in chapter 6. We will then look back over this history as a *de facto* doctrine of children that operates informally in the church and then look forward to propose a more unified, fully conscious, and constructive doctrine of children as a means of grace and provide suggestions for a spiritual practice to accompany it.

Hermann Hesse Burning Leaves
and "A Bit of Theology"

The image of Hermann Hesse burning leaves reminds us of his interest in what he called the "developmental history of the soul." It also evokes the game at the center of his last book *The Glass Bead Game*. We shall return to this game in chapter 8.

Hesse's Nobel Prize for literature in 1946 primarily recognized his novels—*Demian, Siddhartha, The Steppenwolf, Narcissus and Goldmund, Journey to the East*, and *The Glass Bead Game*—about the longing for and search for spiritual maturity from childhood into adulthood and beyond. His considerable poetry with many of the same themes was also acknowledged by this recognition.

Hesse began his last book, *The Glass Bead Game*, in 1931. This was when he settled in for the decade of concentrated effort it took to write his culminating work. It was also the year he married Ninon Dolbin in November and moved into the new house in Montagnola, high above Lugano in the Italian-speaking, southern part of Switzerland.

The Glass Bead Game was completed on April 29, 1942 but the manuscript languished in Berlin for seven months because it was not approved for publication by the Nazi government. It was published first in Switzerland in 1943 and then in Germany soon after the war and received the Nobel Prize in 1946.

Visitors often mentioned observing Hesse outdoors, burning grass and leaves. Zeller includes a picture of him making a bonfire in his biography of Hesse (Zeller 1971, 142), and the Chilean writer and diplomat Miguel Serrano remembered he "was surprised to find Hesse in the garden standing by the fence and wearing a broad-brimmed hat. He was burning grass. He then noticed me and went to open the gate" (Serrano 1968, 20).

As he burned grass and leaves, Hesse daydreamed about a "hundred-gated cathedral of the spirit." A 1936 poem, "Hours in the Garden," elaborated on this. As he watched the ashes of the past filter down through the grate, he could hear music and see the wise harmoniously building a timeless structure of the spirit, like the theologians we shall meet in this book, as they reflect on children.

In 1932 he published an essay called "A Bit of Theology." In it he spoke of "the "developmental history of the soul." Hesse kept his own childhood and youth continually in his mind as he wrote his last six novels. As he said, "My purpose is to delineate that piece of humanity and love, of instinct and sublimation, that I know of from my own experience, and for whose truth, sincerity, and actuality I can vouch" (quoted in Zeller 1971, 8).

The publication of his essay "A Bit of Theology" was in 1932, the same year that Karl Barth published the first volume of his *Church Dogmatics*, when Barth was a professor of theology in Bonn (1930–1935). We shall come to Barth in chapter 6, but for now it is enough to note this and that his study of Anselm, whom we shall meet in chapter 3, was published a few years before in 1930 also while in Bonn. Hesse was beginning his decade of work on *The Glass Bead Game* as Barth worked on the Barmen Declaration of 1934, which led to his dismissal as a professor in Germany when he refused to make an unqualified oath of support for Hitler. Barth returned to Switzerland where he was born and spent the rest of his life there.

In "A Bit of Theology" Hesse wrote:

> ͨ I know it from my own experience and from the documents of many other souls. Always, at all times in history and in all religions and forms of life, we find the same typical experiences, always in the same progression and succession: loss of innocence, striving for justice under the law, the consequent despair in the futile struggle to overcome guilt by deeds or by knowledge, and finally the emergence from hell into a transformed world and into a new kind of innocence. (quoted in Ziolkowski 1965, 55–56) ͣ

Hesse's last six novels examined this triadic rhythm from all sides, especially the second period, which was the most interesting to him as a novelist because of the struggles that take place during that time and when one falls back into it from the third stage. This journey, which has vestiges in all human beings, moves from innocence (paradise, childhood, a time without a sense of responsibility) to the conflicts of adulthood. This conflict cannot help but foster guilt in adults as the awareness unfolds that the ideal cannot be realized. This moves one to despair, which can lead to either "downfall" (self-destructive behavior from drugs to an obsessive compulsive and narcissistic life) or to the "Third Kingdom of the Spirit," which is an experience of a reality beyond the conflicts of morality and law to "grace and redemption" and "faith" (Ziolkowski 1965, 54). Both Hesse's *The Glass Bead Game* and his triadic rhythm of life have, as we said, influenced this book about children and the theologians.

The foundational assumption of this book is that children know God in their nonspecific way and they need to be respected for that. What they need help with from adults is to learn the art of how to identify this experience and express, refine, name, value, and wonder about it in the most appropriate language and action. When children are invited to play deeply in a community of children with God and the scriptures, adults are sometimes astonished to discover how theologically-minded they actually are. Adults who guide such play soon realize that they learn as much from the children as the children do from them. The experience of becoming like children to enter the kingdom and welcoming children to know God is as true and as counter-cultural today as was when Jesus' sayings about children first began to be circulated.

Jesus began as a mysterious presence to his contemporaries. As the first and second generations continued to remember him, he became a text as well as a presence. A "literal reading" of the text is intended here, in the sense that Rowan Williams used that phrase. By this I mean that the rough surface of the texts will not be smoothed over to create a simple, easy-to-grasp summary (Higton 2004, 63). What Jesus said and did concerning children can no more be blended into a harmony or distilled into an essence than the gospels can be, as was attempted by previous generations. This is why so many texts have been reproduced here to read alongside my suggested interpretations. This honors the reader's own ability to interpret them and allows the rough edges of what Jesus said and did to show. It also honors the church as a "community of readers, argumentative and unmanageable, but therefore a community which can give us the gift of a deeper reading of Scripture" (Higton, 2004, 68). That is the overarching hope here.

The revelation of Jesus concerning his relationship with God and our appreciation of that relationship through the Holy Spirit is made manifest by the *whole* life of Jesus from birth to death. While his death and resurrection and his moral sayings have been given great attention over the centuries, his comments and actions concerning children have often been pushed to the edge of theological concern or transposed into superficial abstractions that were given greater authority than the depths their original parabolic form revealed. While many have pushed the parabolic children aside for other and important concerns, this book will focus, perhaps to a fault, only on children, so we ask now—what did Jesus say about them?

Children in the Jesus Traditions

There are four traditions, the "rough edges," about Jesus and children in the gospels. One tradition, a high view, respects children and what they can teach us about mature spirituality. A low view sees children as getting in the way of adults who desire to become true disciples of Christ. In a third tradition, Jesus does not seem to think about children at all! There is a kind of objective indifference, not an indifference that scorns children but one that pays them no mind for the moment because of other concerns that have crowded in to displace them in Jesus' attention. A fourth "rough edge" also emerges from the texts: Children are understood as a means of grace for the continuity of Christ's presence in the church as a source of wonder and creativity.

Matthew, Mark, and Luke include the high and low views of children mixed with some indifference. They add up to a gospel of ambivalence. John, on the other hand, presents a tradition of Jesus that is mostly indifferent. The theme of children as a means of grace stands in the background to all four gospels. It is different from the high view of children, because it is focused on the promise of the generations.

God promised to be with the generations of Abraham (Genesis 15:3–5; 22:17; 28:14), but Jesus broadened this family beyond biological kinship by adopting the children around him. When he blessed and held them he adopted them and made them heirs of his kingdom and part of the benefits and obligations involved in this broader kind of family (Gundry 2008, 154–158). The church has continued because these children have kept coming in each generation to revive it.

Let us now look at each of these four themes—the low view, the high view, the indifferent view, and grace—in more detail. All scripture quotations are from the New Revised Standard Version and they are supplied in abundance, as we have said, to show the rough edges of the texts about children and as an invitation to the reader to join in their interpretation.

A Low View of Children

A cluster of six sayings from the synoptic gospels illustrates the tradition of Jesus' low view of children. This view has drawn approval over the centuries from many theologians, which is certainly understandable. Children are often disruptive to the well-ordered life and single-minded holiness. The responsibilities they place on adults are not always welcome and sometimes are almost impossible to meet.

Most of the time, however, theologians have not spoken about their low view of children directly. Their way of life has disclosed this standpoint. For example, in the seventeenth century a young man named "Christian," the hero in John Bunyan's *The Pilgrim's Progress*, flees his family with his fingers in his ears to muffle their calls to him as he sets out for the Celestial City. It is ironic that all forms of celibacy and cloistered life undertaken to seek the kingdom of heaven exclude the very children that Jesus said show how to enter it.

The first group of passages suggests that one should leave parents, children, family, and fields to follow Jesus and that if this is done there will be a reward now or in the future. This group of sayings may be found in all three synoptic gospels:

> *And everyone who has left houses or brothers or sisters or father or mother or children or fields, for my name's sake, will receive a hundredfold and will inherit eternal life (Matthew 19:29).*

> *Jesus said, "Truly I tell you, there is no one who has left house or brothers or sisters or mother or father or children or fields, for my sake and for the sake of the good news, who will not receive a hundredfold now in this age—houses, brothers and sisters, mothers and children, and fields, with persecutions—and in the age to come eternal life. (Mark 10:29–30)*

> *And he said to them, "Truly I tell you, there is no one who has left house or wife or brothers or parents or children for the sake of the kingdom of God, who will not get back very much more in this age. (Luke 18:29–30)*

Jesus also acknowledged that there would be betrayal and hatred in families for those who followed him in a single-minded way. This reference is found only in Mark, but it fits well with the rest of these hard sayings.

> *Brother will betray brother to death, and a father his child, and children will rise against parents and have them put to death; and you will be hated by all because of my name. (Mark 13:12–13)*

Jesus also told his disciples not to look back, like Bunyan's Christian, to their homes after leaving to follow him. Those responsibilities were at an end. One cannot have a divided mind about this, a single Lucan passage tells us.

> *To another he said, "Follow me." But he said, "Lord, first let me go and bury my father." But Jesus said to him, "Let the dead bury their own dead: but as for you, go and proclaim the kingdom of God." Another said, "I will follow you, Lord; but let me first say farewell to those at my home." Jesus said to him, "No one who puts a hand to the plow and looks back is fit for the kingdom of God. (Luke 9:59–62)*

In addition it is written that Jesus told his followers that conflict with one's family was inevitable if they were going to follow him completely.

In this sense he did not come to bring peace but conflict to families. This reference occurred in Matthew and Luke:

> *Do not think that I have come to bring peace to the earth; I have not come to bring peace, but a sword. For I have come to set a man against his father, and a daughter against her mother, and a daughter-in-law against her mother-in-law; and one's foes will be members of one's own household. (Matthew 10:34–36)*

> *Do you think that I have come to bring peace to the earth? No, I tell you, but rather division! From now on five in one household will be divided, three against two and two against three; they will be divided: father against son and son against father, mother against daughter and daughter against mother, mother-in-law against her daughter-in-law and daughter-in-law against mother-in-law. (Luke 12:51–53)*

In fact, there is some suggestion that Jesus even counseled holding a lower degree of love, or even hatred, for family members. He is reported to have said this by Matthew and Luke:

> *"Whoever loves father or mother more than me is not worthy of me; and whoever loves son or daughter more than me is not worthy of me; and whoever does not take up the cross and follow me is not worthy of me. (Matthew 10:37–38)*

> *"Whoever comes to me and does not hate father and mother, wife and children, brothers and sisters, yes, even life itself, cannot be my disciple. (Luke 14:26)*

Finally, in a very extreme passage Jesus is reported to have said that one should castrate himself for the sake of the kingdom of heaven. This completely rules out fathering children and implies that mothering should also be set aside by his followers. This famous passage occurred only in Matthew's gospel:

> *His disciples said to him, "If such is the case of a man with his wife, it is better not to marry." But he said to them, "Not everyone can accept this teaching, but only those to whom it is given. For there are eunuchs who have been so from birth, and there are eunuchs who have been made eunuchs by others, and there are eunuchs who have made themselves eunuchs for the sake of the kingdom of heaven. Let anyone accept this who can. (Matthew 19:10–12)*

These six sayings and their parallels are enough to give one pause before saying too quickly that Jesus primarily held a high view of children and families. It may be that this low view of children was only meant for his disciples, who were especially called to such a single-minded life. They were to enter the "narrow gate" (Matthew 7:13–14; Luke 13:23–24) and would have no home or family tradition other than being a disciple (Matthew 8:18–22; Luke 9:57–60). This interpretation has been suggested over the centuries to soften these hard sayings, but it may also be that Jesus was misunderstood by his audience or interpreted with an anti-child or anti-family bias, a view held by some in the culture around him. Whatever the cause of these sayings, one must acknowledge that they are present in the synoptic texts and form the basis for a tradition of Jesus' low view of children. Following the authority of this tradition has excluded children and families from the lives of many faithful Christians, as they earnestly sought the kingdom of heaven.

Perhaps you were surprised at the beginning of this chapter to find Bohdan Piasecki's modern painting of the Last Supper instead of Leonardo da Vinci's great fifteenth-century fresco. We are so accustomed to seeing da Vinci's painting, which is truly a masterpiece, that we often don't realize that it represents the low view of children contained in the hard sayings. Piasecki's painting is evocative of a Jewish Passover Seder or an ordinary gathering of the followers of a respected rabbi with their families in con-trast to da Vinci's painting of an extraordinary group of exclusively male disciples for celibate, cloistered adults to comtemplate while dining. With the juxtaposition of these two paintings in mind we turn now to the tradi-tion of Jesus' high view of children.

A High View of Children

The synoptic gospels also suggest Jesus held a high view of children. We shall begin with Jairus' twelve-year-old daughter. Jesus went home with Jairus, a leader of the synagogue, to where a funeral for his daughter was in process. Jesus "took her by the hand and the girl got up" (Matthew 13:25, Mark 5:41-42 and Luke 8:54-55). This child and others were worth healing.

Another example of the high view tradition may call to mind the prophet Zechariah's evocative image of children at play in the streets of Jerusalem to show how it would be when God returns to Zion (Zechariah 8:5). Jesus referred to children at play in the market place. This intriguing situation is found in Matthew and Luke:

> It is like children sitting in the marketplaces and calling to one
> another, "We played the flute for you, and you did not dance;

> *we wailed, and you did not mourn." For John came neither eating nor drinking, and they say, "He has a demon;" the Son of Man came eating and drinking, and they say, "Look, a glutton and a drunkard, a friend of tax collectors and sinners!" Yet wisdom is vindicated by her deeds. (Matthew 11:16–19)*

> *To what then will I compare the people of this generation, and what are they like? They are like children sitting in the marketplace and calling to one another. "We played the flute for you, and you did not dance; we wailed, and you did not weep." For John the Baptist has come eating no bread and drinking no wine, and you say, "He has a demon;" the Son of Man has come eating and drinking and you say, "Look, a glutton and a drunkard, a friend of tax collectors and sinners!" Nevertheless, wisdom is vindicated by all her children. (Luke 7:31–35)*

Sometimes children do not pay attention to what adults tell them to do. That is natural, but the question in this parabolic context is why. If we take a low view of children then these passages seem to compare the adults who do not follow Jesus to irritating children, who are assumed to be unable (perhaps because of defective reason) or unwilling (perhaps because of a diseased will) to listen to what they are told, learn from it, and do what they are told.

If we bracket the children's action, however, and separate it from its interpretative context, it becomes more parabolic. If we also assume that Jesus took a high view of children then these passages suggest that there is something we can learn from children rather than merely taking note of their recalcitrance. Removing the blaming context also allows the following question to arise: Have the children intuited something important about the kingdom of heaven that Jesus is trying to communicate in this indirect way?

Nothing is said about the children misunderstanding the two games proposed, which are probably "wedding feast" because of the dancing and "funeral" because of the wailing involved. There was no controversy about leadership among the children mentioned, something that often breaks down play. Nothing else extraneous to the play of the children is presented in the text that would likely stop the games suggested by the adults. This compels us to ask if there is anything about play *itself* that could have prevented the adult-suggested games.

Play is pleasurable, voluntary, done for itself, absorbing, and has connections with creativity, learning languages, learning social roles, and problem-solving (Garvey 1977). There are also different kinds of play. You can play with words, but words falter when used to say what play is because there is no class of behavior that can be isolated as play. One reason for this is that there is nothing that one can do in a serious way that could not also be done in a playful way. This is because play is part of the non-verbal communication system and is signaled by a smile, a twinkle in the eye, or some other physical indicator, not merely by what is said. People can "talk a good game," even when they can't play it, or they can invite someone to play but not intend to play themselves as a means of deception.

Play is as elusive to define as it is fundamental to our experience, but it can, at least, be divided into two kinds. There is "as-if play" and "what-if play" (Hymans 1992; 1996). As-if play is about assuming adult roles, such as playing funeral or wedding feast. What-if play is about doing or thinking what has not been done or thought before, at least by the individual player.

What kind of play is needed to discover how to enter Jesus' kingdom? A totally new way of thinking is needed, because this kind of kingdom is different from anything "normal" that children might see modeled in the adult world around them. What-if play is needed to know the unknown.

The children in the market place were invited to engage in the as-if play of adult wedding feasts and funerals, but it is what-if play that is needed to know the kingdom. The children in the market place were more profound than peevish when they turned away from the adults' invitation to an inappropriate kind of play to show what Jesus was talking about.

Being like John the Baptist or even Jesus will not help people understand what they must know by their own creative power for themselves about the kingdom. You cannot enter the kingdom by patterning your life after the ordinary adults around you. Ordinary adults don't get it. Jesus used the children in the market place to suggest we need to make a complete break from social convention and think thoughts that have not been thought before if we are to enter the kingdom. In fact it is not so much the content of the thought that opens the door. It is the *process* of the what-if play *itself* that conveys non verbally how to enter the kingdom. Even if you sincerely pretend to be like Jesus or John, that will not work! The kingdom is a matter of creativity, not mimicry.

A second cluster of passages from the synoptic gospels carries the issue of nonverbal communication forward and develops it. Matthew and Mark tell us that Jesus put a child in the midst of the disciples. In Luke he placed the child by his side. Nevertheless, in all three gospels the child remains silent:

> At that time the disciples came to Jesus and asked, "Who is the
> greatest in the kingdom of heaven?" He called a child, whom he

put among them, and said, "Truly I tell you, unless, you change
and become like children, you will never enter the kingdom of
heaven. Whoever becomes humble like this child is the greatest in
the kingdom of heaven. Whoever welcomes one such child in my
name welcomes me. (Matthew 18:1–5)

Then they came to Capernaum and when he was in the house he
asked them, "What were you arguing about on the way?" But they
were silent; for on the way they had argued with one another who
was the greatest. He sat down, called the twelve, and he said to
them, "Whoever wants to be first, he must be last of all and ser-
vant of all." Then he took a little child, and put it among them;
and taking it in his arms, he said to them, "Whoever welcomes one
such child in my name welcomes me, and whoever welcomes me,
welcomes not me but the one who sent me." (Mark 9:33–37)

An argument arose among them as to which one of them was the
greatest. But Jesus, aware of their inner thoughts, took a little child
and put it by his side, and said to them "Whoever welcomes this
child in my name welcomes me, and whoever welcomes me wel-
comes the one who sent me; for the least among all of you is the
greatest." (Luke 9:46–48)

Adults in Rome, Athens, and Jerusalem would have found this saying
of Jesus very strange! It turns the usual roles of adults and children upside
down. The parable is a reversal of the ordinary order of life, but what is
even more important to notice today is that the child said nothing.

The child's eloquently full silence is in stark contrast to the disciples'
pathetically empty talk. If we keep our eye on the child in the midst of the
talking heads and bracket the interpretation of the event, which the gospel
writer has put into Jesus' words, we can see clearly that this is a parable of
action about where to look for spiritual maturity and the inability of words
to communicate it.

Jesus pointed to the child and not to himself. The disciples had already
misunderstood his words. Now he wants them to consider the child's *being*
in itself to guide growth toward spiritual maturity. He wants them to engage
in profound ontological appreciation of children rather than merely talking
among themselves *about* children without really connecting *with* them.

The three narratives are actually quite different. In Matthew Jesus put
the child among the disciples and then spoke to them about changing and
becoming like children. In Mark he sat down, taught them, and then put
a child in their midst as he spoke of welcoming children, while taking the
child in his arms. In Luke he put the child by his side and then spoke in
terms of welcoming children to welcome him and the one who sent him.

Perhaps this kind of talk and parabolic action happened more than once, or perhaps these are different memories of the same event. In any case, Jesus observed that the child is able to enter (or receive) the kingdom and disclose God but that this needs to be shown rather than merely said.

The adult experience of life is larger and more complex than the child's. Does this larger and more complex adult experience add to or detract from the adult's spiritual maturity? The disciples assumed that political savvy added to their maturity and importance. Jesus sidestepped this debate and directed the disciples' gaze in another direction.

He tells them and us that when you receive or welcome one of these kingdom children you also meet him and the One who sent him. This adds to the high view of children because children, like Jesus, are the embodiment of the kingdom "state" of being. This is a very radical thought, but it is even more radical to consider how children communicate this. Isn't it too adult for children? No. This embodiment needs to be shown to be known. It is like play. The meaning is in the action. That is why the children did not speak.

Of course, children can be noisy. Even adults who don't usually pay attention to children will testify to that! The challenge of this passage for adults is whether one has the skill and patience for the ontological appreciation of children. Can one see past the movement and sound and be open to the invitation presented by the being of children to know God?

In another situation, at least in Mark's telling, Jesus was "indignant" when the disciples tried to keep the children away from him. Perhaps they were trying to protect him so he could do something "important" with the adults. Children are not significant in political terms, because they are weak, without funds, and helpless, so they could not help carry the Jesus movement forward. The disciples may have thought that children don't even have the life experience or cognitive ability to understand Jesus' teaching. Some still think the same way today. This event is recorded in all three synoptic gospels:

> Then little children were being brought to him in order that he might lay his hands on them and pray. The disciples spoke sternly to those who brought them; but Jesus said, "Let the little children come to me, and do not stop them; for it is to such as these that the kingdom of heaven belongs." And he laid his hands on them and went on his way (Matthew 19:13–15).

> People were bringing little children to him in order that he might touch them; and the disciples spoke sternly to them. But when Jesus saw this, he was indignant and said to them, "Let the little chil-

dren come to me; do not stop them; for it is to such as these that the kingdom of God belongs. Truly I tell you, whoever does not receive the kingdom of God as a little child will never enter it." And he took them up in his arms, laid his hands on them, and blessed them. (Mark 10:13–16)

People were bringing even infants to him that he might touch them; and when the disciples saw it, they sternly ordered them not to do it. But Jesus called for them and said, "Let the little children come to me, and do not stop them; for it is to such as these that the kingdom of God belongs. Truly I tell you, whoever does not receive the kingdom of God as a little child will never enter it. (Luke 18:15–17)

When we turn our attention away from the adults in this scene and toward the children, something interesting happens. The children, then as today, are not even interested in the adults' political aspirations, their greater experience in life, or their higher stages of cognitive ability. They are not even interested in what *Jesus* is saying! What they are interested in is Jesus *himself*.

The children's intuition about the importance of Jesus for their growth and development was informed by their nonverbal communication system. This kind of knowing is not naïve for the children. It is the state of the art for them. It is only "naïve" when compared to adult thinking that is assumed to be of a higher quality and usefulness. What Jesus does is cast that assumption into doubt. The way that children know is merely different from adult knowing. It is a way of knowing that adults often lose but children can *show* them how to recover it by example. When adults become overly dependent on language they are likely to miss the kind of meaning that children are best at communicating. It is very easy to become over-dependent on language in our highly verbal, tightly scheduled, and multi-tasking culture and miss the best of what children have to teach.

Some might argue that this parable is about the nature of God rather than the nature of children, but if we take a high view of children, rather than considering them unworthy of notice, the relationship between God and children is what draws our attention. The ontological appreciation of the silent child, set in the midst of the talking adults, shows that it is the revelation of God that the child bears silently. Paul is the model for the verbal adult who is unworthy and yet accepted by grace. Jesus' model, however, is the silent child in relationship with God revealing God's presence.

We turn now to the millstone texts. Since children are bearers of revelation for each other as well as for adults, we must take care to balance our responsibilities for their care and upbringing with allowing them to be children who are parables of kingdom entry and bearers of God's presence. Jesus is violently clear about adults not distracting children from their true nature. All three synoptic gospels include a version of Jesus' millstone saying:

> *If any of you put a stumbling block before one of these little ones*
> *who believe in me, it would be better for you if a great millstone*
> *were fastened around your neck and you were drowned in the depth*
> *of the sea. Woe to the world because of stumbling blocks! Occasions*
> *for stumbling are bound to come, but woe to the one by whom the*
> *stumbling block comes! (Matthew 18:6–7)*

> *If any of you put a stumbling block before one of these little ones*
> *who believe in me, it would be better for you if a great millstone*
> *were hung around your neck and you were thrown into the sea.*
> *(Mark 9:42)*

> *Jesus said to his disciples, "Occasions for stumbling are bound to*
> *come, but woe to anyone by whom they come! It would be better for*
> *you if a millstone were hung around your neck and you were thrown*
> *into the sea than for you to cause one of these little ones to stumble."*
> *(Luke 17:1–2)*

These three texts echo Jesus' indignation at the disciples, who hindered the children from coming to him. Matthew connects this saying explicitly with the disciples' discourse on greatness and the silent child placed in their midst. Mark and Luke locate the saying in different contexts, but these different contexts do not change the sayings' meaning or urgency. It is violent language about a matter of life and death.

Some of Jesus' sayings seem to float in and out of different contexts, as if they were taken from a written collection of sayings or an oral tradition and later inserted into the narratives created by the gospel writers. The text about entering the kingdom of heaven is, perhaps, one of the most important of such sayings. Its context in Matthew is the discourse on true greatness (Matthew 18:3), while in Mark and Luke it is when the disciples try to prevent the children from coming to Jesus for a blessing (Mark 10:15 and Luke 18:17). We will treat this saying for the moment as if it were freestanding to see what can be learned from looking at its puzzle directly without any particular context. All three synoptic gospels carry similar versions of this formula:

> *Truly I tell you, unless you change and become like children, you*
> *will never enter the kingdom of heaven. (Matthew 18:3)*

> *Truly I tell you, whoever does not receive the kingdom of God as a*
> *little child will never enter. (Mark 10:15)*

> *Truly I tell you, whoever does not receive the kingdom of God as a*
> *little child will never enter it. (Luke 18:17)*

This appears at first to be like Jesus' other reversals, such as the first being last and the last being first, but this interpretation keeps children "down" conceptually, despite the reversal, because it assumes a low view of children in practice to make the reversal work. This is somewhat like the dean always coming last in a cathedral procession because he is first in importance and everyone knows that.

The reversal in this case is more complex. It is not that the low child becomes high in importance (like an adult) but that the child, whose value as a spiritual teacher is high, teaches the low adult, who is older and is assumed more important, how to enter the kingdom. The irony is that the adult may stay low and unable to touch the kingdom because of an inflated self-evaluation as being higher than children in importance and unable to learn from them. The greatest irony, however, is that adults and children are in the same position with respect to what is ultimate in life and death. Neither is completely in charge. God is.

We turn now to two texts where there is less attestation in the gospels and less direct connection between Jesus and children, but they are still important to understand the tradition of Jesus' high view of children. Both of these texts imply the power of children's intuition. In the first one we find Jesus in the temple. He had just overturned the tables of the money-changers and had been healing the blind and lame when some children saw him. They cried out, "Hosanna to the Son of David." Here is the passage from Matthew:

> *But when the chief priests and the scribes saw the amazing things*
> *that he did, and heard the children crying out in the temple,*
> *"Hosanna to the Son of David," they became angry and said to*
> *him, "Do you hear what these are saying?" Jesus said to them,*
> *"Yes; have you never read,*
>
> > *'Out of the mouths of infants*
> > *and nursing babies*
> > *you have prepared praise for*
> > *yourself'?"*
> >
> > *(Matthew 21:15–16)*

The children had intuited something about Jesus that the priests and scribes had missed. Jesus went on to probe this blind spot and probably quoted the Hebrew scriptures, perhaps from Psalm 8:2, which reads something like this:

> *Thou whose glory above the heavens is chanted*
> *by the mouths of babes and infants . . .*

The children entered Matthew's narrative at the point when the temple was cleansed (Matthew 21:15–16). The temple cleansing context for this event is found in all four gospels, but in Mark 11:15–19, Luke 19:45–48, and John 2:13–17 the children were not mentioned.

We turn now to the other text about children's intuition. It is found in both Matthew and Luke and comments on how things have been revealed to children that "the wise and the intelligent" do not know.

In Matthew this saying comes after John the Baptist's disciples have left to report to him what they have learned about Jesus. In Luke it comes after the joyful return of the seventy. This pair of passages follows:

> *At that time Jesus said, "I thank you, Father, Lord of heaven and earth, because you have hidden these things from the wise and the intelligent and have revealed them to infants; yes, Father, for such was your gracious will. (Matthew 11:25–26)*

> *At that same hour Jesus rejoiced in the Holy Spirit and said, "I thank you, Father, Lord of heaven and earth, because you have hidden these things from the wise and the intelligent and revealed them to infants; yes, Father, for such was your gracious will."*
> *(Luke 10:21)*

After these sayings in both gospels, Jesus reflected on his knowledge of the Father and said that no one knows the Father except the Son and no one knows the Son except those he reveals himself to. This links implicitly to the saying about welcoming children is like welcoming him. He reveals himself to those who know how to welcome children.

We have considered the gospel passages that suggest that Jesus had a low view of children and a high view. We turn now to the passages upon which the tradition of indifference is built.

An Indifferent View of Children

While John T. Carroll, writing in Bunge's *The Child in the Bible*, was surprised to find much about children in Luke (Carroll 2008, 177, 193), I was surprised to find nothing about children in John. It was a relief to learn that I was not alone in this when I read the opening sentence of Marianne Meye Thompson's "Children in the Gospel of John" in the same book. She wrote, "Children are essentially missing from the pages of the Gospel of John" (Thompson 2008, 195).

Jesus, like all adults, did not think about children all the time. There are everyday adult concerns to be taken care of in addition to what children need. Jesus is seen in the gospels traveling, dealing with his followers (including a traitor), facing his own death, and being present to the community on the cross and in his resurrection. His mind sometimes was merely elsewhere.

An example of Jesus' divided attention might be Matthew's version of the Sermon on the Mount (Matthew 5–7). While beatitudes might be construed to be about children and/or child-like adults, the larger portion of the Sermon is about adult concerns such as anger, adultery, divorce, swearing, retaliation, loving one's enemies, almsgiving, prayer, fasting, treasures, clarity of vision, serving two masters, anxiety, judging, profaning the holy, God's answer to prayer, the "Golden Rule," the narrow gate, the test of a good person, self-deception, and being doers of the Word rather than just hearers.

If we were asked which gospel is the gospel of indifference about children it would have to be John. There are no stories about Jesus' birth or childhood. This is also true of Mark's gospel, but in John there are not even any parables or parabolic actions reported that involve children. There is, however, near the beginning of the gospel an event that evokes birth and re-birth. It is the story of Nicodemus, a Pharisee, who came by night and acknowledged Jesus as his rabbi (John 3:1–21). Jesus did not agree or disagree but challenged Nicodemus with a different task than following him as his rabbi. Jesus wanted him "to be born anew." Following anyone, including Jesus, is other-directed. Re-birth comes from within by taking a new and uniquely personal perspective.

> *Jesus answered him, "Very truly, I tell you, no one can see the kingdom of God without being born from above." Nicodemus said to him, "How can anyone be born after having grown old? Can one enter a second time into the mother's womb and be born? Jesus answered, "Very truly, I tell you, no one can enter the kingdom of God without being born of water and Spirit. What is born of the flesh is flesh, and what is born of the Spirit is spirit. Do not be astonished that I said to you, "You must be born from above." The wind blows where it chooses, and you hear the sound of it, but you do not know where it comes from or where it goes. So it is with everyone who is born of the Spirit. (John 3:3–8)*

"Born from above" might also be translated "born anew," and the same Greek word is used to mean both wind and spirit. Being born again into child-likeness may be something like a "second naivete," a concept developed by Paul Ricoeur (Ricoeur 1967), following Kierkegaard, from a philosophical-theological perspective and the approach developed by James W. Fowler, especially in his Stage Five Conjunctive Faith (Fowler 1981, 187–188) in a psychological-theological way. These modern explanations certainly do not exhaust what being "born again" means or how it takes place. This is what makes Nicodemus' response so credible: "How can these things be?"

Today being "born again" is popularly linked to the conversion experience as interpreted and valued especially by two important Christian movements, the Fundamentalist Movement and the Charismatic Movement. Both movements are important correctives for bland, emotionless Christianity that does not take scripture seriously. The intensity of this emphasis, however, sometimes results in a narrowing of Christianity to what Eric W. Gritsch has called "born againism" (Gritsch 1982). Such narrowing squeezes the wonder out of starting all over again without any preconceptions. This is, of course, an impossible ideal, but its lure is what makes Jesus' words to Nicodemus and to us so poignant and challenging.

There is little else in John's gospel that even hints about children except, perhaps, the story of the official from Capernaum—who came to Jesus, fearing for the life of his child with a fever. Jesus said, "Your son will live," so the man went home and was met on the way by his servants with the news that the child's fever had broken and he would live, as Jesus said.

There was also the mention of "a lad" in the story of the feeding of the five thousand who had five barley loaves and two fish (John 6:9), but in Matthew (14:17), Mark (6:38), and Luke (9:13) the loaves and fishes belonged to the disciples. Jesus gave thanks for this offering and distributed it to the crowd. All were satisfied and there was nourishment left over.

When we call the Gospel of John the "gospel of indifference" it merely means that children do not often appear in its pages. This gospel is concerned with adults and their problems, as we have said, so children are merely left out. To say nothing, however, teaches something about children as surely as saying something positive or negative does.

For some reason this gospel also shows Jesus being objectively indifferent or at least distant from his mother. At the marriage of Cana his mother asked him to help replenish the wine, which was running low. He replied, "Woman, what concern is that to you and to me? My hour has not yet come" (John 2:4). He did, however, change the water to wine anyway and the wedding went on in a festive way.

Later his brothers wanted him to go to Jerusalem for the festival of the Booths. They did not believe that he was the Messiah (John 7:5), so, perhaps, they wanted him to become more public to see if it were true. Jesus said that it was not yet time, but he did go in secret and then taught in the temple, which was not secret. He is full of contradictions. Mark tells how there was such a crowd once that he could not eat. "When his family heard it, they went out to restrain him, for people were saying, 'He has gone out of his mind'" (Mark 3:21). It was just after this that Mark tells how he responded to being told his mother, brothers, and sisters were outside asking for him by saying, "Who are my mother and my brothers?" He looked at those sitting with him and said that they were his mother and brothers. "Whoever does the will of God is my brother and sister and mother" (Mark 3:35).

When Jesus spoke to his mother from the cross he said, "Woman, here is your son!" He then said to "the disciple," "Here is your mother" (John 19:26–27). From that point on, John tells us, this disciple, presumably John, took care of Mary in his own home.

These sayings may be rooted in Jesus' stepping back from his natural family to think in terms of what might be called a "kingdom family," one that extends beyond kinship. Everyone is someone's child, but in the kingdom everyone is everyone's child. There is a kind of general indifference here, not antagonism, but a caring that includes a distant formality that is alike for all.

Almost everything Jesus said about children and families involved a kind of ambiguity that runs all through scripture. For example the terms "child" or "children" sometimes means actual children and other times symbolic children, like the adults who are God's children. In addition Jesus is not just Mary and Joseph's son. He is also God's son. This gives a kind of poetic richness to everything Jesus said about children and families, so even Jesus' low view of children must be understood with the implication that kingdom people will care for each other across the lines of biological kinship and love their enemies. This kind of indifference challenged many cultural assumptions about children and families then as now.

We have now considered the traditions of the low and high views of Jesus about children and the apparent absence of an interest in children in John's gospel. We have touched on one of the sources of ambiguity about children in scripture and assumed that grace runs all through the gospels, mentioned or unmentioned, because the Holy Spirit is at work. We turn now to the fourth of the traditions or "rough edges" about Jesus and children.

A Graceful View of Children

At the beginning of John's gospel we hear how Jesus was with God in the beginning and then "dwelt among us, full of grace and truth." He was not accepted in his own home, which may have had something to do with the distant way he treated his family, but to all who welcomed him he gave power "to become children of God." Jesus may have lived with "grace and truth" but he did not say much explicitly about "grace."

Paul was the one who wrote about grace. He used the term (*charis*) in his letters to open or close them. This played on the sound of the usual opening, which might be translated something like "greetings" (*chaire*) and linked it with the sound of the Greek word for "peace" (*irene*). Paul wrote most about grace in his Letter to the Romans (1:5, 3:24, 4:16, 5:2, 5:15, 5:20, 6:1, 15:15). In fact it might be said that the whole letter is a commentary on his salutation, "Grace to you and peace from God our Father and the Lord Jesus Christ" (Romans1:7). God's grace shapes the concept of Christian peace in contrast to the kind of peace maintained by force of arms that was offered by Rome and the *Pax Romana*.

The whole history of theology could be written as a series of debates about the meaning of grace. It defines the quality of the relationship between the Creator and God's creation, especially God's creatures, who have a tendency to resist receiving the gift of grace. In the Roman world the term *clementia* emphasized the forgiveness aspect of God's gift, as in the English word "clemency." Grace is what keeps the church alive as it moves from generation to generation by means of children. It is born anew, over and over again. By grace birth comes physically again and again over the centuries to the People of God and also comes in a spiritual sense to individual lives by surprise from day to day. It takes both kinds of grace to provide even a partial answer to Nicodemus' question.

The Jesus traditions about children then are the high view, the low view, the indifferent view, and the graceful view. These "rough edges" can be summarized by putting the high and low traditions together to give us one of ambivalence. Indifference remains indifference and grace is in the background to all four gospels. One theme that will emerge more clearly as this history continues is ambiguity. In summary we can say that, where children are concerned, the synoptic gospels are the gospels of ambivalence and John is the gospel of indifference. All four gospels are rich with ambiguity about children.

Four Key Strands in the Tapestry

When we look with care at the tapestry of children and the theologians we see "a bundle of a thousand knotted threads which would occupy hundreds of hands for years to disentangle and straighten out, even if every thread did not become terribly brittle and break between the fingers as soon as it is handled and gently drawn" (Hesse 1956, 47). Four key threads that emerge from the history, as we have said, are: ambivalence, ambiguity, indifference, and grace. A brief definition will now be given for each theme. As the vignettes of the theologians accumulate during each historical period the themes will become much more nuanced.

"Ambivalence" is the first of the themes that emerges from the history. It refers to holding two mutually conflicting feelings about a person, place, thing, or action at the same time. It is a psychological term that came into English from the German *Ambivalenz* via Freud, especially as he used it in his *Totem and Taboo* (Freud 1913, 830). Freud said that the originator of the term was Eugen Bleuler, Professor of Psychiatry in Zurich. He quipped that Bleuler knew a lot about this, since ambivalence dominated his response to Freud's new theory of psychoanalysis (Jones 1963, 268). The word became part of the international science vocabulary about 1918 and is used here to indicate the church's delight and aversion, attraction and repulsion, and emotional closeness to and distance from children. It is difficult to tell if theologians have been personally ambivalent about children, but it is clear that when the history of Christian theology is taken as a whole it is ambivalent since it includes both the high and low views of children.

"Ambiguity" is about logic rather than emotions. It refers to the possibility that the word "children" can be understood in two or more ways. Logical misunderstanding contributes to emotional conflicts so it is sometimes important to focus on the logic and bracket the emotions. When ambiguity is combined unconsciously with ambivalence the two themes work together to paralyze our best thinking about children in the church today. This is why these themes need to be separated for analysis and awareness. The pain of unacknowledged emotional and logical conflicts causes resistance to the careful listening and calm caring that are needed to develop a positive doctrine of children for the church.

The third theme that emerges from this history is "indifference." Being indifferent can be neutral but it can also drift into being unconcerned, apathetic, or even turn into a smirk or sneer about children. This is dangerous for a clear-eyed view of children. Besides, if they were considered important by theologians they would speak rather than be indifferent. Still, the term "objective indifference" will be used at times in this book to identify indifference that is more neutral than adversarial.

Whatever one might think about the indifference of theologians to children it is clear that children can be indifferent to theologians as well. For example at Exeter Cathedral in England there is a seated, stone statue of Richard Hooker (1553–1600), whom we shall meet in chapter 4. John Harris created the wonderful painting of the statue with children swirling around it that is on the cover of this book.

Hooker is sitting there with his big hat and long beard, covered with snow. Three choristers of the Cathedral can be seen in their red robes, but more choristers are outside the frame of the painting. Snowballs are flying into the picture from the unseen choristers and flying out toward them. One boy has been hit directly, a burst of powdery white exploding on his head. They are paying Hooker no mind as they play, except as some stone in the snow to hide behind.

The fourth guiding thread in the tapestry is "grace." This term's use in theology has tipped toward a cluster of ideas concerning approval, mercy, and pardon. I would like to stress the pre-Christian, Latin usage as well, which refers to charm and loveliness as well as to favor, kindness, and service to others. Grace is the ability to walk across a room without falling down or the capacity to form a relationship that might not otherwise develop because of undue awkwardness. Grace has as much to do with art and beauty as it does law and punishment in this book. In *Man at Play*, Hugo Rahner, SJ concluded that "the grace of God which 'plays' in the world" is best expressed by the "serious-serene" Christian (Rahner 1965, 104). This is much like the graceful person who will be discussed in the last chapter of this book.

These emerging themes are helpful to guide our reflection, because Jesus never fully described the child that we are to be like to enter the kingdom, nor did he define the child we are to welcome to know him and the One who sent him. This is a blessing. It takes time and patience to get to know children. Most of what they communicate about their spirituality is nonverbal and takes ontological appreciation to fathom. If Jesus had defined the children he spoke of as a means of grace it could have blinded Christians to their reality by smothering them with an authoritative blanket of words.

Conclusion

The people around Jesus, like those in Piasecki's painting of the Last Supper, must have ached when he was gone. Still, his presence remained. For example he appeared at Emmaus, where he was known in the breaking of bread (Luke 24:30–31), and in Jerusalem, where ten disciples had gathered (Luke 24:36–43; John 20:19–25). He was also present in a different way in the wind and fire of Pentecost when "they were all together in one place" (Acts 2:1–4).

Slowly memories began to replace presence, and gratitude crept into their pain. People began to tell stories, remember sayings, and relive the days they spent with him. Knowing the complete structure of his story helped because now it had an ending, even if that ending was an Easter beginning. Finally, people began to write things down and these texts were passed around. By the time Mark's story of Jesus was written, some forty years after Jesus' death, there was still some concern about whether these sacred stories should be written or only told. Mark's story actually begins with the comment that it was really a "gospel," which is an oral announcement. Part of Paul's discussion about the spirit and letter of the law may be related to the concern that was in the air about reducing Christ's spirit to letters painted on parchment or papyrus (Kelber 1983).

The deep gratitude that Jesus' life stirred in people prompted them to seek ways to keep him alive by stories and by celebrating his presence in the community. The church was born in part to do both. This system of relationships in the church was based on adoption into his family rather than biological kinship. It was like being part of his body, as the mystery of Holy Communion suggests.

Among the collected texts there was a variety of passages pertaining to children. The "rough edges" of these themes were allowed to stand rather than rounding them off to a single view. Such openness was also practiced in the way the canon of the four gospels was formed. Having the four perspectives on Christ's life has given the larger story room to breathe over the centuries. The gospel of ambivalence, ambiguity, indifference and grace will increase as the history of children and the theologians unfolds. The *de facto* doctrine, already found in the gospels, will continue to develop as the centuries move toward our time so that this informal doctrine still shapes us.

The proposal about a formal doctrine of children is a matter of knowing what theologians have said but it is also based on experience. The grace children so intensely reveal is the raw energy flowing out from God that can be known by humankind through the creative process. Since it is abundantly clear that people can be creative in destructive ways as well as constructive ways, it is important to realize that grace refers to constructive creativity. This creative energy can be sensed within and in the world around us. The ability to discern grace within and around us and to integrate the two is how we become cocreators with God. The church, *when it is the church*, is the place above all others where grace is discerned and supported and where deeply rooted and constructive creativity reigns.

We began this chapter with Hermann Hesse in his garden. This was because the themes that have emerged from the gospels also fascinated him. He examined them from many perspectives through the characters in his novels. Their spiritual growth showed a pattern. It begins with innocence, which is lost. Then there is the struggle to find justice and overcome the guilt that comes from imperfection. This guilt is managed "by deeds or by knowledge" until there is an "emergence from hell into a transformed world and into a new kind of innocence" (quoted in Ziolkowski 1965, 55–56). When one is able to move through life into such a rebirth as this "new kind of innocence," then one becomes a graceful person. This book is about the role of children in this process.

With these thoughts in mind we conclude this chapter and say goodbye to Hermann Hesse for the time being as he daydreams and burns leaves and grass in his garden. We will meet him again in chapter 8 when we play the game about the *de facto* doctrine, inspired by his Glass Bead Game. One way to clear the way for grace is to become a master of that game. We turn now to collecting the vignettes of theologians, arranged in historical periods, to be the game pieces by which we will play.

In the next chapter we will meet selected theologians from the period when theology was born. Their views of children and the experience they based it on cover the period from about 50 with St. Paul to 500, just after Augustine's death in 430 and the traditional date for the Fall of the Roman Empire in 476.

CHAPTER

2

FROM TEXTS
TO THEOLOGY:
50–500

This statue is both naturalistic and symbolic. The lamb, carried on the shepherd's back, is like a child, but Christ was also the lamb that was slain. God is carrying God's Son and God's Son is carrying the children of God, young and old. Apollo from Greek mythology was also portrayed as a shepherd, so the interplay between Greek polytheism and Jewish and Christian monotheism adds to the layers of symbolic richness and wonder.

The statue was originally from the Catacomb of Domitilla in Rome but is now housed in the *Museo Pio Cristiano* in the Vatican State. It is made of marble and is 39" high but there are 8 1/2" copies for sale all over Rome. The figure of the Good Shepherd was also used in many early sarcophagi for children and adults. Notice that in this representation the lamb's head is turned unnaturally toward the Good Shepherd to hear his voice (John 10:1–18).

◀ *The Good Shepherd* (third or early fourth century)
Museo Pio Cristiano, Vatican Museums, Vatican State

This chapter will discuss six theologians: Paul, Irenaeus, Origen, Chrysostom, Pelagius, and Augustine. They are all male and this maleness will continue throughout the history of Christian theology until our time. This is generally inexcusable but for our particular interest concerning children it is tragic. The development of the *de facto* doctrine of children would have been very different if women had been involved in the official discussion from the beginning. The unrelenting maleness of theology has finally been broken in modern times, so when we come to chapter 7 concerning the contemporary discussion about children, four of the six authors reviewed are women.

You might wonder how "the theologians" were selected for this and future chapters. First, they are of general importance in the history of Christian theology. Second, they are in my judgment key figures in the development of the church's informal doctrine of children in the church. As you will see, some theologians are included who have almost nothing to say about children. Still, the ways they do theology—such as the wonder and playfulness of Cusanus in the fifteenth century—have persuaded me to include them.

This book defines "a theologian" broadly. When the church speaks officially as the church what it says is usually known as doctrine. When a theologian makes an interpretation about how the church believes, or ought to believe, it is more personal and can take at least five forms.

First, theology might be expressed in the arts, such as in Hesse's novels in the twentieth century or the paintings from many centuries that head each chapter in this book. Second, theologians sometimes reflect on their personal experiences, such as Augustine's *Confessions* in the fifth century or Bunyan's *Pilgrim's Progress* in the seventeenth century. A third kind of theology, the one that stays the closest to the scriptures, is found in biblical commentaries. A fourth way of framing theology is to develop a particular theme, such as liberation or the related feminist theologies. A theology of children is sometimes considered to be thematic, but this book will go a bit beyond that to suggest that it fits in the pattern of systematic theology and church doctrine where the doctrine of the sacraments is considered so it can be related to the other classic topics of Christian thought from that location. Finally, theology can be systematic. This form takes a comprehensive view of all doctrines such as God, Trinity, the Person of Christ, Salvation in Christ, Human Nature, Sin, Grace, the Church, the Sacraments and the Doctrine of Last Things. Sometimes the relationships between faith and history and Christianity and other world religions are included as topics, especially today. Thomas Aquinas in the thirteenth century and Karl Barth in the twentieth century are examples of systematic theologians. Each of these five forms of theology have their strengths and weaknesses, but together they help the church formulate and critique its doctrines about the best way to think and live as a Christian.

An example of the broadness of this definition may be found in chapter 7. All of these contemporary "theologians" explore the theme of children in the church. They wrote mostly from a pastoral care or a thematic orientation. Martin Marty is a historian. No major systematic theologian, to my knowledge, has taken up the question of the doctrine of children. This book, which proposes that children are a means of grace, is written by an educator with a special interest in the spiritual development of children. The historical treatment is necessary, however, to uncover the *de facto* doctrine of children that shapes us so we can become more conscious of its limitations to move beyond it.

The proposal that children should be discussed in the context of the sacraments will be presented in this book's concluding chapter, chapter 9. The classical seven sacraments, which may be considered alternatively as important acts of ministry in various parts of the church, provide the struc-ture for a spiritual practice that recognizes children as a means of grace and may be of help to guide future discussions. A formal doctrinal statement about children will take time to develop, but the time to begin this work is now! The *de facto* doctrine of children that presently guides the church is in need of enrichment and refreshment.

The need for enrichment and refreshment is discussed in chapter 8. The *de facto* doctrine of children is an informal doctrine that holds an ambivalent, ambiguous, and indifferent view of children with a hint of grace. The limi-tations of this approach need to be carefully considered and made explicit because it paralyzes our best thinking about the meaning of children and how to care for them as well as what children have to teach adults. Much of what the church says and how it speaks about children today hurts children and undermines families, so this is not a trivial matter.

Despite the limitations of the informal doctrine, children continue to help move the church forward from generation to generation, providing potential for creativity in each age as well as continuity. If this were not true the church would no longer exist, so it is with graceful optimism and delight that we begin the story of the informal doctrine with some of the earliest of the church's theologians.

Introduction to the Period

When Jesus stood before scribes and elders in the high priest's house he was silent, like the child in the midst of the disciples. Peter was outside in the courtyard. He spoke but it was to deny three times that he knew Jesus.

This scene is in all three synoptic gospels (Matthew 26:59–64, Mark 14:55–62, and Luke 22:66–71) with some variations and raises the question about why Jesus refused to present a defence to the charge of blasphemy lodged against him. Was he God? In Matthew's account he broke his silence only to say, "You have said so." In Mark he simply said, "I am." In Luke he said, "You say that I am." Was this blasphemy? It did not really matter. The troublemaker would soon be taken care of, the court thought, and in the garden Peter heard the cock crow.

Why didn't Jesus defend himself? Perhaps, it was because, as Jesus said in Luke's account, "If I tell you, you will not believe; and if I question you, you will not answer." The reality was they had come to convict him so there was nothing he could say that would deter this. On the other hand, some of the theologians in the early church wondered what could be added by words to the testimony of his life. His actions spoke for themselves, as did those of the martyrs.

Origen was one of the theologians who pondered this question. In the beginning of his *Contra Celsum*, a book that argued against what the philosopher Celsus had said against the Christians, Origen even wondered if a verbal defense of the faith would weaken the testimony of Jesus' life (Evans 2007, 5). He decided to speak up because the philosophers might lead people away from the truth rather than toward it. We will have more to say about Origen in a moment.

There are at least three things that make this period very different from the church today. In the first place, the community was still working out what theology was and the nature of the church it served. Second, for three-fifths of this period Christians were under threat of persecution. Third, the Christians of the East and West were not formally divided. These three topics set the stage for discussing the six theologians selected to represent this period.

Emerging Theology

Today we refer back to the classical doctrines of the church. During this period these doctrines were being worked out. The place of children in the developing church was not given much formal thought except in terms of baptism because theology was largely embodied. The greatest advocacy for truth was when faithful Christians were martyred. In those days questions about the *meaning* of children were not central to the concerns of the community. Furthermore, moving children to the center of theology was impossible to think about because there was no systematic theology yet to have a "center"! The centering of the community was around Christ's presence, mediated directly in religious experiences or by the memories of those who had known him and the stories that were recounted, as well as by the growing number of texts.

What the community did discuss, however, was how to balance the authority of the oral tradition with the growing collection of texts, now beginning to be cited as an alternative means of revelation to the direct experience of God. The community was also forced to face the need for unity despite the healthy diversity that kept the movement creative and growing. Questions of unity had to be faced as both a practical and theological matter.

The expression of personal experiences of Christ and their interpretation needed to be balanced with what the community decided as a whole. The distinction between doctrine and theology began to be more clear and the relationship between theology and philosophy began to be worked out. A critical moment for this book was when the role of the sacraments began to be discussed. What were they and how should they be regulated as the church spread out across the Mediterranean world and beyond?

By the fourth century major decisions had been made about the content of the faith by the great councils. Once doctrines began to be established the theologians were guided by them but continued to think about them. This process has never stopped. The church is always reforming (*semper reformanda*), to borrow a watch-word from the Reformation.

Persecution and Privilege

Today the place of the church in our culture is largely one of indifference. During its early centuries, however, the extremes of persecution and privilege pertained. For about three of the first five centuries of the church the threat of persecution prevailed. Children saw family, friends, and respected leaders in the community choose to remain publicly Christian despite their death by martyrdom. This meant that people like Paul, Irenaeus, Origen, and countless others risked their lives when they called themselves Christians. By the time of Pelagius and Augustine, however, it was not only safe but often politically advantageous to be a Christian.

For children this meant that they lost their parents or were martyred with them. Tertullian (c. 150–155), the first major theologian to write in Latin, wrote two short books to his wife to advise her not to re-marry after his death. Children in general are a burden and distract from the life devoted to God, he argued, but more specifically one might be tempted to deny the faith for their sake when faced with martyrdom. Legends and a whole literature developed in the church that are full of poignant scenes, such as in the *Martyrdom of Perpetua and Felicity*, where mothers leave their children behind to die as martyrs. Others gave up their children to go on pilgrimages or to enter the monastic life. This literature has been surveyed by O. M. Bakke (Bakke 2005, 260–279).

The persecutions came about because the Romans merged religion and politics in a way that made the worship of the emperor the most important symbolic act of political unity. Christians often prayed for the emperor and supported the Roman government, but would not acknowledge that the emperor was God. When they were put in the intolerable position of having to make a sacrifice to the emperor many refused. They did not seek martyrdom, but if it came, it came. Martyrdom was a way to be like Christ, after all, and it formed a deep and powerful union with Christ because it demanded all one had to give: life itself. Martyrdom was also a kind of social responsibility to the community of Christians, because it gave hope and showed the community that being a Christian mattered. It was proof that God existed and was powerful. Such a choice for death to embody the truth was also supported by a long philosophical tradition, looking back to the death of Socrates in 399 BC.

Persecutions began early in the life of the church and they began in Rome. The local persecution of Nero in 64 may have contributed to the deaths of Peter and Paul, but it certainly killed many other Christians. They gave their lives away as a gift for truth during the early centuries of this period. Ignatius of Antioch was condemned toward the end of Trajan's rule in 117. He was taken to Rome, where he was thrown to the wild beasts. Seven of his letters are known to exist. One of them was to Polycarp, bishop of Smyrna, who was martyred in 156. Justin Martyr, as his name implies, was another Christian leader who was killed. He lived in Rome at various times and addressed his *Apology*, a formal defense of Christianity, in 153 to the Emperor Antonius Pius himself! It argued that the true God had been known before Christ but that the divine Logos was known best in him. This is why Christians worship Christ and not the emperor. They have not broken any other laws so they are not criminals. He was martyred anyway in Rome about 165.

When Irenaeus was a young man, sometime about 155 or 156, he saw and heard Polycarp at the "royal court" in Smyrna. Polycarp had actually known some of the apostles. His love of truth, his calm commitment, and his way of being a bishop had a great influence on the young Irenaeus. When Irenaeus moved to Celtic Gaul (now France) he became involved in the church there. In 177, while he was carrying an important letter to Rome, Pothinus, the old bishop of Lyons, died in prison. Despite the persecution in Lyons, Irenaeus returned to the city to succeed Pothinus as bishop. It is likely that he too was martyred some time later.

It is important to tell this part of the story, because today it is largely forgotten and because it explains the priorities of some of the early theologians whose writings may seem indifferent to children. What has gone unrecorded is how the children felt as they saw these leaders and family members standing as martyrs for the truth of Christianity. That communicated something to them that was vivid, frightening, and yet truthful. Some of them, as mentioned above, joined their parents in martyrdom.

It was the persecution of Septimus Severus in 202 in North Africa that took the life of Origen's father in Alexandria and drove Origen's teacher, Clement, from the city. In 222 there was an anti-Christian uprising in Rome during which Pope Callistus was killed. It was not until 250, however, that the first truly universal and systematic persecution began under Decius (249–251). As it swept through the empire, Origen was imprisoned and tortured. He died shortly after his release.

Valerian, who was emperor from 253–260, renewed the attacks on Christians in 257 and 258, but he was captured by the Persians in the East while on campaign. His son left the laws on the books but they were not actively enforced, so things became mostly quiet for Christians in the empire for about forty years until the persecution of Diocletian in 303.

Diocletian was of humble origin and a soldier. When he became emperor he proved to be a great administrator and reorganized the empire. The growing numbers of Christians meant that he either needed to include them politically, as Constantine would do later, or break their power, which he attempted to do. A series of edicts made life very difficult for Christians. They lost books and property and sometimes their lives, but it was Diocletian's fourth edict in 304 that made life very dangerous. They were forced to make sacrifices to the emperor. As in the days of Decius' systematic persecution, some fifty years before, many were once again martyrs but also many "lapsed" by denying the faith.

The tide against Christianity began to turn in April of 311 when toleration for Christians was engineered by Constantine. At the battle of the Milvian Bridge, which spanned the Tiber just north of Rome, Constantine carried the cross as his emblem into battle and defeated his rival for power. This enabled him to declare the so-called Edict of Milan in 313, which established freedom of religious observance for all. In addition he provided money for churches, made political appointments that included Christians, and took an active part in theological deliberations among the bishops until his death in 337. It was Constantine who ordered and paid for the Council of Nicea in 325, which began the series of definitive, general councils during that century. The empire's political establishment of Christianity culminated in 391 when Emperor Theodosius made Christianity the exclusive religion of the empire and banned all pagan ritual. The toleration of Constantine gave way and the violence that Rome had used against Christians was now used by Christians against pagans and unorthodox Christians.

The establishment of the Christian religion favored the growth of the bishops' power, but this was also enhanced by the decay of the empire's administration. The empire's decline left a power vacuum in some cities and even whole regions of the empire, which the bishops filled. The empire had reached its peak in geographical terms by the time of Trajan's death in 117, when it began to decline. Among the many Christian bishops who stepped into the political gaps left by the crumbling empire was Augustine, whom we will come to at the end of this chapter.

The Eastern and Western Church

Today the Eastern and Western churches are formally divided. During the early centuries of the church they were unified, although there was stress and strain caused by the different cultures and languages involved and, as always, the personal ambitions of bishops and cities. The relationship between Christians in the eastern, Greek-speaking and western, Latin-speaking parts of the Roman Empire during this period was relatively open. The theologians traveled back and forth, theologically and geographically, between East and West, on foot, by donkey, in carriages, and by ships, powered by oars and sails.

There may have been no formal division between the eastern and western church but cultural differences played a role in the way children were treated, although this had not yet hardened into theological positions and liturgical practice. In general children were more accepted and assumed as part of the church in the East and there was less concern about their original sin than in the West.

Examples of communication between East and West are many. The Greek-speaking church leader and theologian Justin Martyr lived at times in Rome and the Greek-speaking bishop and theologian Irenaeus lived in Celtic Gaul, which is now part of France. Latin-speaking theologians like Augustine lived in North Africa while other Latin-speaking theologians lived in Palestine, such as Jerome and Pelagius in their latter years. Both Greek-speaking and Latin-speaking bishops met in counsels together to give classical meaning to the fundamental nature of God, Christ, the church, humanity, the nature of salvation, and other fundamental matters during this period.

The last general council of Eastern and Western Churches, at least in the view of the Eastern Church, did not take place until almost three centuries after this period when the Seventh General Council met in Nicaea in modern day Turkey in 787. This is the city where Constantine had first called the bishops of East and West together in 325. The absolute separation politically took place in 1453, when Constantinople fell to the Islamic armies, which carried their flag all the way to Vienna, which was besieged in 1529.

When this period began Jesus was moving back and forth along the River Jordan, occasionally through Samaria, and most infrequently (if ever) along the sea route, where encounters with Roman soldiers made matters uncomfortable and sometimes dangerous. He encountered trouble in Jerusalem and was crucified, died, and was buried. Somehow he remained present to his disciples and others as the resurrected Christ, as he is present with us today, despite his death.

Paul was one of those to whom Jesus appeared after his death. This took place when Paul was traveling from Jerusalem to Damascus and this experience changed his life. He went from being a kind of "Jewish Hitler," seeking to stamp out the Followers of the Way, to becoming one of them himself. He carried the Christian message to the Mediterranean basin, including Athens and Rome. Others carried it beyond.

We began this story with Jesus and the children. It continues now with the earliest theologians. What did they think about children and what experience did they base their views on? We will begin to answer this question with a discussion of Paul.

Selected Theologians

The Apostle Paul (6 BCE–65 CE)
Children Are Less than Adults

Paul's presence was considered by himself and others to be an important way to convey apostolic authority and power. He had not known Jesus personally in Galilee or Jerusalem, but could mediate the presence of the living Christ because of what happened to him on the road to Damascus. This was conveyed in three ways. First, he traveled to the churches he founded and supported them by his presence. He also sent an apostolic emissary when he could not come personally. He also conveyed his presence by the text of letters, which were likely passed around and read aloud. He did not limit himself to passing on collections of sayings or telling stories about Jesus, but in addition presented his own thematic thinking about God and Christian living. How did he see children fitting into his theology and what did he base that on?

Paul's experience with children is not something of interest for most Pauline scholars. There is also almost no information to base any conclusion on. All we know of his childhood was that he grew up in Tarsus, a trading city on the coast of the Mediterranean Sea in what is now southwestern Turkey. He went to study Torah in Jerusalem, and later, after experiencing Christ on the road to Damascus, traveled mostly in the Greek-speaking world of commerce among the cities at the eastern end of the Mediterranean to advocate for the way of Christ. He was probably a Roman citizen and used his Roman name, Paul, when he traveled, rather than, Saul, his Jewish name. Finally he was taken to Rome as a prisoner and may have traveled on West to Roman Spain before his death in Rome, which tradition tells us was probably about the year 65. His letters to young churches, most of which he founded, contain some of the earliest theological writing in the church.

In his letters there are no revealing stories recorded by himself or by others about him with children. He is more famous for thinking that it is better to marry than "to burn," which is not a ringing endorsement of family life. Besides, he had little time for domesticity, even if he had been so inclined, because he was single-mindedly intent to travel to "the ends of the earth" to spread the good news of Christ. He was determined to run this race well, all the way to the end.

One of the most famous and important of Paul's writings is his hymn to love (1 Corinthians 13). This famous passage, read at most Christian weddings, is part of a letter written to encourage the Corinthians to be more mature and authentic in their love for each other and to grow up theologically. Paul wanted them to give up their "childish" ways.

There is an important difference between being "childlike," which Jesus counseled as the way to enter the kingdom, and being "childish," a trait that Paul wanted people to grow out of. Someone who is childish inappropriately acts like a child. An example is being irresponsible or when adults affect a sing-song voice and condescending manner to communicate with children. Someone who is childlike remains appropriate for an adult but can bring the gifts of children—such as wonder, playfulness, and creativity—to any situation.

When Paul's hymn to love is considered from the point of view of children it does not seem to appreciate that children are able to love without guile, hope without qualification, and be faithful. The brutal fact is that if children do not have these qualities they will fail to thrive and probably die! Faith, hope, and love are not limited to mature adults.

Paul gave voice to his culture when he spoke only occasionally about children, but what is most interesting is how different his opinion of children was from the tradition of Jesus' high view. Jesus counseled giving up "adultish" ways to become like children to enter the kingdom of God. Paul wanted them to become *more* adult.

Paul may never have heard or read the Jesus sayings and parables about children or the stories about his relationships with them that later found their way into the gospels, but we don't need to make excuses for Paul. He also was making a valid point. Children do, indeed, need to grow up and be more adult and the congregation in Corinth probably needed to do just that, but what is missing in his view of children was the paradox that while children need to grow up to be more adult, adults need to grow up to be more childlike. It is the loss of this intriguing paradox, which is present in what Jesus said, that set the Pauline course for the theology of children in the centuries that followed.

Paul was mostly concerned about the adults in the new churches he founded and that they come to understand what had happened to him on the road to Damascus. Being "in Christ" seemed to be the crux of the matter for him. In his letter to the Galatians he wrote: "There is neither Jew nor Greek, slave nor free, male nor female, for you are all one in Christ Jesus" (Galatians 3:28). This soaring affirmation, however, did not mention the polarity between children and adults. Was this because it was insignificant for him or merely unnoticed? Children were probably just taken for granted, as they were by most of his contemporaries. They were always around in families and along the roads, as he hurried on to the next missionary outpost.

Paul was certainly not against children, but they could not think like adults, which prevented them from acting like adults. What he missed was that the love he advocated (I Corinthians 13:4–7) does not include anything that a child cannot do, at least as we think about children today. In fact, they are likely to love more naturally than adults, who often develop an astonishing ability for duplicitous, loud talk about love that he critiqued as "a noisy gong or a clanging cymbal."

His first letter to the community at Corinth also included other references to children that have a negative ring to them. For example when Paul compared children and adults in terms of the spiritual versus the material, he used the child as an example of what is less spiritual (1 Corinthians 3:1). When he contrasted children and adults in terms of knowledge (1 Corinthians 13:11) the child was the example of less knowledge. He also said, "Brothers and sisters, do not be children in your thinking; rather be infants in evil, but in thinking be adults" (1 Corinthians 14:20). In this narrow context he appears to advocate for being innocent, a quality he calls attention to in infants, but puts that down as unrealistic because of the need for right thinking in adults to manage their life experience. His linking of life experience with evil and adult thinking with salvation is puzzling because he clearly understands that people, including himself, often do what they know is wrong and don't do what they know is right. This is also puzzling because the positive innocence of infants he notes here does not fit with his general view of human nature as sinful.

Paul, or his disciples, also mentioned children when reflecting on their relationship to the people in the church at Thessalonica, the capital of the Roman province of Macedonia. They could have "made demands as apostles of Christ," but instead they were gentle, "like a nurse tenderly caring for her own children" (1 Thessalonians 2:7). The assumption is that children are helpless and need care. This reduces the relationship with children to their dependency. The adult helps and the child is helpless. This is realistic but it also neglects children's abilities to wonder, to play and to be creative.

To the Galatians (4:3) he wrote that the pre-Christian period in a person's life should be compared to the present time with Christ, by saying that the heir takes full power and possession over his inheritance by adoption. Before this legal vesting, however, one is like a child, a slave to the elemental spirits of the universe.

Paul (or a follower) wrote to the church of Ephesus about unity in Christ by saying that "We must no longer be children, tossed to and fro and blown about by every wind of doctrine, by people's trickery, by their craftiness in deceitful scheming" (Ephesians 4:13–14). The congregation needed to grow up in order to "speak the truth in love" and grow into the head of the body, which is Christ. Again, childhood is something to grow out of on the way to a more positive adulthood.

Paul (or the Pauline tradition) also argued that fathers are to teach their children. This should be done without anger and children are to obey (Colossians 3:18–4:1). What is the basis for this obedience? It appears to be male authority. Where are faith, hope, and love in this kind of relationship? He does not say.

All of the passages referring to households need to be read in the context of the culture Paul lived in. A household not only included an extended family but slaves who helped run the home and the business usually attached to it. This complex of home and business needed strong leadership, which was centered in the father, although the mother and father each had their own spheres of responsibility. All the members of the household needed good organization and leadership for the household to be a success. The children's task was to do what they were told and carry out the jobs that they were assigned like everyone else after about the age of seven.

Given the way households were organized and run, Paul (or the Pauline tradition) could use the management of children as part of the criteria by which to measure good leaders in the church. In 1 Timothy 3:4 we find that a bishop must be able to "manage his own household well, keeping his children submissive and respectful in every way." Deacons were also to be able to "manage their children and their households well" (1 Timothy 3:12).

In a letter to Titus, Paul, or someone writing in his tradition, advocates for appointing elders in every town of Crete, where Titus was at the moment. They needed to be people, married only once, who have children who are believers (1:6). These passages about the qualifications of church leaders carry with them an implicit view of children that is limited to them being creatures to be managed, nothing more.

In summary we can say that Paul paid little mind to children except for noticing that they needed teaching and control. Obedience is the solution to their immaturity and no trait attributed to them was something that we would consider positive today or that Jesus valued children for. They do not even appear to have had, in Paul's view, the ability to trust, to hope, or to love. Paul had a low or at least a very narrow estimate of children. There was nothing they could teach adults except by way of a bad example.

Looking at Paul's theology through the narrow window of his view of children does not reduce the enormous scope and significance of his life and writings. It merely assesses what he wrote about children. Like the majority of theologians we will encounter in this story, there was little said about children and little experience of children to inform what was said. Most importantly, what was said seems to have little awareness of Jesus' high view of children.

With Paul, the Christian movement is seen shifting from its Jewish origins into the world of Hellenistic Greek thought. As other Greek-speakers carried the gospel into the Latin West the welcome was more dangerous than warm. Still, the community kept growing and leaders kept coming forth, such as Irenaeus, to whom we turn now.

Irenaeus (c.125–c.200)
Children Are Developing Creatures

When Irenaeus was a young man he lived in Smyrna, a Roman administrative city on the road between Ephesus and Pergamum. The city was by the sea about the coastal midpoint in what we now call Turkey. He met Polycarp there, the bishop who was later martyred. Polycarp had a profound influence on him. Eusebius, the ancient church historian, tells us that Polycarp had spoken with John face to face and with others who "were eye-witnesses of the word of life and all the words which he heard were in harmony with the scripture" (quoted in Osborn 2005, 172).

After a time Irenaeus left Asia Minor and moved to Rome. He then moved on to what today is called Lyons and is today the third largest city in France. In those days it was called Lugdunum and was a Roman administrative center. The Roman forum sat on a hill in this largely Greek-speaking trading community at the confluence of the Rhone and Saone rivers. In 177 Irenaeus left Lugdunum to travel to Rome with a letter for Eleutherus, bishop of Rome. His journey "for the peace of the church" is why he was away when Pothinus, bishop of Lyons, died in prison. Irenaeus took his place as bishop when he returned.

Nothing is known about Irenaeus' experience with children. He does not seem to have been married. The reason he is included in this brief history of children and the theologians is because his theology's main image is growth, which he said can be seen in children, wheat, and other parts of God's creation. Each flaw is really a happy fault (*felix culpa*), he argued, because it stimulates growth.

Osborn wrote concisely about the kind of growth that Irenaeus placed at the center of this theology:

⌐ The growth of man towards God is governed by the ideas
of childhood, testing and habituation: the infant Adam rises to
maturity (*dem* 12), engages in a contest which ends in fellowship with God, and is made accustomed to God throughout his
long pilgrimage. At the same time God is made accustomed to
man and declares his goodness at every stage (3.20.1). God is
not reluctant to share his goodness and guides his creature in a
way which is everywhere harmonious. (Osborn 2005, 198) ⌐

God did not abandon Adam and Eve when they lost their innocence.
God cared for them instead and showed them the way forward out of Eden
toward eternity. When they were filled with terror, Irenaeus tells us, God
replaced the rough fig-leaves they used to cover their guilt with the soft-
ness of animal skins (Osborn 2005, 104, 219). The perfection in this theology is not at the beginning but at the end of time and was brought about
because God became human so humans can be like God.

Iraeneus was a seeker of truth, like the Greek philosophers, and in him
"Athens and Jerusalem meet at Patmos, as surely as the two great rivers
meet at Lyons and flow on as one stream. The transcendent realities of
the Athenian philosophy are transmuted by the prophets and patriarchs of
Jerusalem. Greek love of truth and beauty remains; but the Platonic scaf-
folding comes down" (Osborn 2005, 263). Iraeneus' theology combined
philosophy and scripture with his mystical vision, a vision like John experienced on the island of Patmos off the west coast of Asia Minor which
resulted in the Revelation to John, the last book in the Bible.

Iraeneus' vision of the final completion of God's creation also evoked
children to express it. God's artistry in the world "conveys a mystery because
on the one hand it is progress and growth (4.4.1; 4.9.3; 5.12.4), while on the
other hand it is a return to childhood (*dem* 46, 96) because God's word has
become a child like us (*coinfantiatum*) (4.38.2)" (Osborn 2005, 198–199).

In terms of our study, Iraeneus looks back to Jesus' high view of children and looks forward to nineteenth century theology and the Romantic
poets. The poets especially resonated with the idea of the culmination of
adulthood in a kind of mature and informed childhood state. An example
is Novalis (1772–1801), a German poet who thought that human beings
move from childhood to adulthood and then on to mature childhood. He
advocated for the ideal of the "true synthetic child" for humankind, which
is someone more clever and wiser than most adults yet also playful like a
child (Osborn 2005, 199, note 8). This is somewhat like the view expressed
by Hesse in his "A Bit of Theology" referred to in chapter 1.

A final link between children and Irenaeus' theology returns us to the importance of martyrdom in the lives of the early Christians. Irenaeus talked about how martyrdom strengthens the children when they see adult leaders make this gift of their lives. Martyrdom sends God's power back to God, which is made visible in this sacrifice that children can understand. Furthermore, the growth of humankind is not possible without tribulation, he argued, and children can understand that as well in these moments of revelation, despite their fear and loss.

Irenaeus put the reality of martyrdom into a very physical metaphor. He quoted from the letters of Ignatius of Antioch, probably written during his journey toward his own martyrdom in Rome between 100 and 118. Ignatius wrote that he would be ground like fine flour for the feast of the king. He continued this thought and spoke of himself as "the grain of Christ, to be ground by the teeth of wild beasts and to become the pure bread of God (5.28.4)" (quoted in Osborn 2005, 242). Irenaeus was probably martyred in Lugdunum about 200.

Irenaeus was one of the first to use scripture alongside the oral tradition with equal respect. He used two criteria to test the truth of his work (Osborn 2005, 122). Is it logically coherent? Is it aesthetically harmonious?

We turn now to Origen, who was also deeply interested in texts. He was born in Egypt when Irenaeus was about sixty years old and still the bishop of Lyons with about fifteen years yet to live. His indirect view of children, as seen in the central metaphor of his theology, was a very positive one.

Origen (186–251)
Children Are Symbolic of Something Else

Origen was born into a Christian family, despite his Egyptian name, which means "Son of Horus" in Greek (Crouzel 1989, 4, note 11). He was the oldest of seven children and grew up in Alexandria, one of the most cultured cities in the Roman Empire. His father was martyred when he was about seventeen years old and Origen prepared for martyrdom all the rest of his life. He was a serious Christian in a time of persecution, so he got rid of his secular books as a distraction to the holy life and, following Matthew 19:12, probably castrated himself or had a physician perform the operation, as was sometimes done during his time. This cut him off from ever fathering children (Crouzel 1989, 9, especially footnote 32) although some, such as Rowan Williams, have said this part of his history is "highly suspect" (Williams 2004, 133). What is certain is that in his later years Origen interpreted Jesus' admonition to become a eunuch "for the sake of the kingdom of heaven" in a less literal way. He also changed his mind about owning books and assembled one of the most extensive libraries in the Christian world.

Origen was a complex human being rather than a plaster saint. He was about equal parts a philosopher, an interpreter of scripture, and a master of the spiritual life. This interpretation was originally advanced by Jean Danielou just after the Second World War (Danielou 1955, ix) and will structure this vignette of Origen and his thoughts about children.

Origen continued the process of integrating Greek philosophy with Christian theology to make it more palatable and plausible to pagan critics. He argued for a fall of the soul before creation, which accounted for the human longing to return to God and the presence of evil in the world. Children were not interesting to him as a philosopher since they were not yet challenged by sexual passions, the danger of misused reason, the longing to return to God, or a corrupted will. They were almost a null category for him, which he thought of as a kind of purity. This purity, however, did not equip children to move beyond the transitory, physical aspect of the world they were involved in. Origen wanted children to become involved in the world of ideas that lay beyond this transitory world. That took, he argued, adult thought and discipline.

Origen was also an interpreter of scripture. He was famous for his *Hexapla*, a work, usually in six columns, which compared the language of the Hebrew Testament with a Greek transliteration, using the Greek alphabet as a guide to pronunciation, and four Greek translations in parallel.

He made careful, literal interpretations of scripture, but also found important symbolic meanings. For example, in his *Commentary on Matthew* Origen argued that becoming like a child is like when Jesus put his own body to death. This spiritual maturity as the nullification of the body is like a "little child who has not tasted sensual pleasures and has had no conception of the impulses of manhood." He went on to write, "the same might also be said in regard to the rest of the affections and infirmities and sicknesses of the soul, into which it is not the nature of little children to fall, who have not yet fully attained to the possession of reason" (Menzies, 1965, 484). When Origen defines the child in terms of what he or she does not have—sensuality, sexuality, reason, and will—he defined away the adult powers that can get them into trouble, but he also defined away the tools that children might use to find their way home to God.

The above interpretation was "too simple," however, according to Origen, so he added another level of interpretation: "whether as dogma, or for the sake of exercise, so to speak, let us also inquire what was the little child who was called by Jesus and set in the midst of the disciples"

(Menzies, 1965, 485). The child is actually the Holy Spirit, he argued, "set in the midst of the reason of the disciples of Jesus." To receive such a child is to receive the Holy Spirit, Jesus, and God, since all three are inseparable. Children were symbolic of the Holy Spirit, so he valued them for that characteristic rather than their own unique existence.

Finally, Origen was a master of the spiritual life. His attitude toward *real* children seemed to follow the negative Jesus tradition. They got in the way of an adult's struggle to return to God. In *An Exhortation to Martyrdom* he wrote, "And you, Ambrose, who have a wife and children, brothers and sisters, remember the saying, 'If anyone comes to me and does not hate his own father and mother and wife and children and fathers and sisters . . . he cannot be my disciple" (Origen 1979, 69). He went on to remind the reader that "it is not the children of the flesh who are the children of God (Romans 9:8)," because such earthly ties impede the soul's return to God by martyrdom or other means. As a Platonist, it seems to me, he followed the aphorism that the only way to know God is for like (the Image of God) to know like (God). The return to God required a rigorous attempt, drawing on all the capacity of reason and self-discipline of the adult, to first uncover the *Imago Dei* and then be guided by it to become God-like.

Children, then, were also considered to be a symbol of the uncomplicated and pure state that adults need to move to from their corrupted state so that they can be with God. Real children were a hindrance to the holy life of adults, but they did have some usefulness. It was mainly as a symbol for the Holy Spirit, which was important because it is by the power of the Holy Spirit that one moves forward toward perfection to be with God. Children then are instrumental as symbols for adults to find their way back to the kingdom of God, which is somewhat like what Jesus said in a parabolic rather than a philosophical way.

About a century after the death of Origen, Chrysostom, another Greek-speaking theologian, was born. During the century between the death of Origen and the birth of Chrysostom the church had gone from being persecuted to being established and important politically. The church's first imperial benefactor was Constantine, who died in 337, about a decade before Chrysostom's birth.

One of the many enormous changes that Constantine presided over was the splitting of the empire into two administrative parts, East and West. The capitol of the East was the "New Rome," Constantinople, named after its founder. The division of the empire into Greek-speaking and Latin-speaking parts for administration also contributed to the division of the church into similar parts. The church was still one when Chrysostom was born but the differences in language, culture, and theology made future unity unlikely and present co-existence problematic. This was evident during the great church councils that Constantine began at Nicea in 325, which hammered out key Christian doctrines during the fourth century and were roughly contemporary to Chrysostom's lifetime. We turn now to his view of children and the experience it was based on.

John Chrysostom (c.349–407)
Children Are Like Wax for Forming Proto-monks

John Chrysostom was an ascetic, preacher, and bishop. The name "Chrysostom" (Goldenmouth) was applied to him in the fifth century (Kelly 1995, 4, note 11). This reputation was founded on the quantity and quality of his many surviving sermons.

He was born into an upper class family in Antioch, along the seacoast of what is today known as Syria. His father died soon after his birth, leaving his wife, then about twenty years old, to raise John alone. Like many Christian women of independent means, she chose not to re-marry. John was trained in Greek rhetoric and literature, probably at the school of Libanius, a well-known pagan and professional orator. He was baptized on Easter Sunday, probably in 368, when he was about nineteen years old.

About 371 an effort was made by the church in Antioch to have him ordained. He refused. This made his friend Basil and those promoting him for ordination angry. Basil had even relied on John's promise that they would be ordained together. About a decade later he wrote that he had refused because he felt unworthy. In any case for this reason and the lure of the ascetic life he decided to retire to a semi-communal, monastic life for about four years, probably living in the barren cliffs of lime and chalk on Mt. Silpios near Antioch. He then withdrew further into a cave alone for two more years, mostly standing and seldom sleeping, during which time he is said to have memorized the newly canonized Christian scriptures. His health finally broke down completely and he returned to Antioch (Kelly 1995, 26–35).

Soon after returning to the city, he wrote several works including *Against the Enemies of Monasticism*, which defended monks against attacks by outraged, wealthy families whose sons had turned their backs on their family responsibilities to become monks. He argued that the city was full of corruption, so monks were the best teachers of young boys. Monastic training helped the young ascetics know God so they could return to their homes, like well-trained athletes, and reform their families and society. His harsh and uncompromising stand for monasticism was tempered by pastoral experience during the next decade by which time he would write again about families and the education of children.

Chrysostom was ordained priest in 386 when he was about thirty. In a fertile period from 387–397 he wrote two very important treatises. The first was *Concerning Priesthood*, which justified his refusal to be ordained some twenty years earlier and described the complexities and spiritual dangers of being a priest. The second was *On Vain Glory and How Parents Should Bring up Children*, which advocated for religious training at home primarily by the father rather than monastic training. Parents, he wrote, are like artists who paint on a blank canvas, sculptors who give shape to shapeless stone, or those who impress their seal on formless wax. They should not only teach their children the discipline of the ascetic life but also biblical stories so they can identify the lessons to be extracted from them. One should begin with tame stories and only later tell fearful ones. It was his view that the idea of hell should not be introduced until at least fifteen years of age.

The education of young girls was finally mentioned in the last paragraph of this long treatise. Kelly summarized this paragraph as follows: "Just as boys get excited by sex, so their sisters find pretty clothes and expensive jewelry irresistible; their mothers should keep these temptations well out of their way" (Kelly 1995, 86). Chrysostom was clearly more interested in and had more experience with the education of boys than girls.

John began to preach as soon as he was ordained priest and used an allegorical and typological approach to the Greek Bible. He emphasized practical applications for living the pure life and his many digressions were held together by his passion. A little over nine hundred sermons survive (Mayer and Allen 2000, 7). Henry Chadwick, author of *The Early Church*, wrote that John's writing and preaching was "the most readable and edifying" of all the church fathers (Chadwick 1967, 186).

Few children listened to his sermons, although he encouraged their attendance. His style was to "upbraid the offender and explain to him the error of his ways" (Mayer and Allen 2000, 39). He aroused tears, laughter, and scorn in his listeners, and he attacked Jews, games, the theater, and any frivolity of behavior or dress with righteous anger. This approach began in Antioch and continued in Constantinople, where he was taken secretly by Imperial order to be installed as bishop in 397.

John was bishop in the New Rome for about six years, usually in controversy with other bishops, the clergy of the region, visiting monks, the upper classes of the city, and the emperor's family, especially the empress.

The rest of the population, however, supported him, and the first time he was exiled by the emperor they rioted. The uproar was so significant that he was immediately recalled, but he was exiled for good in June of 404 (Kelly 1995, 282–285).

The questions prompted by evil in the world and its relation to baptism have involved theologians since the beginning of the church, but by the first half of the third century onward (and probably much earlier) children regularly received baptism and holy communion (Bakke 2005, 282). There is something faintly amusing yet touching about the debates that took place around Chrysostom's lifetime. Elizabeth A. Clark has written: "I doubt that at any time before or after the first three decades of the fifth century were a group of celibate men so concerned with babies. Whether 'babies-in-theory,' or flesh-and-blood babies, is difficult to judge: the passion with which they detail the sufferings and death of infants, their shrieks and wails upon receiving the baptismal water, might suggest the latter" (Clark 1991, 283). Chrysostom concluded that infants may have inherited physical death from Adam's fall but not sin. This was in contrast to Augustine's later view that the fall caused both original sin and mortality. Augustine's view set a new course for theology in the West, but Chrysostom and Eastern theologians in general had more confidence in the human ability to cooperate with God to create the holy life.

When Chrysostom was a young man he found that strict discipline helped his spirituality to mature. His retreat of some six years allowed him to advance toward becoming a priest with integrity. He therefore urged parents to provide the same discipline for their children that he had found so useful for himself. Perhaps he viewed his own childhood as if he had been like wax, imprinted by baptism, self-discipline, and God's grace. His Christian identity, like a seal, moved him with great urgency and generosity to want the same for as many children as possible, but this same urgency caused him to try to impose the life he found helpful for himself on others. Instead of urging the journey of discovery for others he dictated, sometimes with charm and other times with vitriol, the conclusions that he had arrived at for himself.

Pelagius (c. 350–c. 418)
Children Have Strengths for Spiritual Growth

There is no evidence that Pelagius spent much time with children. In fact nothing is known about his early years. He was not married, it appears, and was involved in the spiritual direction of adults rather than children. It is important to meet him, however, to know him as a person as much as possible—rather than as a vague, negative idea—because he helped sharpen the definition of the low view of children in theology by advocating for a high view of human nature.

Pelagius was born not long after 350. This was about the same year that Chrysostom was born (c. 349), but Pelagius entered this life at the other end of the known world in Britain and outlived Chrysostom by about a decade. Pelagius traveled to Rome when he was about thirty, and made his home there peacefully until he was about sixty, working as a spiritual director. Everyone, including St. Augustine, the vigorous opponent of his ideas, considered him to be a virtuous human being.

It is a striking coincidence that at around 383 Pelagius, Jerome, and Augustine might have all been in Rome at the same time. Chrysostom was ordained in Antioch just three years later. Augustine returned to North Africa in 388. When the Visigoths sacked Rome in 410, Chrysostom had already been dead three years and Pelagius was in North Africa or, perhaps, was already in Palestine to be with other Roman refugees. Jerome had been in Bethlehem since 386 and led a monastic community there, while continuing his studies and translations until his death in 420.

In 413 Pelagius wrote a letter to Demetrias, the teenage daughter of an illustrious Roman family. Her family too had fled Rome, so she took the veil from Bishop Aurelius of Carthage in North Africa. Her family requested two of the foremost masters of the spiritual life they knew to advise her. One was Pelagius (a trusted family friend) and the other was Jerome (the renowned ascetic) of Bethlehem (Kelly 1975, 312).

Pelagius wrote to Demetrias:

> ❧ When I have to discuss the principles of right conduct and the leading of a holy life, I usually begin by showing the strength and characteristics of human nature. By explaining what it can accomplish, I encourage the soul of my hearer to the different virtues. To call a person to something he considers impossible does him no good. Hope must serve as guide and companion if we are to set out on the way to virtue; otherwise, despair of success will kill every effort to acquire the impossible . . . . Once something has been shown possible, it ought to be accomplished. The first foundation to be laid for a pure and spiritual life, therefore, is that the virgin recognize her strengths. She will be able to exercise them well once she realizes she has them. (Burns 1981, 40–41) ❧

This sort of supportive and optimistic teaching outraged Jerome and Augustine because it assumed that human beings could participate in their own redemption. They held that redemption was totally dependent on God's grace. Jerome obliquely reminded Demetrias about this in his letter to her. He wrote that Pope Anastasius "had crushed the hissing sea-serpent, but rumour had it that its poisonous offshoots were still alive and active in certain quarters" (Kelly 1975, 313). This inferred that Pelagius' views were close to those of Origen, the "hissing sea-serpent," and should not be followed because they were heretical, which was only partly true.

Augustine had begun his attack on Pelagius by about 412 with his treatises *On the Spirit and the Letter* and *On the Merits and Remission of Sin and the Baptism of Infants*. This began a controversy that would last the rest of his life, even though Pelagius died about 418, some twelve years before Augustine. Roman aristocrats Melania and Pinianus, who were acquainted with Augustine, urged him to break off his campaign because they had met Pelagius in Palestine and found his doctrine and sincerity to be sound. Instead Augustine refuted Pelagius' letter to Demetrias sentence by sentence (Burns 1981, 61–108) and argued that original sin had so corrupted reason and the will that it was impossible to do what Pelagius counseled.

Augustine's "victory" over Pelagius was accomplished by his many anti-Pelagian treatises and church council diplomacy, which made the word "Pelagian" a convenient term of general abuse in the Christian church. Many outstanding theologians have, nevertheless, held a Pelagian or optimistic view about human nature and Rees has suggested that the following may be numbered among them: John Cassian in the fifth century; Erigenia in the ninth century; Alexander of Hales, Peter Abelard, Duns Scotus and Thomas Aquinas in the twelfth and thirteenth centuries; William of Ockham in the fourteenth century; Melanchthon, Arminius, and probably Erasmus in the sixteenth century; John Wesley in the eighteenth century; and Teilhard de Chardin in the twentieth century (Rees 1988, ix).

Rees also made the striking observation that while sermons may be anti-Pelagian, arguing for depravity and total dependence on God's grace, the church's pastoral care, prayers, and hymns are Pelagian, encouraging people to have hope, to make good ethical choices, and to use their willpower to live well, loving God and their neighbor. This is a good tension to acknowledge and celebrate, it seems to me, since both extreme views are wrong when they stand alone and both are right when they stand together.

Theology in the Greek East was not involved in this Latin controversy. Origen had made room in the East for the will and reason to guide the soul back to God, even though some had considered him a heretic. This more optimistic view was also assumed in Chrysostom's advocacy for the ascetic

training for children. He thought it would have an effect if it were begun
early enough. Gregory of Nyssa (c. 331/40–395) summed up this view in
his *Sermon on the Sixth Beatitude*, which may, perhaps, be considered to
speak for the Eastern Church:

> ◌ However, would the Lord really command us to do some-
> thing that is beyond our nature and issue a commandment
> whose enormity oversteps our human capacity? That is not pos-
> sible. He would not order naturally wingless creatures to become
> birds, or creatures fitted for life on dry land to live under water.
> If in all other cases his ordinances are adapted to the capacity of
> those who receive them, and he forces no one beyond nature, we
> may then conclude by logical inference that the reward which is
> offered in this beatitude ("Blessed are the pure in heart, for they
> shall see God.") is not beyond hope. (Burns 1981, 31) ◌

Pelagius was in more congenial company in the East, but this controversy continued to hound him and he probably died in the deserts of Egypt
in seclusion as a heretic. Perhaps, someone, wherever he died, was able to
overlook this and offer him the Holy Communion of *viaticum* to give him
spiritual food for his final journey. In the meantime his high view of human
nature had been largely overcome by the low view of Augustine to whom
we turn now.

Augustine (354–430)
Children Are Sinful without God's Grace

Augustine was seventy-five years old and dying in 430 when the Vandals
were at the gates of Hippo, where he had been bishop for thirty-five years.
The siege growled around him, as he stayed alone in his room with God and
copies of the Psalms of repentance placed on the walls to prepare him. In his
latter years he had been working on his *Reconsiderations* (*Retractationes*),
which must have meant a lot to him, because to review the contents of his
library, even excluding his letters and sermons, was not easy for an elderly
man. James J. O'Donnell notes, "Given the physical demands of ancient
reading—dealing with bulky, handwritten manuscripts—we must assume
both an intense interest on Augustine's part, not to say self-absorption,
and a heroic memory for what he had said and where he had said it"
(O'Donnell 2006, 318).

His *Reconsiderations* did two things. First, it made the identification
of his works easier and more certain in the Middle Ages and second, it
confirmed his identity as an author, the teacher and defender of the faith.

Some have suggested that his *Reconsiderations* be considered the second part of his autobiography (O'Donnell 2006, 317–319). The first part, found in his *Confessions*, was about what he left behind when he was ordained; the second part was about his life as a bishop. We will focus mostly on the first part of his autobiography to try to understand what his experience with children taught him to say about them when he was a bishop.

Augustine's experience of children was very different from that of Paul, Origen, Chrysostom, or Pelagius. He was married for approximately fifteen years (372–387) and a father. He was born in Thagaste, only about forty miles south of Hippo, where he later became bishop. He lived all but five years of his long life in this region of Roman North Africa and was the child of a devoted, Christian mother and a religiously indifferent father. He had a sister and two brothers and his father was baptized at his death in 370 (Clark 1984, 46), when Augustine was about sixteen.

He remembered in his *Confessions* that he was beaten and shamed as a boy. He also remembered stealing pears for no reason and later counted that as evidence of original sin. When he was seventeen he went to Carthage, the major city in the region, to complete his education in Latin literature and rhetoric. It was there that he was set on the philosophical path (the love of wisdom) by reading Cicero's *Hortensius*. He also joined the Manichaeans, who believed that good and evil were separate and opposing forces in the universe, and he was married.

Augustine and his unnamed wife lived together in "concubinage," which today would mean an unmarried relationship, such as with a mistress. In Augustine's world it meant something else. "Concubinage of this kind was a traditional feature of Roman life. Even the Catholic church was prepared to recognize it, provided that the couple remained faithful to one another" (Brown 1969, 62).

Augustine, his wife and son lived in Rome and then Milan from approximately 383–388. His mother, who had been tricked into staying behind in North Africa, joined them in Milan anyway and continued to work for her son's conversion and advancement. His wife was sent back to North Africa so he could marry a rich, young girl from a good family to establish his career as a teacher of rhetoric. Augustine complained that his wife was "torn away from my side because she was a hindrance to my marriage" (Augustine 1991, 109). He recorded nothing about *her* feelings or future except that she said she would never re-marry. She just disappeared. He also never married again, writing in the *Confessions* that "I was never a lover of marriage but a slave of lust" (Augustine 1991, 109).

The child of his marriage was named Adeodatus, a Gift of God, but

Augustine also referred to him as "my natural son begotten of my sin" in his *Confessions* when he described their preparation together for baptism. This ambivalence was also expressed later in the same book when he praised his son as a dialogue partner in his book *The Teacher*, like a proud father, and then wrote "For I contributed nothing to that boy other than sin" (Augustine 1991, 163–164).

In 387 Augustine and Adeodatus were baptized by Bishop Ambrose in Milan on Easter Sunday. That same year, when he was thirty-three and Adeodatus about fourteen, his son lost his mother, when she was sent back to Africa, and his grandmother, who died in Ostia, the seaport of Rome, as she was about to return to Africa herself. The question of the effect of silencing of Adeodatus' tears for his grandmother by his father has been examined by Donald Capps, who links the shame the father experienced as a child with the shaming of his son's grief (Capps 1995, 21–36). Augustine almost cried in public himself, referring to "something of the child in me," but was restrained by the silencing of Adeodatus. Later Augustine wept in private, remembering the tears his mother had shed for him, and as he said in his *Confessions* his "heart was healed." He did not mention how his son finally dealt with his grief, if at all (Augustine 1991, 174–176).

After staying in Rome for much of the next year Adeodatus and his father returned to North Africa, where Augustine hoped to set up a monastic community in Thagaste, probably on the property he had inherited. Adeodatus lived for about three more years and then died around the same age his father had been when he married. He, like his mother, disappeared textually except for being mentioned in the *Confessions* as a child and in *The Teacher* as a youth. The young man appears in the pages of *The Teacher* as a respectful and playful conversation partner with his father.

Augustine also learned about children apart from his family. Chadwick tells us that throughout his life Augustine studied infant behavior to better understand human nature (Chadwick1986, 68–69). He was fascinated by Job 14:4–5, which in the Greek *Septuagint* stated that no one is pure from sin before God, not even an infant of one day (*Confessions* (Augustine 1991, 9).

Babies may seem innocent, he thought, but the "feebleness of infant limbs is innocent, not the infant's mind" (Augustine 1991, 9). If the infant were stronger and had language then the child would show evidence of sin. Martha Ellen Stortz called this view of infancy "non-innocence," because the Latin word Augustine used was *in-nocens*, which literally means "not harming" (Stortz 2001, 82–83).

Augustine could not remember his own sin from infancy, although he did remember it from childhood, such as when he stole pears for no apparent reason. He filled in the gap in his earliest memories by making observations of infants around him, such as this one from the *Confessions*:

> I have personally watched and studied a jealous baby. He could not yet speak and, pale with jealousy and bitterness, glared at his brother sharing his mother's milk. Who is unaware of this fact of experience? Mothers and nurses claim to charm it away by their own private remedies. But it can hardly be innocence, when the source of milk is flowing richly and abundantly, not to endure a share going to one's blood brother, who is in profound need, dependent for life exclusively on that one food. (Augustine 1991, 9)

This dramatic story is to persuade the reader that children are born evil, so God—who is all-powerful, all-good, and all-knowing—cannot be considered to have created the evil in us. Neither could evil come from a competing force since that would imply the dualism of the Manichaeans, the heresy of his youth that he was eager to show he had left behind. Besides, if evil came from another source then it would limit God's power, knowledge, and goodness. Evil likewise does not come from the stars, as some had held, for the same reason. Neither did it originate in some sort of pre-creation event like the fall described by Origen and other Platonists. Evil came from Adam's disobedience in Eden, which all humankind has inherited. Augustine thought this inheritance was transmitted sexually, which was plausible in his day, but not necessary to his theory. Since evil is not created, what is it? It is a privation of goodness—like when a tree rots, a shirt is torn, a person becomes sick, or Adam disobeyed God.

Since all are infected with original sin, God chooses from among the equally undeserving to bestow grace on a few. This grace is irresistible but not coercive, a very fine distinction. It is not possible to know God's reasons for choosing some and damning others. It may not even be reasonable, such as when God chose Jacob (Israel) the Trickster, over his dutiful brother Esau. Even those chosen, however, find it impossible to live well without grace, because one cannot distinguish *caritas* (appropriately directed, self-giving love) from *cupiditas* (misplaced love such as loving money as an end in itself rather than as instrumental to *caritas*), so we remain restless until we rest in God, as Augustine is famous for praying.

Augustine had formulated something new. His interest in children, his reason, and his reading of Paul had framed children as utterly evil and predestined. This idea dominated the old bishop's later years until he died, but his low view of children still lives today. Still, one wonders what would have happened if Augustine had picked up the baby he reported observing and gently rocked the little one? What if he had patted the baby's back and the baby burped? Perhaps "the evil" he saw in the infant's "glaring" was caused by gas or some other discomfort. It is certainly clear today that the thought process he imputed to the infant was unlikely. Of course, we cannot hold him responsible for modern views of developmental psychology, but we can hold him responsible for his brilliant and sonorous distinction between *caritas* and *cupiditas*. What if a little *caritas* for the infant and the woman nursing the two babies had been shown? Would that have changed the course of theological thinking about children? His early view of human nature—as shown in *The Teacher*, *Christian Teaching*, and *Free Choice of the Will*, a book Pelagius and the Pelagians had quoted over the years in support of their doctrines (O'Donnell 2005, 318)—was not as set on the child's deformity by original sin as in his last years.

In Book 14 of his great work *On the Trinity*, he wrote, "Human nature is great, but because it is not the highest reality it could be corrupted; . . . nevertheless because it has a capacity for the highest reality and can partake in it, human nature remains great" (Augustine 1984, 336). He also wrote in a letter to Dardanus that children "possess" God before they "know" God. He summarized this idea by saying that "We affirm, therefore, that the Holy Spirit dwells in baptized children although they do not know this. They are unconscious of Him although He is in them . . . like a covered spark awaiting increased age to be enkindled" (Augustine 1984, 416). There are many sides to Augustine.

He was a bishop for thirty-five years, which meant that he presided at the daily liturgy and preached several times a week. Some eight hundred sermons survive. He taught converts and provided spiritual direction in person and by letters, of which some 218 still exist. He administered the diocesan real estate and acted as judge in the bishop's court. He did all this while struggling against the Manichees (387–400), the Donatists (400–412), the Pelagians (412–430) and always the pagans. In addition he remained a contemplative and a writer, which nourished his other activities.

In a sermon on Psalm 121 he wrote, "A soul tied by an earthly love has, as it were, birdlime on its wings and cannot fly. Once purified of the course affections of this world, extending, as it were, its pair of wings and freeing them from every weight, it flies with them, that is, with the two commandments of the love of God and the love of neighbor (following Matthew 22:40). But where, however, does it direct its flight if not toward

God, since it rises by loving" (Augustine 1984, 231)? This is what he most aspired to for himself and for others, as he lived and died a bishop, caring for souls and defending the church.

Conclusion

We have looked at six theologians during this first period of the church. They share a low to medium view of children's value. Paul usually referred to children as bad examples of mature thinking and spirituality, so they need to be well brought up in the Lord and church leaders should be rated in part by how they manage their children. Irenaeus had little to say about real children, but since his thinking focused on growth and since children were one of his central metaphors for growth, children play an important but indirect role in his theology. In this sense he had a symbolic view of children. Chrysostom was also interested in the growth of children and focused on what and how to teach them virtue and discipline. If one begins early enough and if one is assiduous enough, then children will grow up to be worthy Christians. He had a low but optimistic view. Pelagius also had nothing to say about young children, but he thought that human beings in general could participate in their own spiritual growth. This challenged and helped clarify Augustine's theory of original sin. It is ironic that Augustine, the only person in this group who had actually lived in a family with a child, was so pessimistic about them. He advocated tirelessly in his old age for children coming into the world helplessly and permanently infected with original sin except for those whom God chose to save.

Irenaeus and Pelagius are more optimistic about growth than Paul, Origen, or Chrysostom while Augustine is consistently pessimistic except for the in-breaking of God's grace. This view rubs against some of his writings. In *The Teacher*, for example, he implies that good teaching can make a difference, but why bother in his predestined world? The saved are saved and the unsaved are doomed.

There is some ambiguity in the way this group thought about children. Irenaeus and Pelagius used the term "children" only in a vague way, limited at best to illustrations. Origen explicitly noted his symbolic usage of the term in his exegesis of Matthew where "child" is a symbol for the Holy Spirit. Augustine wrote about his own childhood and made observations of real infants. This was employed by rhetorical skill, sometimes achieving real beauty, to convince the reader about his view of original sin. Apparently he felt that he had been beyond saving so he was astonished that God had redeemed him anyway. He wanted people to know that was possible.

Indifference was shown by all of these theologians. Only a very small part of their complete works was devoted to children. Chrysostom probably wrote the most about children because of his interest in their education. Pelagius wrote nothing about children and Irenaeus barely mentions them except in metaphor. Augustine's tremendous literary output makes the *Confessions* and *The Teacher*, classics that they are, only a small portion of his whole corpus of some five million words in Latin. It could not have occurred to any of these theologians to write a theology of children, because they were too occupied with other things, including the invention of theology itself.

Obviously all of the theologians in this chapter are men. This has been mentioned before but it will be mentioned once more. Men and women, mothers and fathers, grandmothers and grandfathers all need a voice in this story, but most of these voices are not there. The experience base for writing a theology of children is very shallow during this period and will continue to be shallow until the sixteenth century, when Protestant clergy began to marry. It was then that some theologians began to know children directly in their own homes.

Today change about the voices involved and the experience base for a theology of childhood is taking place before our very eyes! In the contemporary discussion, as reviewed in chapter 7, there are mothers, fathers, grandfathers, grandmothers, and even a great-grandfather involved.

Finally, grace is evident during these first and uncertain centuries of the church. This is clear because the church continued! Whatever theologians said or did, children found ways to extend the church into future generations. God must have been gracefully present in the families and church that nourished these children so they could carry the church forward into the Middle Ages to which we turn now, focusing on the Latin West.

CHAPTER

3

LATIN THEOLOGY
AND THE SCHOOLS:
500–1500

During the Middle Ages the image of children was subsumed into the portrayal of Christ as a child. In this painting the infant is presented to the viewers by Mary. The founders of the Franciscan and Dominican friars are standing alongside Mary's throne, perhaps contemplating the Mother and Child, but they are not looking at them. The only figure looking at the child is the angel on the upper left. Mary is dressed in black, perhaps anticipating the death of her son, as she holds the infant crowned with light. Each of the three males has a golden nimbus, while Mary does not.

The child is looking to the viewer's left and is turned that way as he sits on his mother's knee. His blessing is in that direction as well. His face is not that of a baby. It is of an undetermined age since, after all, he is the Logos, who was with God at the beginning. Nothing was made without him (John 1:1–5). The intimacy and warmth of the lamb, carried on the Good Shepherd's shoulders, has become the Logos to be adored from a distance.

◄ *Madonna Enthroned with Child, St. Francis, St. Domenic and two Angels,* Cimabue (1340–1302)
Galleria degli Uffizi, Florence

T his chapter covers a thousand years. That is almost half the entire story, but this period saw little theological thought about children. There was, of course, nothing "middle" about the Middle Ages to the people who lived then. They were concerned about having enough food to keep from starving before spring. They hoped for good weather so the roads could be used and their crops would grow. Prayers were offered to save them from the plagues. They made their way in the dark with candles and cooked on an open hearth. Marauding bands were a threat and a passing army or waves of pilgrims a disaster. There was always the grim danger of childbirth with the loss of so many mothers and infants. Most people worked the land and the families had about five to eight children, though about half died by age five. Still, the children kept coming to carry the age and church forward. With life expectancy hovering around forty years or less, the church was about half what we today would call children and youth.

Four theologians have been selected from this period to be consulted about children. They are Anselm, Abelard, Thomas Aquinas, and Nicholas of Cusa. They lived from the eleventh to the fifteenth centuries, which is the last half of the period, but they come from traditions that were forming when the age began. Anselm was a Benedictine monk. Abelard was a teacher, who for a tumultuous time directed the cathedral school in Paris, and was later a monk. Thomas was a Dominican friar and university teacher, mostly in Paris, Rome, and Naples. Nicholas was a priest, a bishop in Germany, and finally a cardinal in Rome. None of these theologians came into daily contact with children. The idea of children no doubt stayed on the periphery of their thinking, if they thought about them at all. This was an age of theological indifference toward children, but this lack of awareness does not tell the whole story, as we shall see.

Introduction to the Period

Some context is needed for our four theologians, so we will sketch in the church traditions they came from, the part children played in the church's crusades, and the church's involvement in education to set the stage. We turn first then to the introductory themes of the church, the crusades, and the schools.

The Church

The year 476 marks the traditional date for the "Fall of the Roman Empire." The last Roman emperor was Romulus Augustus (475–476). He was deposed by Odoacer, who in turn was driven out of the region to restore imperial control by a huge army led by Theodoric. Theodoric the Great (493–526) was king of the Ostrogoths, a Germanic (Gothic) people from the northeast of today's Italy. He had been raised as a hostage in the court of Emperor Zeno at Constantinople. Still, he adopted some traditions of ancient Rome, but made his capital at Ravenna, which had been declared the capitol of the Roman West in 401 by Eastern rulers. This city on the eastern coast of the Italian boot was filled with the sensibilities, domes and mosaics of the East, as well as Theodoric's own mausoleum. It is also where Dante lived his last two years and died in 1321.

During Theodoric's rule the rather chaotic ascetic tradition in the Western Church was reformed by Benedict of Nursia (c. 480–c. 547). About 500 he became a hermit in a mountain cave east of Rome at Subiaco. By the traditional date of 529 he had founded his monastery on a hill, Monte Cassino, about halfway between Rome and Naples. That is where he died, but his Rule has continued to guide monks—who prayed, worked, and studied together in permanent, self-contained, and self-supporting communities—to the present day. These communities slowly grew into islands of art, order, thought, work, and prayer in the turmoil of the Middle Ages. By the time that Charlemagne was crowned Holy Roman Emperor at St. Peter's in Rome in 800 the Benedictine communities had spread across Europe and England. During the eleventh, twelfth, and thirteenth centuries these monks and nuns had became the wealthiest, most venerated, and most learned part of the church. This was the tradition that shaped Anselm.

Christians participated in the government of Theodoric. The most famous and learned of these was Boethius (c.480–524), born about the same time as Benedict. He was concerned that leaders in the Western Empire were no longer bilingual in Greek and Latin, so he set out to translate important Greek works into Latin and carried on other writing projects alongside his administrative tasks.

Boethius was also concerned about the unity of the Eastern and Western churches. The papacy in Rome was not yet strong, so he worked, as a lay person, to keep the two sides in good communication. The aging and disillusioned Theodoric, an Arian Christian, suspected him of betrayal and interpreted these efforts as treason. While Benedict prayed in the solitude of a monastic cell, Boethius found himself in a jail cell.

As Boethius awaited his execution in Pavia, a short distance south of Milan, he meditated on his death. His symbolic dialogue partner was a woman, Philosophy herself! She sent away all kinds of medicine except for reason and guided Boethius, as recorded in his *The Consolation of Philosophy*, toward the love that heals and holds together the universe: "If Love who rules the sky/ could rule your hearts as well" (Boethius 1999, 46). This is a theme that Dante (1265–1321) picked up almost eight hundred years later as his *Commedia* drew to a close. In the last lines of the *Paradiso*, as the poet's "power failed the lofty phantasy," Dante's desire and will "were revolved, like a wheel that is evenly moved, by the Love which moves the sun and the other stars" (Dante 1975, 381).

Theodoric also executed Symmachus, another able Christian administrator, and the pope as well. The Roman state and the whole study of philosophy virtually disappeared after Theodoric until the Carolingian renaissance of the ninth century. Meanwhile the *Consolation* survived. It was copied and read widely in German and French translations. Alfred the Great (849–899), king of Wessex, had it translated into English and Chaucer made a translation of it about 1380. Queen Elizabeth (1533–1603) also undertook its "Englishing."

Boethius had helped keep philosophy alive, which is the tradition that Abelard grew out of in the twelfth century. His love of reason expressed itself in the study of logic. Boethius' interest in the unity of the Eastern and Western churches also disappeared after Theoderic but like philosophy it also revived from time to time. In the fifteenth century Nicholas of Cusa was involved in discussions between the Eastern and Western churches.

The church in Rome survived Theoderic and began to grow stronger and more organized under Gregory the Great (c. 540–604), born almost twenty years after the death of Boethius. Like Boethius, he came from an old Roman family. His family had vast estates in Sicily and a home on the Caelian hill in Rome. Gregory gave away his inheritance to create monasteries and became a monk about 574.

Gregory the Great was probably trained as a lawyer and was made prefect, the chief administrator of the city of Rome, when he was a little over thirty. By this time, however, Rome had shrunk almost to a village, surrounded by mountainous ruins. In 590 the clergy and people of Rome declared him to be their pope. He had hoped to live the contemplative life, but as pope he brought financial responsibility and far-sighted organization to the land holdings and organization of the papacy. He also wrote prolifically in an age when the ability to read was dying out. In addition he reformed church music along the lines of what we now call "Gregorian chants." Gregory even expanded the church by sending out missionaries, as far away from Rome as the British Isles. Under his leadership the church moved forward through the continuing chaos of the empire's decline to renew its calling and identity. Gregory's reforms set the church on a course that was reinforced by Gregory VII in the eleventh century and prepared the way for the church culture in which Anselm, Abelard, Thomas, and Nicholas of Cusa, also known as Cusanus lived.

The decline of Rome's political power and culture continued in the West. By about 800 the Latin language had already ceased being used for general communication and was limited to use as the international language of scholars and the church. The church's influence also declined, but a reformation was begun again by the Cluniac Order, founded in Burgundy in 910. This new and highly centralized monastic order advocated widely for the church's reform, and in 1059 the College of Cardinals was founded to remove the election of the pope from the bickering families in central Italy and put it into the hands of leading churchmen. A member of the reforming party was Pope Gregory VII (Hildebrand).

Hildebrand (c. 1020–1085) was a diminutive (5' 4 ½" tall) and visually unimpressive person, but he had a powerful intellect, great firmness of will, and enormous courage. He worked hard to make his vision of the church a reality, because, as he argued, a church riddled with the same flaws that society has, can hardly reform it. He was one of the most interesting people in the Middle Ages and resolutely separated the clergy from the laity by requiring celibacy for the clergy and higher standards for their piety and education. He increased the political power and wealth of the church by centralizing church government and the influence of the pope. Church law was codified and he established a policy of papal authority over sovereigns. The reforms of Gregory VII were important in general but their focus also helps explain the theologians' indifference to children.

The Crusades

The crusades were the major economic, religious, and political events of the twelfth and thirteenth centuries. They began with the call to arms by the pope, Urban II, in 1095 during the synod in Clermont, in what today is eastern France. The shout, "God wills it," set the church on this course.

Jonathan Riley-Smith closed his important study of the crusades by arguing that the theology on which crusading rested passed out of currency in the late sixteenth and seventeenth centuries. The idea of holy war was replaced by the concept of the just war. This meant that violence came to be regarded by most theologians as no longer morally neutral but as something intrinsically evil. It could be justified only as the lesser of evils. Christ also ceased to be identified with a single political system so that by the eighteenth century it no longer seemed reasonable to regard crusades in any way except "with a mixture of sorrow and contempt" (Riley-Smith 1987, 255).

It is still hard, even from today's historical perspective, to define what a crusade was. Geoffrey Hindley's broad definition is, perhaps, the most helpful. The term refers to the various kinds of bloody religious violence over a thousand-year period. It began about 635–42, when the Arab armies conquered the Byzantine provinces from Egypt to Syria, and ended when the Catholic Spanish Armada sought in 1588 to convert Protestant England by arms (Hindley 2003, xv–xx). The crusade that is of particular interest for this book, however, took place in 1212 and had its origins in France and Germany. It was the crusade of children.

In May of 1212 a shepherd boy, Stephen, appeared at St. Denis in Paris and demanded to see King Philip. He had a letter from Jesus Christ, he said, to deliver to the king. The king received him and told him to go home, but Stephen, barely fifteen years old, preached his own crusade, and by the end of June perhaps tens of thousands of children, no one knows for sure how many, started walking south toward the coast at Marseille. The adult crusades had all failed, Stephen announced, because the adults lacked faith. The children's crusade, he preached, was completely faithful. They would rely on God to feed them and even to open the sea, as God did for Moses, so they could walk to Jerusalem. The sea did not open and those who survived mostly turned back and walked home. Some children, however, accepted the offer of free transportation in ships to the Holy Land. After the ships set sail, news slowly reached Marseille that the children had been sold as slaves.

In the same year (1212) a peasant boy in Germany, Nicholas, also called for a children's crusade. He led his company of young people through Germany and over the Alps. Their destination was Genoa, where the sea was to open for them as well. It did not. Most of the children remained in Genoa, unable to face the journey back over the snowy Alps. A few went on to Rome with Nicholas, their child leader, to see the pope. Nicholas III, who four years earlier had called for the Albigensian Crusade in Southern France (1208), told the children to go home and serve the church by becoming monks when they were older.

The vision of Stephen and Nicholas was extraordinary. It combined naïveté with tragedy for both the children who perished and the adults who allowed this to happen. These crusades still raise the question today about what it means to be a fool for Christ. How foolish can one be without balancing it with Christ's other warning to be as wise as serpents? Can children know the difference? Not many theologians, if any, asked such questions during this period.

The Schools

Anselm, Abelard, Thomas, and Nicholas of Cusa all benefited from and became teachers in the church's educational institutions. The rise of the cathedral schools was especially important. They existed along with the monasteries as places of education and grew into the great secular universities. The abbots and bishops had helped keep education alive in the Latin West by means of the cathedral schools after the barbarian migrations of the fifth century, despite the loss of many books and the inability of most to read. Some secular schools survived, especially in Italy and for a time in Gaul, but they disappeared in the sixth century.

The bishops' schools took in children about the age of seven until about the age of eighteen when the boys were asked to become priests. Choristers were also trained at choir schools to provide music for the cathedrals. It was not until the eleventh century that the towns began to support their own schools to teach boys reading, writing, and arithmetic because this was useful for business. These municipal schools began in Italy and spread all over Europe by the fourteenth century. Girls were usually educated at home to equip them for managing households.

One of the most famous cathedral schools was at Notre Dame in Paris, which gave birth to the University of Paris—chartered in 1200, some fifty years after Bologna, the first university in Europe. While Bologna concentrated on law, Paris seemed interested in everything and during the thirteenth and fourteenth centuries was the most famous university in Northern Europe. The University of Oxford apparently arose out of a migration of disenchanted students from Paris to England in 1167 due to disagreements about the price of books, clothing, and lodging. The University of Cambridge resulted from a similar migration from Oxford. "By 1500 there were seventy-seven universities in Latin Christendom" (Artz 1958, 316).

The rise of the cathedral schools and the universities alongside the monasteries developed two kinds of theology. This has been elaborated on by Emero Stiegman, following Jean Leclercq. These two kinds of theology differed in the way the sources were treated, the goal of scholarship, and the method (Stiegman 2001, 29–130).

The source of theological knowledge for both the cathedral schools and the monasteries was scripture and patristic manuscripts, but the goal for the monks was to use the texts for contemplation. Their method included singing them in their liturgical life and using them as an aid for an oral pastoral tradition to guide their lives. The schoolmen were much more interested in the texts themselves and their analysis. They developed a method of disputation to discover the truth in them. Scholastics sought to understand God while the monks sought God's presence. Sometimes these two goals were unified, as in the case of Anselm.

Neither group, however, had much experience with children and neither was inclined to discuss the meaning of children in their contemplation or study of texts. With these background themes in mind we can now turn to the four theologians: Anselm (1033–1109), Abelard (1079–1142), Thomas (1224–1274) and Cusanus (1401–1464). We begin with Anslem.

Selected Theologians

Anselm (1033–1109)
Children Are Gifts to the Monastery

Anselm was born in Aosta in 1033 on the Italian side of the Great St. Bernard Pass. After he became archbishop of Canterbury many years later he told Eadmer, an English monk of Canterbury who was his close companion and biographer, about a vision he had when he was a child. Anselm remembered climbing a mountain and coming into the presence of God in his court. God was alone with his steward. Everyone else was gathering in the harvest since it was autumn. God asked him in a friendly way who he was, where he came from, and why he had come. The boy Anslem answered as well as he could, then the steward was told to bring him bread and when he ate it he was refreshed (G. R. Evans 1989, 3).

When Anselm was fifteen he knew he wanted to become a monk, but the local abbot would not admit him without his father's consent. After his mother died, he and his father fought. Anselm renounced his patrimony, gathered his possessions, and in 1056 crossed the Alps by the Mont Cenis pass and walked into the Rhone valley. He then traveled across what is today France into Burgundy and finally arrived at the Abby of Bec in Normandy.

Anselm was about twenty-six when he arrived at Bec. He had been drawn there by the fame of Lanfranc's (?–1089) teaching and the external school of the monastery, over which he had presided as abbot for about twenty years. Anselm found what he had been looking for and became a monk in 1060. He was elected abbot in 1078 and by that time Lanfranc had moved to England, where he had been appointed Archbishop of Canterbury in 1070, following the Norman Conquest by William in 1066.

Until Anselm became abbot, a period of nearly twenty years after his arrival, his life was a peaceful balance of prayer, spiritual direction, teaching, and writing. His two great meditations on the nature of God were written during that time. The *Monologion* explored the theme of faith seeking understanding, while his *Proslogion* defined God as that which nothing greater can be conceived, which demonstrated by logical necessity that God exists, since the concept that God exists is greater than the idea that God does not. He worked out these ideas with his students.

His relationship with his students can be seen in part by the atmosphere that permeates his writings. He did not develop his ideas in public disputation, as was done in the schools and universities later in the Middle Ages. His approach was to have conversations with students to sharpen his thoughts, which were then used as a literary device (Southern 1990, 114). It is G. R. Evans's view that the "Master" and "Pupil" roles were collaborative, as they reflected together seeking the truth in this process (Evans 2001, 95) and that one can hear in his written dialogues "the echo of real queries put by the pupils" (Evans 1989, 39). This method was expressly defined in the first words of his *Monologion* as "talk among friends," an approach he never departed from by choice (Southern 1990, 118) These discussions with serious and respectful students in the abbey did not prepare him for the contentious disputation that was forced on him by Roscelin, a teacher of Abelard, who was apparently more interested in controversy than in truth (Evans 2001, 98).

Anselm followed Lanfranc to Canterbury and was consecrated archbishop himself in December of 1093. During the troubled time when Anselm was archbishop, he was sent into exile twice but continued to write and completed his third masterpiece, *Cur Deus Homo* (*Why the God-Man?*) from 1095–1098. In this treatise he "deduced the necessity of the Incarnation from the nature of God and the need to protect the rational beauty of the universe which He had created" (Southern 1990, 227). This masterpiece also had nothing to do with children.

It was during this time that Urban II made his call for the first crusade at Clermont in 1095. Clermont is also where Blaise Pascal was born in June of 1623. We shall meet him in chapter 5 and Anselm's work will appear again when Karl Barth is discussed in chapter 6.

As we said, there was nothing about children in any of Anselm's theological masterpieces, but he was concerned about them. Monks usually had little to do with children, but by this time the custom of "donating" children to monasteries was firmly established and the rearing of these children was a necessity that usually involved harsh treatment. Anselm's view of how to care for these children was unique for his time. Richard Southern, the distinguished Cambridge scholar, has written:

> On no issue was he more remote from his own age than in his opposition to the insensate brutality with which monastic teachers, no doubt imitating the rest of the world in this, treated the children under their care. His similes of the growing tree which requires freedom for growth rather than restraint, and of the goldsmith who works by gentle pressure and a discreet evocation of the desired shape, rather than by heavy hammer-blows, belong to a train of thought which only found full expression in the romantic theories of the nineteenth century. (Southern 1990, 446)

G.R. Evans, also a scholar of Anselm at Cambridge, has added:

> Anselm was a gentle if firm master in the spiritual life. One abbot complained to him that the boys in his house were incorrigible and perverse. The more they were beaten the worse they became. Anselm exclaimed that he was rearing men to be nothing but brutes. If a tree is planted and then confined on every side so that it has no room to grow, will it not become twisted and knotted? If these boys are hedged in with fear and deformed by constant blows they will grow twisted inside with resentful thoughts. Of course they reject the teaching which could help them grow. They must be formed with encouragement and the gentlest and most carefully judged of blows if any are needed, as a goldsmith would form a leaf of gold into a beautiful figure. The soul inexperienced in the love of God needs kindness, compassion, loving forbearance, so that it may grow strong enough to bear tribulation patiently and love those who hate it. Thus Anselm won the abbot to see his fault by reasoning and by illustration. (G. R. Evans 1989, 7)

In addition, Anselm always seemed to find time amid his writing projects, prayer, and administrative responsibilities to teach and inspire the young men who came to work under him. He was interested in the next generation even if he had little opportunity to work directly with young students.

Anselm was strict with the young people he mentored. He demanded obedience but thought that "the wax of youth was alone fit to take a new impression, being neither so soft as to lose, nor so hard as to repel, the imprint of the seal" (Southern 1990, 446).

Anselm was forty-six and already internationally famous for his writing and manner of life when Abelard was born in 1079. A new way of thinking was about to be born and Abelard was to contribute to it, but our main interest is about what he though about children and the experience he based that on.

Peter Abelard (1079–1142)
Children Are a Bother to the Serious Theologian

Abelard was born in Le Pallet, about eight miles to the east of Nantes in Brittany, which is now part of France. He was the first-born and had a sister and three brothers. His father was the lord of a castle, inherited from his mother's side of the family, but Abelard renounced his inheritance as the eldest son and became a wandering scholar, preferring "the weapons of dialectic" to the sword and axe of the knight. By the time he was in his early twenties he had made a name for himself as a teacher of logic and by age thirty-six (1115) he was master of the Cathedral School in Paris. This is where his life took an abrupt turn.

Among his students was a brilliant, young, and already famous scholar by the name of Heloise. Nothing is known about her parents, but she had grown up in the Abby of Argenteuil just northwest of Paris on the river Seine. She was the niece of Abelard's colleague, Fulbert, also a canon at the Cathedral of Notre Dame. Uncle Fulbert, who may have actually been Heloise's father, was furious when he discovered that Abelard was having an affair with her.

To avoid further conflict, Abelard sent Heloise from Paris to his extended family in Brittany, where she gave birth to the baby resulting from their liaison. The baby was called Astralabe, the name of a new instrument of medieval science used to understand and meditate on the heavens, usually spelled "astrolabe." This is a bit like naming a child "Telescope" in the time of Galileo in the seventeenth century or "Computer" today. There was something clever about the name, but one wonders how the child felt, as he grew older. His parents were almost always absent. They lived apart and far away. All he had was the name they gave him and it was of a thing instead of a person.

When Heloise returned to Paris after the baby was born she and Peter were "secretly" married though it was immediately known and

caused another scandal. By this time she was about eighteen and he
was about forty. Abelard sent Heloise away again, perhaps, to spare her
further scenes with Fulbert, since the husband and wife could not help
seeing each other. Their love seemed more painful and problematic after
marriage than before.

Heloise went to the convent at Argenteuil where she had spent
her childhood. Abelard visited her there and Betty Radice tells us they
made love in a corner of the convent refectory, the only place they could be
alone. She went on to say, "What he had in mind when he made her wear
a postulant's habit no one can know, unless it was to give greater protection from Fulbert, but it was a disastrous thing to do" Abelard and Heloise
2003, xxiii).

The situation grew worse. One night the agents of Fulbert woke
Abelard from his sleep and, as he wrote later, "cut off the parts of my body
whereby I had committed the wrong" (Abelard and Heloise 2003, 17).
By this time in history a eunuch had become an object of ridicule, lacking
any of the dubious honor it had held in Origen's time. The problem had
become so wide-spread by the Council of Nicea in 325 that the castrated
were barred from the clergy (Burge 2003, 149). The history of castration
and the kingdom of heaven is complicated, as Laura Engelstein's book
shows. It concerns the eighteenth century Skoptsy (the self-castrated) sect
in Russia, which continued into the twentieth century until it disappeared
during the Stalinist Terror (Engelstein 1999).

Abelard had taught in his ethics that intent was the most important
part of the ethical act. Heloise fully agreed with him. She wrote, "Wholly
guilty though I am, I am also, as you know, wholly innocent. It is not the
deed but the intention of the doer which makes the crime, and justice should
weigh not what was done but the spirit in which it is done" (Abelard and
Heloise 2003, 53). She never repented for her love, which she experienced
as pure in its intent.

The net result of these events was that Heloise became a nun and
abbess while Abelard became a monk. He was also an abbot for a short
time, but that was a disaster and he ultimately left the abbey to continue
his teaching. The general interest in his castration, however, did not disap-
pear and the link to Origen did not go unnoticed because Origen was read
by twelfth-century scholars in Latin translations. Abelard even took the
trouble to distinguish his case from that of Origen. He wrote:

> ↄ Yet Origen is seriously to be blamed because he sought a rem-
> edy for blame in punishment of his body. True, he has zeal for
> God, but an ill-informed zeal, and the charge of homicide can

be made against him for this self-mutilation. People think he
did this either at the suggestion of the devil or in grave error but,
in my case, through God's compassion, it was done by another's
hand. I do not incur blame, I escape it. (Abelard and Heloise
2003, 83) ↩

The questions of marriage and children for true philosophers and
theologians came up in the letters that passed between Abelard and
Heloise. Heloise, as Abelard wrote in a letter to a friend, put the question
like this:

> ↪ But apart from the hindrances to such philosophic study con-
> sider, she said, the true conditions for a dignified way of life.
> What harmony can there be between pupils and nursemaids,
> desks and cradles, books or tablets and distaffs, pen or stylus
> and spindles? Who can concentrate on thoughts of Scripture or
> philosophy and be able to endure babies crying, nurses soothing
> them with lullabies, and all the noisy coming and going of men
> and women about the house? Will he put up with the constant
> muddle and squalor that small children bring into the home?
> (Abelard and Heloise 2003, 14). ↩

Abelard was famous for his book *Yes and No* (*Sic et Non*), which provided no conclusions to a famous collection of 158 problems for students
of theology—only what the authorities had said, which often conflicted.
When it came to children, however, he and Heloise were clear (Gilson 1960,
20–36) Children are unthinkable for great philosophers, like the pagans
Theophrastus or Seneca, or for theologians, like Jerome or Paul, because it
takes one's full commitment without any distractions to think or pray without ceasing. Both Abelard and Heloise agreed on this (Gilson 1960, 20–36).

Abelard's teaching career ended when Bernard of Clairvaux
(1090–1153), one of the most powerful religious leaders of his age, succeeded
in having his works condemned at the Council of Sens in 1140. Abelard was
about sixty-one at the time and growing weary of conflict. It was then that
Peter the Venerable, Abbot of Cluny, received Abelard into his care at the end
of his life. He wrote to Pope Innocent II requesting that Abelard be allowed
to stay "so that no one's intervention shall be able to disturb or remove him
from the home the sparrow has reached or the nest the turtledove is so happy
to have found" (Abelard and Heloise 2003, 216). He died in 1142.

Heloise died in 1164 and she was buried with Abelard at the Paraclete,
where he had been buried twenty-two years earlier and where she had continued as abbess. In 1204 an anonymous writer wrote "when her dead body
was carried to the opened tomb, her husband, who had died long before

her, raised his arms to receive her, and so clasped her closely in his embrace (quoted in Burge 2003, 275). Their bodies were moved several times over the ensuing centuries until today they rest together once again in Paris, where it all began, in the cemetery Père Lachaise under an elegant stone canopy.

Neither had paid much notice to their child, who was raised by Abelard's extended family. Abelard wrote at least a draft, which survives, of a letter of advice to him, the "Song (or Poem) for Astralabe" *Carmen ad Astralabium*), when the boy was about seventeen. His mother also wrote on his behalf to Peter the Venerable to find a position for him after Abelard died, but there is little other mention recorded of him by his parents. Astralabe apparently became a monk and was finally the abbot of the Cistercian abbey of Hauterive from 1162–1165 in what is now the Swiss Canton of Fribourg (Burge 2003, 270).

The moving and perplexing story of Abelard and Heloise shows their antipathy toward children in general and their own child in particular. It was their love for each other and Abelard's vocation as a philosopher that mattered to them, not their child. Abelard and Heloise must be counted at least as strongly indifferent to children as we turn now to the next century and Thomas Aquinas.

Thomas Aquinas (1224–1274)
Children Have the Potential to Grow

During the High Middle Ages, 1000–1300, the population of Europe grew once again after having declined with Rome's fall. City life also thrived once more. To respond to this new situation the church authorized in the thirteenth century a new kind of monk. They were called friars. They traveled and lived in cities. The Franciscans and the Dominicans were the leaders in this movement and their work complemented that of the monks who were cloistered in the countryside, such as the Benedictines. Our focus here will be on the life of Thomas Aquinas, who was donated to the Benedictine abbey of Monte Casino as a child and then became a Dominican friar as an adolescent—traveling the rest of his life mostly between Naples, Paris, and Rome to study and teach theology.

Thomas was probably born in the family castle of Roccasecca (now in ruins) near Aquino midway between Rome and Naples, in about 1224. His family was large, wealthy, and established. He was the last of eleven children and the youngest of the four boys, so it was natural for him to be given as an oblate to the nearby Benedictine monastery, where his cousin was Abbot, when he was about five years old.

Roccasecca was in the kingdom of Naples, ruled by the Emperor Fredrick II who was opposed to Pope Gregory IX's political aspirations for the region. Monte Casino became a focus of imperial-papal rivalry and Fredrick's troops occupied the abbey in early 1239. It was about that time that Thomas was sent by his parents to study at the University of Naples that had been founded by Fredrick. Thomas probably lived in the Benedictine house there for a time, but by about age fourteen he had found the Dominican teachers to be the most interesting. They were teaching something new—the pagan, Greek philosopher Aristotle (384–322 BCE), the Islamic philosopher Averroes (1126–1198), and the Jewish rabbi Maimonides (1135–1204). These resources proved to be important for Thomas as he matured into a theologian.

The Dominican life appealed to Thomas, so he joined the Order sometime about 1242–1244. His family disapproved and resisted this, but he persisted and left home to study with Albert the Great in Paris and Cologne before returning to Paris in 1256 to begin his teaching at the university. He spent the rest of his life in study, prayer, teaching, and writing.

Like most medieval theologians, Thomas had little experience with children. The handbooks for confessors known as penitentials, used from about the sixth century to the twelfth century, never mentioned children before age seven as sinners needing pastoral care, so priests had no professional reason to be concerned with them.

A *summa* or summary was a standard genre for medieval writers to write about theology, law, and medicine from about the twelfth century. When Thomas wrote his *Summa theologiae* for seminarians, he knew they would not likely see children except when they baptized them as infants until they began to hear their confessions as a prelude to their first communion. Even within the monastery, contact with children was limited for the average monk to prevent abusive relationships from developing. There was also a tendency among theologians to rely on authoritative texts rather than actual experience, so even if one were interested in children there would be no need to be engaged with them personally. The authoritative texts were what mattered to interpret them properly.

Still, one wonders what monks remembered from their own early days in the monastery. Did they feel anger, even despair, at having been separated from their families? How did they cope with monastic child rearing that for the most part was cruel and brutal, only occasionally being more humane when people such as Anselm were involved?

When Thomas wrote about children, Augustine's doctrine of original sin cast a shadow across the page from eight hundred years before, but

Aristotle (384–322 BCE), who lived almost sixteen hundred years before, balanced this with a more optimistic view. Aristotle's books on matters from ethics to biology had been lost to the West for centuries, but they were kept alive by Islamic philosophers and were being translated into Latin from Greek and Arabic during Thomas' lifetime.

Thomas found ways to fit Aristotle's view of children as creatures full of uncultivated potential with scriptural advice about them, and Augustine's view of their fundamental evil, derived from Adam's fall. He did this by his interpretation of God's grace. Cristina L. H. Trania noted that "Thomas envisions grace as completing rather than correcting nature. Thus he tends to emphasize children's potential for spiritual growth with the aid of grace rather than, like Augustine, their incapacity for true devotion and virtue in the absence of grace" (Traina 2001, 106).

In *De malo* (*Concerning Evil*) Thomas argued in Question V, Article 3 that some have said that children who die without baptism suffer torment "from their privation of the vision of God" but others say they do not. Aquinas concluded, " But combining the two positions, we can hold a middle position" (Aquinas 2003, 240–241). The separated souls lack the supernatural knowledge that faith implants but they do not have a disordered will so one cannot grieve about what one never had. "It belongs to natural cognition that the soul knows that it is created for happiness, and that happiness consists of attainment of the perfect good." That perfect good is beyond natural cognition. "And so the children's souls do not know that they are deprived of such a good, and they accordingly do not grieve. But those souls possess without anguish what they have by natural knowledge" (Aquinas 2003, 241).

Brian Davies sums up:

> Aquinas takes people born in original sin simply to be people in need of grace—a need shared by their physical ancestor and consequently passed from him to them . . . . He also maintains that there can be no question of there being pains and suffering due to original sin on the part of those who inherit it and who die before making any choices. In writing on original sin, St. Augustine insists that babies who die before baptism suffer accordingly in hell—a view that St. Anselm also accepts. According to Aquinas, however, the fate of babies who die before baptism can only be assumed to be whatever counts as less than what is gained by those who choose to accept what God offers to people in Christ. And this, so he argues, need be anything but unpleasant. Quite the contrary. (Davies 2003, 49)

Original sin is essentially to be in need of what God is doing in Christ. This is why Thomas had an optimistic view of children's potential and their ability to receive grace to help shape their lives through an education in virtue.

Following Paul, Thomas also taught that children owe their parents obedience and that fathers were in charge of their households. At the same time he made some remarkable counter-cultural assertions as well. Perhaps they came from his struggle with his own family about becoming a Dominican. When children reach puberty, he argued, they can act against their parents' wishes in three cases: their donation to holy orders, their marriage, and if their parents advocate evil acts. These exceptions to Paul and the culture around him may seem to be commonplace today, but they were almost unthinkable in the thirteenth century, especially the idea that children could marry without their parent's permission. Arranged marriages were the basis for political and business agreements.

Thomas was in Paris during 1270 when attacks were renewed on the Dominicans and Franciscans. One charge was that they admitted "boys" to their orders. The Dominican constitution expressly forbade the reception of boys under the age of eighteen and a statute of Innocent IV required a year's probation and that no one could enter religious life until the age of fourteen, the commonly accepted age for puberty among boys. (Puberty was thought to take place at twelve among girls.) Weisheipl follows this controversy carefully and concluded, "Thomas defends the acceptance of boys before the age of puberty, because the things we learn in childhood are more firmly inculcated within us. Thomas undoubtedly had in mind his own experience at Monte Cassino where he had been an oblate" (Weisheipl 1974, 271).

As his life drew to a close, Thomas moved from Paris to Naples, where he was at work teaching and writing by 1273. On St. Nicholas' Day, 6 December 1273, something extraordinary happened to him while he was saying mass. Friar Reginald of Piperno (d. 1290) was with him. Reginald was his usual server during mass as well as his secretary and constant companion. He thought that Thomas had a mystical experience, but a more rigorous, biological view has been taken by Weisheipl, a fellow Dominican and leading Thomastic scholar today. His conclusion is that Thomas must have experienced a stroke or nervous breakdown.

When interpreting this experience much depends on whether Thomas could no longer write or whether he chose not to write. Assuming a choice, he may have realized that the whole edifice of his thought had been built on a false assumption or logical mistake, but he never said. We might conjecture that he realized that God's presence is all we need to know. This is a kind of knowledge that is as open to children as it is to learned theologians. There is much conjecture about this event, but all that is really known is that he never wrote again and said that his writing seemed like straw to him. He left his great *Summa* unfinished (Weisheipl 1974, 320–323) and died about three months later on the way to the Second Council of Lyons by the order of Pope Gregory X.

Thomas shared many of the common views of the Middle Ages about women, the heredity of slaves (who were sometimes thought of as if they were children), a narrow rationalism that did not fully integrate the emotions with the body, and the male dominated hierarchy in the family—all severe limitations from a modern point of view. He also had a low view of infants' abilities.

Perhaps, it was Thomas' great esteem for reason that caused him to take a low view of infants because of their irrationality and ignorance of life. Children were not models of spiritual perfection for Thomas. This view was in contrast to the popular medieval devotional traditions. The Cistercian cult of the Child Jesus, for example, honored simplicity as wisdom rather than ignorance. Trania has expanded on this by saying "Some mystics and visionaries of both sexes imagined themselves as infants nursing at the breast of Jesus or of Mary; in a fascinating twist, a number of nuns envisioned themselves suckling the infant Jesus" (Trania 2001, 128–129, cf especially note 105). Thomas was not enthusiastic about any of this.

Thomas, however, took a middle view when it came to children, but there is also a sense in which he was indifferent to them. When all the questions of his great *Summa Theologiae* are reviewed no major question was asked about children. Are they a means of grace? Do they reveal how to enter into spiritual maturity? Does welcoming them open one to God? Children enter into his theological thought process only in "scattered" places and in "oblique" ways, as Trania notes, which counts as one of the "deepest flaws in Thomas's teachings on children" (Trania 2001,132).

Thomas also did not comment in any extensive way about the interests and needs of children as a moral issue. He might have commented on the widespread abandonment of children in his time or discussed them generally as moral agents, although, as we said, he thought they should make their own decisions about entering religious orders, marrying, or obeying a commandment by a parent to do something immoral.

In summary, when we think of Thomas it is hard not to think of grace, for it is grace that for him completes the human being's natural gifts and

enables children to develop into people of mature spirituality in cooperation with their natural gifts. This view was unlike both the Pelagians and
the Augustinians, who seemed to want their human beings either self-
determined or defiled with no middle way, like the one Aquinas took.

In the next century famine, freezing weather, and the Black Plague
ravaged Europe and the population declined again. In the fifteenth
century there was a re-awakening of classical learning and a measure of
prosperity. It is in this century that we meet Nicholas of Cusa.

Nicholas of Cusa (1401–1464)
A Childlike Player with Words and Images

When I walk into the church *San Pietro in Vincoli* (St. Peter in Chains) in
Rome I walk down the center aisle to see the chains of St. Peter and then
turn to the right to look at Michelangelo's famous statue of Moses. Most
everyone does that. On the way out, however, I like to move to the right
and sit for a time by the place where Nicholas of Cusa was buried. If you
do that and find a top lying on his grave you will know that, perhaps, I have
just been there.

Why a top? Nicholas loved to play with images and paradoxes about
God. The top is both. God is like the spinning top, which is more at rest
the greater its motion. The name of the book in which the top metaphor
was used is also playful. It combines the verb "to be able," *posse*, and the
verb "to be," *esse*, to make the Latin neologism *possest*. Both words are
verbs because God is action but God is more. God is possibility (*posse*)
and specific actuality, which "is" (*est*) as the infinitive of *esse* also shows.
Other examples of Cusanus' playful theology may be found in the bowling
game with a wobbly ball he refers to in *De ludo globi (On the Ball Game)*.
There is also the beryl or transparent stone in *De beryllo*, and the quizzical
geometry of the Infinite Line and the Maximum in *De docta ingnorantia
(On Learned Ignorance)*.

Nicholas was named cardinal in 1448 by Pope Nicholas V and his titu-
lar church was *San Pietro in Vincoli*. That is why he was buried there, but
his heart was literally buried in Germany at Kues, where he was born, just
across the Mosel River from its twin village Bernkastel. This second grave
site is also in the floor but this time it is in the chapel of the St. Nikolaus
Hospital in Kues, which he funded for old men. There is also a triptych,
which includes a painting of Nicholas holding out his old, arthritic hands
in prayer. Most of his beloved and remarkable fifteenth-century library is
also housed there.

Nicholas studied at the University of Heidelberg and then went to the University of Padua to earn in 1423, what we might think of today, as a doctor's degree in canon law. He became a canon lawyer, a lecturer, active in councils, the pope's special envoy, and worked for the reconciliation of the Eastern and Western churches. When he was returning to Venice from Constantinople in 1437 he had an experience at sea, perhaps a visionary experience, which brings us to the question of Nicholas of Cusa and children. To explore this indirect theme in his work we will look at his *De docta ignorantia* (*On Learned Ignorance*) written in 1440 and *De apice theoriae* (*On the Summit of Contemplation*) written in 1464 just before he died.

The first book contains reflections on one of his most famous ideas, the coincidence of opposites. This is a kind of juxtaposition that children make and accept. They do not have the need that adults do to resolve opposites, to merge them, or to round them off in any way. The coincidence of opposites allows for the harmony of the opposites without losing their contrariety, which was the logical point Nicholas wanted to make about God.

He used another bit of childlike whimsey when he wrote about God as Maximum, which is both hidden and revealed. Seeking God is like a game of hide and seek. Cusanus understood this from his own longing and journey to know God in a personal way. He had sought God for decades and then was found by God during his experience at sea. God's presence is both unfolded (*explicata*) in the universe and enfolded (*complicata*), but this fact cannot be known, like knowing a specific tree and calling it by its generic name. The unfolding and enfolding of God in creation must be experienced nonverbally and personally, which is a kind of knowing children are quite comfortable with. In fact they trust their senses and the rest of their non-verbal communication system more than language. This sometimes gets them into trouble logically when compared to adults but other times it gets them out of trouble theologically.

Cusanus talks about access to learned ignorance not as learning something discrete and namable in ordinary language, but as being with God. Learned ignorance is neither ignorance nor knowledge but goes beyond both. It is being informed by wonder, by the act of contemplation, by a kind of receptivity—whatever one might call this ability—to know the mystery of God's presence. He gave the theme of wonder special attention in his work (Nicholas of Cusa 1997, 42–43, 48, 87, 223, 228, 253). This is also an ability clearly open to children, perhaps even more amply than to adults.

Nicholas loved to play with words. He attempted to catch his readers by surprise by his striking images and quirky language so they could be struck with wonder and move in spite of themselves toward becoming learnedly ignorant. Children do this naturally, but adults need to be caught off guard to wonder and he took special delight in stimulating this means of knowing God in his readers.

In 1497, the year of his death, Nicholas wrote *De apice theoriae* (*On the Summit of Contemplation*). H. Lawrence Bond summed up this work as being "no mere tinkering or fine tuning of terminology. For Cusa, this work is intended to complete, to finish, and to redirect his earlier speculations, although not to contradict them" (Nicholas of Cusa 1997, 70). How did he sum up? He began again to play with words.

Nicholas moved on from his conclusion in *De possest* to speak in his last book about how God is *Posse ipsum* (*Being Able Itself*). This raises the question for the reader that was asked by Peter of Erkelenz in the dialogue, "But since earlier you already said much about *Possest* and explained it in a trialogue, I wonder why this does not suffice?" (Nicholas of Cusa 1997, 294).

The answer in part given by the Cardinal in the dialogue was that "nothing can be more powerful or prior or better" for "that without which nothing whatsoever can be, or live" (Nicholas of Cusa 1997, 294). This new term, however, is even more difficult to translate. Bond finally decided to try "*Posse* Itself," a mixture of Latin and English for the purely Latin *Posse ipsum* that becomes awkward in English as "Can-Itself." He hoped to keep the "direct and fluid power of the verb" in this way (Nicholas of Cusa 1997, 332, note 20). The point is that all potentiality is in God and that implies that God's action and God's ability to act are the same. There is no need to add any words to "*Posse* Itself" when speaking of God.

Children are good at intuiting this naturally, Nicholas argues:

> ❧ What child or youth does not know *Posse* Itself since each says one can eat, one can run, or one can speak? Nor is there anyone with a mind who is so ignorant that one does not know, without a teacher, that nothing is unless it can be and that without *posse* nothing whatever can be or can have, can do or can undergo. What young boy or young girl, when asked if they could carry a stone and having answered that they could, when further asked if they could do this without *posse*, would deny it emphatically? For the youth would consider the question absurd and superfluous, as if no one of sane mind would have doubts about this, that anything could be made or become without *Posse* Itself. (Nicholas of Cusa 1997, 295) ❧

Children, like adults, can know the Creator by participating in the creative process of the universe as creatures. Near the end of the dialogue the Cardinal says:

    ℘ In activity or in making, the mind sees most certainly *Posse*
Itself appear in the *posse* to make of the maker, in the *posse* to
become of the makeable, and in the *posse* of the connection
of both. But there are not three *posses*, but rather one and the
same is the *posse* of the maker and of the makeable and of their
connection (Nicholas of Cusa 1997, 302–303). ℘

Cusanus does not like the term "trinity," so Bond translates what
Nicholas thinks might be a better word as "unitrine." This is because, as
Nicholas said, following Augustine, if you have to count, you don't know
what God is yet.

The whimsy of Nicholas' word play and the wonder it causes shows
that what he wants to convey is that to know God one must wonder and
when you do wonder, God's presence as Maker can be known by children
and adults alike.

Where then does Nicholas of Cusa fit into our categories of ambivalence, ambiguity, indifference, and grace? He says almost nothing about
children directly, but when he speaks of God to adults he invites them to
play as if they were children. He does not present a high view of children
directly, but his playful invitation suggests it indirectly. He bequeathed a
hospice for old men where they could be cared for, worship, and read in his
library, but he also left hints for everyone who will listen that being child-
like is a way to know God.

Conclusion

Anselm, Abelard, Thomas, and Cusanus worked out their theological
thoughts with young men. They did not meet children in their daily lives
so their writing did not naturally bring them into focus. They were also
part of a culture that saw children in a very different way than our own.

In 1962 Aries' *Centuries of Childhood* was published in English.
Historians immediately began to look for evidence to counter his assertion
that in the Middle Ages people did not have a concept of childhood. The
"discovery" of the idea of childhood as a transition period between infancy
and early adulthood, he argued, would have to wait until the fifteenth, sixteenth, and seventeenth centuries. Others argued that there was evidence
in the Middle Ages that there was a concept of childhood.

Texts about law in the Middle Ages treated children with special sensitivity to their restrictions and the training of monks also made allowances

for children's diet and need for rest at times. Medical texts usually included something about infant care. The Hippocratic tradition was still used and it divided children into three stages: *infantia* from birth to age seven, *pueritia* from seven to twelve for girls and seven to fourteen for boys, and *adolescentia* from twelve to twenty-one for girls and fourteen to twenty-one for boys. Still, most people could not read these texts, so for them pictures of swaddled babies and children playing were communicated by church windows, carvings, or when children were referred to in sermons. Pope Leo the Great, for example, preached in the fifth century that "Christ loved childhood, mistress of humility, rule of innocence, model of sweetness" (quoted in Heywood 2001, 15). Yes. There was an awareness of childhood in the Middle Ages.

Still, when children were portrayed they were usually seen as sinful or as saints. The little saints were seen as a *puer senex*, a child who already thought like an old man, which the paintings of Christ also depicted, as well as that Christ existed before the world as part of the Holy Trinity so was of an age that is really beyond our ability to comprehend or depict in any simple way.

What is most likely, it seems to me, is that what we think of as "childhood" did not exist. This seems obvious, because there were no experts on childhood like in our juvenile legal system. There were no pediatricians, child psychologists, early childhood educators or other specialists to define this period of development. Instead one went from being taken care of by mothers and nannies as infants to an apprenticeship for adult tasks as soon as ability and opportunity allowed. Working for one's father in the fields or for one's mother in the home was one avenue into adulthood. Two others were an apprenticeship as a knight or monk. The historian Doris Desclais Berkvam has observed that there may have been a concept of childhood in the Middle Ages but if there were it was "a consciousness of childhood so unlike our own that we do not recognize it" (quoted in Heywood 2001, 14). The indifference of the theologians may have been related to this more fluid and less formal view of children during their time as well as their general lack of theological interest.

Whether there was a concept of childhood in the Middle Ages or not, grace broke through in the undefined spaces of child development. One has to ask what prompted Boethius and Benedict to move in such different directions? Why did Gregory the Great give up his inheritance and become a monk and then give up the life of contemplation to become pope? Why did Gregory VII move into a life of service to the church? These are unanswerable questions except for the human experience that the theological term "grace" attempts to identify, express and communicate. By grace the church moved forward through people like these. In a time when theologians were indifferent to children, the children still found ways to carry the values and spirit of the church to a new generation.

Anselm was an Italian who walked across France to find his spiritual home at Bec. Abelard left home to be a scholar when he was born to be the lord of a castle. Thomas, an Italian, was given to the Benedictines to stay near home and as an adolescent became a Dominican friar who moved between Paris, Rome, and Naples teaching, studying, and writing. Nicholas was a German who died in Italy and was buried in Rome, even if his heart was buried in his German home. God laughs and plays.

Something graceful and unexpected happened again and again. Then in the sixteenth century grace danced in to keep the church creative and relevant once more. Protestant clergy married and become involved with young children in their own homes, when the pastors were willing. Our conversation now shifts in the next chapter to three theologians during the sixteenth century who were willing.

CHAPTER

4

A REFORMATION OF
THE EXPERIENCE BASE
FOR KNOWING CHILDREN:
1500–1600

In the sixteenth century real children came into view, both in this painting and in the homes of the Protestant theologians when they married. The children flow out of the green and natural setting in the painting's upper left to populate Bruegal's (c. 1524–1569) canvas with their play and games. By Edward Snow's count, forty-six games are represented (Snow 1997, 199).

The painting is organized in a large "X," which crosses near the center where two children, riding piggyback, are trying to pull each to the ground. This is the point where the conflicting forces in the painting also struggle with each other. The children can't return to their lush and verdant infancy but if they move up the narrowing and darkening street to the right they will be blocked at the end in a dismal play-less world. If they move along the

Children's Games, Peter Bruegal (1560) ▶
Kunsthistoriches Museum, Vienna, Austria
(Erich Lessing / Art Resource, NY,
Kunsthistorisches Museum, Vienna, Austria)

fence to the lower left they will continue to play but the adults there to guide them seem lost in children's games. When the eye moves to the lower right of the painting's visual logic, the children are playing at adult tasks, which may become the happy reality of true adult vocation, where play survives outside the painting's frame.

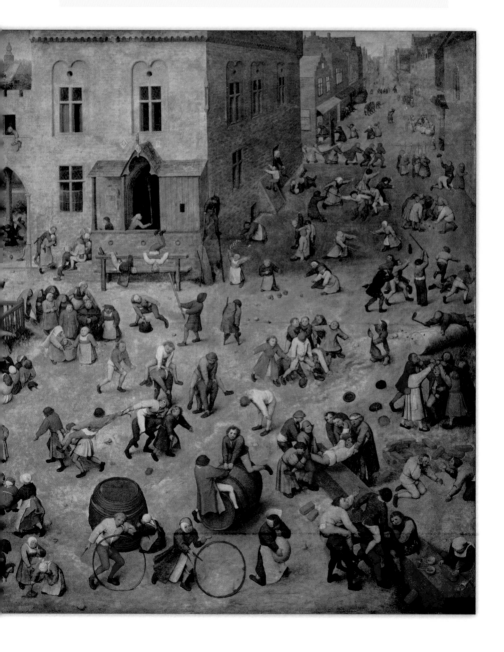

If you were to look at a map showing the religions of Europe in 1500 it would be all Roman Catholic. By 1600 the religion of Europe was divided into four major parts—Catholic, Lutheran, Calvinist Reformed, and Anglican. All of Spain, Portugal, and Italy remained Catholic. Much of France and eastern Europe did too. There were also pockets of Calvinist worship in France and Switzerland and of Calvinist and Lutheran worship in eastern Europe. All of Germany and Scandinavia had become Lutheran.

The situation off the coast of Europe in the British Isles was likewise greatly changed. The Church of England became Protestant instead of Catholic, but there were still areas of deep Catholic and Calvinist allegiance in the realm. Anglicans were mostly present in the middle and south of England, but this was mixed with Calvinist and Catholic areas of influence. The north of England was primarily Catholic. Ireland was also Catholic with small groups of Anglicans along the east coast. In Scotland there were Catholics and Calvinists with a few Anglicans living by the sea in the south.

Introduction to the Period

We will examine three Protestant reformers who lived during this century of enormous theological change—Martin Luther, John Calvin, and Richard Hooker—to see what they had to say about children. All three were married and had children or step-children, but their characters, languages, and cultural differences varied, as did their reactions to children in their lives and in their theological writing. These were contentious times among Christians, when differences were stressed, usually violently, more than commonality sought, so these three leaders went their own ways, despite their common reaction to Rome and experiencing children in their homes.

Limiting our focus to three Protestants shifts our attention away from Roman Catholic reform, which, it must be stressed, was also underway during this century, so we will begin with a few words about the Catholic interest in children in terms of the sacraments and catechesis. "Catechesis" is a term that originally meant oral instruction, but in this century its meaning was narrowed primarily to printed books and concise summaries of doctrine for children. Eventually it inferred a "catechism," like the Baltimore Catechism some older readers from the United States may remember.

The change from oral instruction to printed books began with Johananes Gutenberg of Mainz in the middle of the previous century. He printed a papal proclamation in 1454 and just two years later published his first bible. By 1520 there were more than two hundred different printed editions of the Bible in existence in many languages. The new medium of print carried great authority, as television does today, and became a means for promoting instruction. This instruction in turn emphasized the differences of religious opinion much more rapidly than ever before, as books and pamphlets proliferated.

It was also in the fifteenth century that Jean Gerson (1363–1429) took the lead among Roman Catholics for the religious education of children. He had been the chancellor of the University of Paris, but in later life he devoted himself to teaching children in Lyons. It was he who probably developed the first catechism for children. It was written in language children were likely to understand and was first presented in the form of posters to be placed in public places. As printing became more available, it was published as a teaching manual.

In the sixteenth century Roman Catholic educators of children were pushed into greater activity by their own reforms and by the publication of Luther's *Shorter Catechism* for "the young and simple people," as well as other Protestant catechisms, such as Calvin's in Geneva. All of these printed texts included questions with answers to be memorized so children could understand, or at least parrot, their families' and religious leaders' interpretation of Christian theology, scripture, and worship.

Peter Canisius (1521–1597) developed a Roman Catholic shorter catechism in Latin (*Catechismus minimus*), which was translated into German. Luther visited the parishes and schools in Saxony in 1528, which prompted him to prepare his *Small Catechism* for the laity and the *Large Catechism* for the clergy. Years later Canisius published another version of his "shorter catechism" that had the words divided into syllables to make the mastery of the text easier for children.

The urgency of educators during this period was for children and adults to get their doctrine right. Their souls were at stake, the reformers on all sides thought. This approach emphasized the rational ordering of Christian thought to educate children, but it was done at the expense of diminishing the importance of the great narrative and symbols of their faith. Sermons, carvings, windows, and other objects in churches and other public places had been used to present the story of Christianity and its heroes. This was replaced by the concepts of doctrine and formal written instruction.

In some Protestant churches the images of the great narrative were broken up and painted over so words from scripture could be painted on the walls instead, like huge pages from printed books. An example of this was in 1524 in Zurich. Zwingli headed a committee that removed all statues and other images from the city's churches. "In Zurich," he wrote, "we have churches which are positively luminous; the walls are beautifully white" (quoted in Miles 1985, 103).

After the Council of Trent, which met off and on from 1545–1563, Roman Catholic doctrine was reformed and this reform reached Rome with the election of Paul IV (Caraffa 1555–1559). He was still an Italian prince but served the church first and turned Rome into a more serious place, doing away with many church abuses and promoting Catholic piety. The Council of Trent had ordered, and Paul IV supported, the idea that parish priests should conscientiously teach the children under their care and promote their obedience to God and their parents. This view spread throughout Catholic Europe as the decades of the century unfolded.

The archbishop of Milan, Charles Borromeo, followed up on this new vision by establishing the Confraternity of Christian Doctrine, approved in 1571 by Pius V, and setting up schools. In addition, Robert Bellarmine's catechisms, written for the Papal States, also became widely influential to help make the religious education of children a priority.

The questions in Bellarmine's catechisms avoided abstractions and put the questions in the *children's* mouths rather than the adults, which changed the dynamic of the teaching relationship. By the end of the six-teenth century these reforms began to influence the Roman Catholic approach to children through Catholic missionary work, including South and North America, India, Japan, China, and elsewhere.

The Roman Catholic clergy who taught children and provided their pastoral care still were not married, but it has never been entirely clear whether a direct experience of family life is always necessary to understand children well. This seems very likely, at least to avoid over-romanticizing or over-demonizing children or their parents, but there have always been those who have had a special gift for working with children and families despite lacking this dimension of personal experience. Interest, empathy, and the memory of one's own childhood go a long way to inform those who work with children, whether they are married or not. This is one reason why the shift in the theologians' experience of children did not bring about a uniform change in Protestant theology. Luther, Calvin, and Hooker provide us with three examples of the diversity that resulted instead.

Selected Theologians

Martin Luther (1483–1546)
Children Are God's Little Jesters, a Mixture of Law and Gospel

In the sixteenth century scientists were making discoveries about the heavens and the earth while ships were plowing through the seas to discover new lands. It was in this context of creative ferment that Martin Luther stepped forward and nailed his Ninety-five Theses, to the north door of the Castle Church in Wittenberg on All Saints' Day, October 31, 1517. This dramatic event may be legend, but what is historically certain is that he sent a copy of his theses, which still exists, to his ecclesiastical superiors for debate, and the forces that caused the Reformation crystallized around him.

Luther was born in Eisleben, where he would die, during a visit to mediate a dispute involving the counts of Mansfeld some sixty-three years later. His father was the son of a farmer but became a businessman, beginning as a copper miner and then leasing a pit to oversee for himself. This enabled him to send Martin to the university when he was eighteen years old to study law, but this did not go as his father planned. In 1505 Luther entered the monastery of the Augustinian monks in Erfurt.

The Augustinian monks, in all their varieties, traced their tradition back to Augustine of Hippo in the fifth century. When Augustine returned from Milan to Thagaste, his home in North Africa, he and some friends set up their own community, based on poverty, study, and prayer. After he became bishop he continued to support monks and nuns, and a letter has survived that he wrote to a group of nuns to restore harmony in 423. Mary T. Clark tells us that the letter is authentic but that "in recent years" Augustine's Rule for Men has been discovered. This is the text she used and commented on in *Augustine of Hippo: Selected Writings* (Augustine 1984, 481–493).

The nuns and monks influenced by Augustine fled North Africa during the Vandal invasion around the time of his death and settled in northern and central Italy. A formal Rule was developed in 1243 and the next year Pope Innocent IV collected the various communities of monks into the Order of St. Augustine. In 1256, during the "Grand Union," other communities were added by Alexander IV, who declared the Augustianians to be a mendicant order. This order spread across Europe and became active in the cities and universities. The Augustinians in Erfurt had established "a fraternity in honor of St. Anne," which reached out into the community beyond the monastic walls (Oberman 1989, 130).

Unlike Thomas Aquinas, Luther had *not* been donated to a monastery as a child. He entered as a young man and had to overcome the resistance of his family to stay there. The precipitating factor for his entry was a vow he made to St. Anne when he was almost struck by lightening. He was returning to the university to begin his law studies after a visit home. St. Anne was the patron saint of the miners Luther grew up with and of people in any kind of distress, so it was natural for him to pray to her.

On July 17, 1505, just two weeks after the storm, Martin knocked at the gate of the monastery of the Augustine Hermits in Erfurt and asked to be allowed to begin the process to become a monk. He was accompanied by some friends who had been present at a farewell party the evening before. The doorway he entered was not to an ordinary monastery. This group of about fifty monks lived in the famous Black Monastery, which was the *studium generale* of the Saxon Reform Congregation, the only one in the region until a second study center was attached to the University of Wittenberg just the year before in 1504 (Oberman 1992, 130).

Hans Luder, Martin's father, was angry that his son would throw away a university education in law to enter a monastery, but in 1507, when Martin celebrated his first mass as a newly ordained priest, his father bestowed on the monastery a generous sum of twenty gulden. Luther persisted and in 1512 he became a doctor of theology at the University of Wittenberg.

Political forces then swirled around him. In August of 1520 he published his *Address to the Christian Nobility of the German Nation* and in October *The Babylonian Captivity of the Church* was printed. In December he burned *Exsurge Domine*, the papal bull that threatened excommunication, before the Elster Gate in Wittenberg. In 1521 at the Imperial Diet of Worms he declared that unless he were convicted by scripture and plain reason he would submit to neither popes nor councils. His famous statement—"Here I stand, I cannot do otherwise. God help me, Amen"—may be legendary, but he had plainly placed scripture above the pope. For Luther there would be no passive reliance on Rome's interpretation of God's revelation. He would use his own reason and interpretation of tradition to make his translations, write his commentaries, and worship God.

In January of 1521 he was excommunicated by Pope Leo X and summoned to the Diet of Worms. He refused to recant and was declared an outlaw, which meant that anyone could kill him without punishment. Elector Friedrich the Wise arranged for him to be "kidnapped" and hidden at the

Wartburg Castle for a time. In 1522, despite the danger of the imperial ban
and the clear instructions of his prince, Luther returned to Wittenberg,
where he resumed his lectures and in 1524 abandoned his religious habit.
It was there he spent most of the rest of his life.

To this point children had played no role in his theology, but now
Luther rejected the idea that some occupations were religiously superior
or merited more grace than others. Instead, he proclaimed the priesthood
of *all* believers, including those who were married as well as those involved
in what he emphasized was enforced celibacy. Celibacy might be received
as a divine gift, he thought, but it could not be forced. When Luther married—perhaps to make a theological point, or as he said "in defiance of
the devil" (Oberman 1992, 278 and 280)—he learned that life in a family
is vastly different from life in a monastery. What he had spoken about in
theory from 1520–1525 to other monks and nuns who were thinking about
becoming married, became a fact for him personally.

Martin Luther married Catherine (Katharina von Bora, 1499–1552) in
1525. She had entered the convent in 1508, and had taken her vows in 1515.
She then fled the convent and traveled to Wittenberg, where she sought
shelter with the family of Lucas Cranach the Elder, a friend of Luther's.

Cranach was a well-known painter who made at least five portraits of
Luther, but for purposes of this book it was his painting that shows Jesus
surrounded by happy women and children in contrast to the dismayed and
angry disciples muttering in the shadows that deserves mention. It was
painted in 1538 and has the same theme and compositional form as a painting by Emil Nolde done in 1910. Both versions of this scene may be found
at the beginning of chapter 7.

When Catherine and Martin married she was twenty-six and he was
forty-two years old. Pastor Johannes Bugenhagen presided and the wedding was held on the evening of June 13, 1525, at the Black Monastery. It
was a quiet ceremony with a few friends. Melanchthon, Luther's cautious
colleague, was worried that the marriage would ruin the whole cause of the
Reformation. He was not invited.

The Black Monastery was the very monastery that Luther had entered
as a young man in 1505, twenty years earlier. Now it was the site where
the "reformation" took place in Luther's experience of children, because
his former monastery became the home of the Luther family. This home
and other properties were provided as pay by the elector who also made
Martin and Catherine a wedding gift of one hundred gulden in cash, but
the renovation of the Black Monastery used up the entire sum. Kate took
over managing the whole enterprise, despite her six pregnancies during

their first decade of marriage. Their finances were especially tight, but she made a brilliant success of family life.

Luther's critics considered the Reformation to be caused by his lust for women in a negative way, but he considered sexual attraction in a positive way. His view was that those who are ashamed of marriage are also ashamed of being human so they try to improve on what God has given them. He interpreted Genesis 2:18—when God said, "It is not good that the man should be alone; I will make him a helper as his partner"—as meaning that God generated sensuous delight in marriage rather than forbidding it. He wrote, "This is the Word of God, by virtue of which . . . the passionate, natural inclination toward woman is created and maintained. It may not be prevented by vow and law. For it is God's Word and work" (quoted in Oberman 1992, 273–274).

The Incarnation itself also points to the value of the whole human being. When John wrote, "And the Word became flesh and lived among us" (John 1:14) he meant "flesh" and not "spirit" or "church." There would be no portrait of Christ or God's creatures by Luther from only the neck up. To limit the definition of the person to the intellect and the spirit, Luther thought, was a perversion of Christianity.

This holistic and celebratory view of human nature expressed by Luther not only made his Catholic critics nervous but also his Lutheran followers. Oberman notes that "The tendency to make him 'respectable' . . . explains why one of Luther's most revealing and engaging letters has been all but suppressed" (Oberman 1992, 276). Oberman referred to a letter in December of 1525 that Luther wrote to his friend Spalatin, whose wife was also named Catherine. He greeted him on his wedding day, reflected on when he would hold his wife and embrace her, and then wrote "On the evening of the day on which, according to my calculations, you will receive this, I shall make love to my Catherine while you make love to yours, and thus we will be united in love." (quoted in Oberman 1992, 276).

What Luther learned from family life had a great deal to do with the talent, intelligence, competence, and energy of Catherine, whom he called "My Lord Katie." Luther learned that while the routine of childcare appears to "that clever harlot, our natural reason," to be insignificant, distasteful, and despicable, it is in reality "adorned with divine approval as with the costliest gold and jewels" (quoted in Strohl 2001, 140).

As Luther and Kate awaited the birth of their first child they were not alone. A monk had married a nun. People waited to see if a two-headed monster would result from this most unsacred of unions. Little Johannes, however, was born strong, and as Luther said, he was a good eater and drinker, *"homo vorax ac bibax"*!

Luther's experience of children and family life changed him. He and Catherine had six children—in 1526, 1527 (died at eight months), 1529 (died at thirteen years), 1531, 1533, and 1534. After 1529 Luther's sister's children were added to their household, as well as students. Students joined him for "table talk" in his home as much as in the lecture hall. Catherine's aunt "Muhme Lene" had her own room and two of Catherine's nieces were also living in the house. There was also a steady stream of visitors, both friends and those who showed up to meet the "great man" and, no doubt, to ask him favors. No one really knows except perhaps Catherine, who had to manage and pay for it all, how many people were actually living in the former monastery at one time.

Luther may have advocated for the biblical "headship" of the family by the father, but his life displayed a partnership between husbands and wives. Luther respectfully and playfully also called his wife "Mr. Kathy" and made fun of husbands who thought themselves above washing diapers and making beds alongside their wives. He made her executrix of his will, which was unheard of in those days, and heir to all his modest property (Ozment 2001, 30–37). It was from this foundation in personal experience that he attacked the anti-marriage and anti-feminist sentiment in the writings of ancient philosophers and medieval clergy.

Luther argued that there are four critical duties for parents. They are to form children in the true faith as they mature, to provide the sacrament of baptism for infants, to attend to children's education for vocation, and to provide them with a suitable spouse in a timely fashion (before lust intrudes). At the same time he seemed genuinely to enjoy the company of children and called them "God's little jesters."

Children, like all people, are simultaneously justified and sinful, Luther argued. They are, as he put it in Latin, *simul justus et peccator* (Strolh 2001, 134). The sin, which deformed our nature at the fall, continues to ensnare us, but we can hear God's command as Law and God's promise as Gospel to help us cope with the sin everyone is involved in. This view compelled Luther to be sure that the teachers of children were mature, seasoned confessors of the evangelical faith and responsible members of their own families and communities. He wanted children to be aware through the lives of these mentors of the faith that both Law and Gospel were available for them to counteract the original sin they were born with.

His last years were full of ailments and sadness. His beloved daughter Magdelena died in 1542, which saddened him. Finally, at his last lecture he said, "I am weak. I cannot go on." Still, he went on and made his final visit to Eisleben. At dinner he suffered angina pectoris but still ate well and was in good spirits. There was pain and sweat, but he went to bed. At 2:45 AM he became pale. His feet and nose became cold and he died. Luther was carried back to Wittenburg where he was buried.

Heiko A. Oberman noted that his last concern was for his pregnant wife. Little Elizabeth would not be born until five months after his death. He prayed, "Lord God, I thank Thee for having allowed me to be a poor beggar on earth. I leave no house, property, or money. But you gave me a wife and children, I commend them unto Thee. Feed, instruct, and preserve them as Thou hast preserved me, O Thou Father of children and widows" (quoted in Oberman 1992, 322).

Luther had a high view of children and he learned from them. He also knew them as specific children with a unique potential for a graceful life. They were for him creatures full of a wonder that he warmly responded to. Children were real and not symbolic for him, but he also knew they carried original sin with them and with that a need for grace. In conjunction with this view of human nature he also advocated for children to be well-educated and cared for with love and responsibility because he was convinced that if supported properly they could grow into responsible Christians by God's grace. When Luther died in Germany, John Calvin was about thirty-seven years old and living in Geneva. We turn to him now and his thoughts about children.

John Calvin (1509–1564)
Children Are Evil but Need Care

Luther was loud. Calvin was quiet. Both were controversial. Luther was German. Calvin was French. Luther spoke expansively about his inner life. Calvin did not. Neither developed a theological system. Luther stressed themes such as Law and Gospel while Calvin's so-called system was what John Dillenberger called a wheel without a rim, a hub full of spokes, and some spokes were longer than others (Bouwsma 1988, 276, note 100). What Abelard and Heloise so objected to about children, Luther reveled in. John Calvin did not go that far, but he did marry and felt a responsibility to provide for his own stepchildren and the children of others. The journey he took toward a family was as complicated as Luther's was.

Calvin was born at Noyon in Picardy, one of four or possibly five boys. His mother died when he was about five and his father soon remarried and sent young John to a neighbor to be raised. At age twelve John was sent to the University of Paris, where he finished the arts course and earned a master's degree in 1528. This was just as Ignatius Loyola, the future founder of the Jesuits, was arriving at the university.

Before Calvin was twenty his father, who had intended his son for theology, had a quarrel with the Noyon cathedral chapter and decided that John must become a lawyer instead. John dutifully went to the University of Orleans to study law, and to Bourges, but while he was there he also became interested in the new humanist learning and studied Greek. John graduated in law, but his father had already died in 1531. He was now his own master, so he embraced the new humanistic learning, continuing in Greek and learning Hebrew as well. His first book, *Commentary on Seneca's Treatise on Clemency*, was published in April of 1532, but it showed little evidence of his maturing interest in religion.

Sometime between 1532 and 1534, "Calvin experienced a 'sudden conversion'" (Walker 1959, 349), yet Bouwsma has argued that Calvin experienced no cataclysmic event but gradually realized that he was not only a follower of the new humanism but also of Luther's theology, incomplete though he thought it was (Bouwsma 1988, 10–11). It is, perhaps, best to follow the editors of Calvin's Institutes to say that "we cannot be certain of the stages through which he came or of the date of what he calls his 'sudden conversion.' (Calvin 2006, xxx). We shall leave "sudden conversion" in quotes and say that the preceding decade of his life 1523–1533 was a stirring and dangerous time in which he thoughtfully participated. In his Commentary on the Psalms Calvin himself wrote that "God subdued my heart to teachableness (quoted in Calvin 2006, li).

When Calvin traveled home to Noyon in 1534 to resign his Roman Catholic benefices, he was imprisoned there for a short time because of his Protestant leanings. The king, Francis I, was by this time attacking the "Lutherans," so matters became too dangerous for Calvin to remain in France. By New Year's Day of 1535 he was safely in Protestant Basel.

The year 1536 was important for Calvin. By this time he had moved from Basel to Geneva, after being threatened with divine wrath by Farel if he did not come help him champion the Protestant cause. Geneva by then was a small city of about 10,300 people but it was swelling with Protestant refugees, like Calvin, from France (Graham 1978, 106).

The year 1536 was also the year that Calvin published the first edition of *The Institutes of the Christian Religion*, which included a letter to the French king, whom he thought misunderstood the French protestants and he said so. The first edition was only about 6-1/8" x 4" so it could be easily hidden. He continued to revise his masterpiece all his life until the last edition being in 1559, about five years before his death. About the

1559 edition he wrote "Although I did not regret the labor spent, I was never satisfied until the work had been arranged in the order now set forth" (Calvin 2006, 3).

It was also in 1536 that the Roman Catholic priest and humanist Erasmus died. Only the year before his close friend Sir Thomas More (1478–1535), another humanist and Chancellor of England, had been beheaded by Henry VIII for denying the king's supremacy in spiritual matters. The humanistic spirit of classical learning and optimism, like that of Erasmus and More, had by this time been muted by the violence of religious conflict. Erasmus' *Praise of Folly, Encomium Moriae,* punning in Latin on his friend's name, had been published in 1511. Its laughter and wonder now seemed tepid and irrelevant, as religious controversy heated up and boiled over. By this time Luther had been married for eleven years.

It was providential that life in Geneva was not easy for Calvin. The city government expelled their two main pastors, Calvin and the older Farel, in 1538. Calvin was invited to Strasbourg, where he worked with Martin Bucer. Bucer had a great influence on him, as they ministered to a congregation of French refugees together for three years. Bouwsma suggests that he was probably happier then than at any other time in his life (Bouwsma 1988, 21). This was partly because of the harmonious balance between pastoral duties and his work on an expanded version of *The Institutes,* but this was also when he met and in 1540 married Idelette de Bure, a widow with two children.

Calvin was recalled to Geneva with his bride in 1541. He and Idelette had at least three children together, but none of them survived infancy. He got married to her when he was about thirty-one years old and he was only forty when she died in 1549. His grief at her death "suggests how important the marriage had been for him" (Bouwsma 1988, 23).

To speak of children in Calvin's theology involves a discussion about original sin. The Doctrine of Original Sin, championed by Augustine, was affirmed by Calvin to explain sin without diminishing God's sovereignty as all-good, all-knowing, and all-powerful. It was also biblical, he argued, and true to experience, since some who knew of the Gospel's benefits still rejected it.

He wrote in *The Institutes* (and it was carried unchanged in all editions) that "Even infants bear their condemnation with them from their mother's womb; for, though they have not yet brought forth the fruits of their own iniquity, they have the seed enclosed within themselves. Indeed, their whole nature is a seed of sin; thus it cannot be but hateful and abominable to God" (Calvin 2006, 1311, 4.15.10). God, nevertheless, chooses to save some though none deserve it. This seed argument is also used in a positive way. "To sum up, this objection (Calvin is referring to the argument that infants are incapable of either repentance or faith.) can be solved without difficulty: infants are baptized into future repentance and faith, and even though these have not yet been formed in them, the seed of both lies hidden within them by the secret working of the Spirit" (Calvin 2006, 1343, 4.16.20).

Sometimes Calvin can be very positive toward children. He wrote " 'Out of the mouths of babes and sucklings thou hast established strength' Indeed, he (Calvin is referring to David in Psalm 8.2.) not only declares that a clear mirror of God's works is in humankind, but that infants, while they nurse at their mothers' breasts, have tongues so eloquent to preach his glory that there is no need at all of other orators" (Calvin 2006, 55, 1.5.3).

At other times his views are chilling. In Book 3, concerning the Holy Spirit, Calvin argued that God loves children but appears angry to frighten them with "a voluntary fear that befits children" (Calvin 2006, 557, 3.2.12; 573, 3.2.27). God also tests them, as he did his own Son (Calvin 2006, 702, 3.8.1) and uses his rod to make them "obedient and teachable" (Calvin 2006, 706, 3.8.6). In spite of the love Calvin attributed to God—which is masked by anger, testing and the rod—God still passes over some and condemns them, which he does "for no other reason than that he wills to exclude them from the inheritance which he predestines for his own children" (Calvin 2006, 947, 2.23.1).

Calvin's ambiguity is nowhere better illustrated than in his commentary on the 23rd Psalm. He wrote, "By the metaphor of the shepherd, he (David) praises God's care; he means that God's care for those who are his own is like the solicitude of a shepherd for the sheep entrusted to him" (Calvin 1958, 260). At first this sounds like words of comfort and then it is realized that if you are not one of the elect, one of God's own, then you are outside the flock and the comfort of the shepherd's care and sheepfold.

In the next century Calvin's followers, the Calvinists, were less ambiguous about election and declared the double logic of God both saving and damning people. In the Westminster Confession of Faith, adopted by Parliament in 1648, the assertion of double predestination reads like this:

> ↶ Others, not elected, although they may be called by the ministry of the Word, and may have some common operations of the Spirit, yet they never truly come unto Christ, and therefore cannot be saved: much less can men, not professing the Christian religion . . . And to assert and maintain that they may, is very pernicious, and to be detested. (*Westminster Confession of Faith*, chapter X "Of Effectual Calling" 4, 1646 Edition) ↷

Calvin himself, however, moved the text of his own consideration of predestination, Bouwsma tells us, from the doctrine of providence to the doctrine of salvation in his final edition of *The Institutes*. He had always opposed speculation about God's secrets and thought that if predestination is understood in the context of faith it could evoke gratitude and inspire confidence. This made the doctrine useful for salvation, he thought (Bouwsma 1988, 173). Still, while predestination may have evoked gratitude and inspired confidence for some it also inspired arrogance or despair for others.

Despite his views on original sin, election, and predestination, Calvin remained concerned about the health and education of the children in Geneva as if they were all among the elect. At the same General Council, May 21, 1536, which abolished the Roman mass and established the Reformation in Geneva, it was also resolved that a "learned man" be paid to direct education in the city and that "each person be bound to send his children to the school and to make them learn" (quoted in Graham 1978, 146). In 1559 Calvin also succeeded in establishing a new academy, which became known all over Europe. "This new institution served initially as a training ground for Reformed pastors, but from its early days many of the magistrates supported (and fought for) a broadening of the curriculum" (Pitkin 2001, 180–181).

Calvin seems to have been interested in the details of children's lives from outlawing the use of peashooters in school to the building of balconies to keep them from falling out of windows. This broad involvement with children made Calvin "more appreciative of the positive character of children, dwelling less on their sinfulness than some of his forebears (such as Augustine) or successors (such as Jonathan Edwards)" (Pitkin 2001, 169).

While Calvin may have had experience with children as a pastor and educator he probably had little experience with them at home. Nothing is known about his relationship with the two children of his wife's first marriage. Idelette de Bure brought into their marriage a daughter named Judith and a son, whose name is not known. As his wife lay dying in 1549, Calvin promised her that he would care for his stepchildren. After her death he wrote in a letter to Viret, April 7, 1549 from Geneva: "Although the death of my wife has been exceedingly painful to me, yet I subdue my grief as well as I can. . . . I have been bereaved of the best companion of my life . . ." (Calvin 1960, 91–92).

Usually, however, Calvin's references to children were symbolic. Pitkins wrote that his "application of the image of 'children' to his followers in the Reformed faith conforms to the largely symbolic character of children in most of his writing, especially his extensive and influential commentaries on Scripture" (Pitkin 2001, 160–161). He once wrote, "And yet I have myriads of children throughout the Christian world" (quoted in Pitkin 2001, 160), so his children were primarily the adults he had reared in the Reformed Tradition.

Calvin interpreted Psalm 127:3 as an assurance to parents that children are a "heritage of the Lord." On the other hand, he wanted to ensure that children show respect and obey their parents and all authority in the city. Children who cursed or disobeyed their parents were to be executed, unless parents had failed properly to instruct them. This law may misrepresent Calvin's views about the balance between love and discipline for raising children (Pitkin 2001, 173, note 41), but the death penalty *was* legislated and it had biblical authority behind it to support death as the appropriate punishment for striking or cursing one's father or mother (Exodus 21:15, 17; Leviticus 20:9). There is no evidence that this law was ever enforced against children. The death penalty, however, was enforced for blasphemy if the person appeared to be unredeemable. The most famous example was the Spanish physician Servetus, a critic of Calvin and the Holy Trinity. He was burned at the stake in 1533.

Both Luther and Calvin advocated for original sin and children's damnation, but they also worked for children, as if all children were numbered among the elect. This was the opening wedge in an implicit gap, an inconsistency, that was beginning to show among theologians between their low view of children's nature and an optimism about their upbringing.

Calvin's direct involvement with children in a personal, family situation was not as extensive as Luther's or even Hooker's, but he was still open to making children a part of his life. In 1557, some eight years after his wife died, he invited his brother's four young children into his home while he helped his brother concerning a divorce from his wife, who had been banished from the city. Calvin at times seemed to disapprove of harsh treatment for children or their abandonment, despite their original sin or lack of election and in spite of the death penalty in Geneva for cursing or disobedience to one's parents. Children had less malice than their elders, he thought, which was something their elders should copy. He commented on this in his interpretation of 1 Corinthians 14:20 where "Paul urges believers to be children not in understanding but in malice" (quoted in Pitkin, 2001, 165).

Calvin's view of play had special implications concerning children. When children play they express what is authentic and spontaneous. That is good, he thought, but when adults play roles in the theater they wear masks and project an artificial role, which he condemned. Calvin's personal emblem was a hand offering a heart with the words suggesting openness and purity (*Prompte et sincere*). It was children's lack of guile that he admired and resonated with (Bouwsma 1988, 178–179).

On the other hand, in the *Institutes* he argued "Observe and heed all these words which I command you, that it may go well with you and with your children after you forever, when you do what is good and pleasing in the sight of your God" (Calvin 2006, 371, 2.8.6). He then quoted Deuteronomy 12:28 and argued that obedience is better than "playfulness of the human mind," which takes people away from God's Word. Moses had to "restrain such wantonness."

When Calvin is compared to Luther we find a less high view of children and less experience with them. When we turn to Richard Hooker we will find that despite his involvement with children in his own family his theological writing was largely indifferent to them.

Richard Hooker (1554–1600)
Children Are Part of the Natural Law

When Elizabeth took the throne in 1558 Richard Hooker was about four years old. He lived all the rest of his life under her rule. The Protestant Reformation had come to England with Elizabeth's father, Henry VIII, but the realm had been returned to Catholic rule under Mary Tudor. She, like Elizabeth, was one of Henry's daughters, but was executed by Queen Elizabeth. The Elizabethan Settlement, a balancing of Roman Catholic and Protestant religious and political interests, made the continuing reformation possible in England during the sixteenth century. This broad conception of the church was something that Hooker helped establish. He mapped out a middle way between Calvinist Geneva and Catholic Rome, which placed the existing controversies in a larger framework, to help create rather than merely consolidate what would later be called the "Anglican" approach to the Reformation.

In 1554 Richard Hooker was born in Heavitree, a village about two miles outside of Exeter. "Bloody Mary" was on the throne. Luther had already been dead in Germany for about eight years and Calvin, now forty-five years old, was a widower living in Geneva. Ignatius Loyola (1491–1556), the founder of the Jesuits, was sixty-three and would live only two more years.

It is not clear whether Hooker's mother and father were married, but his father left the family for good to make a career in Ireland when Richard was about eight. His uncle, John Hooker, a leader in the public affairs of Exeter, saw to it that little Richard went to grammar school in Exeter and then on to college with the sponsorship and financial help of John Jewel, Bishop of

Salisbury. Richard moved to Corpus Christi College, Oxford, at about age 15. Philip Secor has written that "The college quadrangle the young Hooker now entered would become the physical and emotional matrix of his life for the next fifteen years and his intellectual fulcrum until he died in 1600" (Secor 1999, 63). John Rainolds (1549–1607)—a young, bold, brilliant, and outspoken Calvinist—was Hooker's tutor. He was about five years older than Hooker and guided him through his academic career.

The curriculum was still largely a medieval one. Hooker read Boethius for logic, arithmetic, and music theory (considered a branch of mathematics). The work of Peter Abelard was consulted on the scholastic mode of argumentation. Philosophy was read, especially Aristotle, and so were the scriptures and theology, including the work of the new Protestants. Latin, Greek, and Hebrew—Hooker was later appointed deputy Regius Professor of Hebrew at the University—were learned and used. Hooker earned his MA in 1577 and became a fellow of the college the same year. In 1579 he entered holy orders as a deacon and later would become a priest.

The year 1584 was a turning point for him. He was now about thirty and had always been short of money, so it was some comfort to be appointed to a parish part-time at St. Mary's in Drayton Beauchamp. He probably went there on weekends and for special occasions. He also was appointed to preach at St. Paul's Cross—a massive, eight-sided, lead-roofed, wooden pulpit in the yard of St. Paul's Cathedral in London. It was his first moment on the national stage and was probably when he met his future wife, Joan Churchman, for he stayed at the Churchman home while in London.

In 1585 Hooker returned again to the national stage but in a more permanent way. He was appointed Master of the Temple, which made him rector of a church that was a boisterous place, built in the twelfth century by the Knights Templar and modeled on the Holy Sepulcher in Jerusalem. Under Henry VIII it was taken over by the crown and leased to lawyers, who converted the grounds into residence inns, halls, and study areas for law students, barristers, politicians, judges, and the powerful in the realm. This is where the famous debates between Walter Travers and Hooker took place.

On Sundays Hooker would conduct the Church of England liturgy with a homily and holy communion in the morning. In the afternoon Travers would climb into the pulpit without any liturgical flourishes and move immediately into his flamboyant and dramatic sermon to refute whatever Hooker had said in the morning. In the next century Thomas Fuller described this running debate as "the pulpit spake pure Canterbury in the morning and Geneva in the afternoon" (quoted in Secor 1999, 181).

Travers was removed from his post by the queen and the archbishop of Canterbury rather summarily in 1587.

Richard Hooker was married to Joan Churchman in 1588, a significant date in English history. The last Roman Catholic crusade, the Spanish Armada, sailed against Protestant England and was destroyed, mostly by the weather. Meanwhile the Hookers lived in the Churchman home and for the first five years of their marriage a baby was born each year. Joan was one of the some 25 percent of the girls in London who could read and write and her family was a prosperous one. The Hookers continued to live at the Churchman home as Richard worked on his *Laws of Ecclesiastical Polity*, after resigning as Master of the Temple. The Preface and the first four books of *The Laws* were published in 1593, a year of plague in London during which some ten thousand people perished. By this time there were four little girls in the house. The first-born child, Richard, had died soon after his birth.

In 1595 the parish at Bishopbourne became available and Hooker was appointed. This was his dream come true. The rectory was large and comfortable for his family and Canterbury Cathedral was only three miles away with its library and learned colleagues. While Hooker made his daily rounds as a parish priest he was finishing Book V, which was devoted to the worship and pastoral care of the Church of England. The 1597 edition of *The Laws* included the now completed Book V. The Hookers' last child, Edwin, was born and died soon afterward in their new home.

Hooker died in 1600. He was forty-seven and died well before what was considered "old age" in those days (Secor 1999, 322). His death came in the rectory with his family around him and under the pastoral care of Adrian Sarvaria, a distinguished colleague from Canterbury, who called on him often during the Bishopbourne years. The notes and manuscripts for the last three volumes of *The Laws* began a life of their own at his death and were not published until many decades later.

What did Hooker write about children? One way to answer this has been provided by Philip B. Secor and Lee W. Gibbs. They published selections from Hooker's writings (Secor and Gibbs 2005) on 124 primary themes. The theme of "children" was not included although there were a few selections referring to "children of God," pregnancy, and marriage. If we read *The Laws of Ecclesiastical Polity* (Hooker 1888) directly with children in mind, however, a bit more may be found.

The first four books provide the foundation for *The Laws*. Laws in general, including natural and divine law, were considered in Book I and it was concluded that they are founded on reason. Book II considered the nature, authority, and adequacy of scripture as a means for knowing the truth. Book III outlined the scriptural basis for worship and government and Book IV defended the liturgical practice of the English church. In these first four books the terms "child" and "children" were used about thirty-one times. In most cases the terms refer to human beings in general such as in the phrase "children of men" or "children of Israel." Other times "children" is used in a literal way, like saying that the Gentiles did not circumcise their children (4.11).

Hooker did, however, touch on some matters relevant to the nature of children. They can know God by the Spirit, as the prophets did, but they lack reason, which most people need to employ to understand religion (Preface.1). Children also have an "eagerness of their affection" that is opposed to being reasonable. This leaves children open to being drawn into various religious enthusiasms. These characteristics can be a danger to them (Preface.3). It is not logical to argue against this danger that "God hath chosen the simple" or that "Christ's own Apostle was accounted mad" (Preface.3) to support unreasonable religion, because this argument uses reason to prove that reason is not authoritative, which is a self-contradiction.

Children are deficient in knowledge as well as reason. Angels have "full and complete knowledge" while children are "without understanding or knowledge at all" (1.6). Still, children can "grow by degrees" until they become "even as the angels themselves." Here Hooker anticipates Locke's (1632–1704) idea of the child as a clean slate or *tabula rasa* by saying that "The soul of man being therefore at the first as a book wherein nothing is and yet all things may be imprinted." He also compared the place of reason in stones, plants, and animals to human beings and concluded that human beings have the power to move beyond their ability to know by the senses, which they share with animals, to a higher kind of knowledge (1.6).

Education and instruction can aid in the child's growth, so that "our natural faculty of reason is both the better and the sooner able to judge rightly between truth and error, good and evil," but it is sometimes difficult to know when the growing child is responsible enough to use "reason as sufficieth to make him capable of those laws whereby he is then bound to guide his actions." Knowing when this moment occurs in individual children is something that "common sense" can determine better than the philosophers (1.7).

The origin of the knowledge of natural law (1.8) is a relationship with God, which children can experience. The laws of nature are discovered by reason but some can also be known by all. Even a child of two days can know what people have known forever, merely by being human (1.8). There is much more to learn after infancy, however. We come into the world naked in mind as well as body, but our families help us clothe our bodies and minds with what is needed to live well (1.10). Judgment can eventually develop so that a mature youth can even be moved to seek his or her own baptism (3.1).

Hooker's defense against attacks on the liturgical practices of the established church in Book IV used the metaphor of a child with a knife. It has been argued, he wrote, that some liturgical practices are considered dangerous, like giving a child a knife. The remedy is not to take the knife from the child. How would the child then learn to use it upon reaching the age of discretion? In addition to the harm that is done to the child by removing established liturgical practices, like a dangerous knife, this removal robs everyone of that liturgical help (4.12). No. Removing such practices "quite and clean" is not the answer. Reasonable education and oversight is a better solution.

Book V, which is longer than the first four books taken together, was a commentary on *The Book of Common Prayer*. What Hooker made explicit is how the theological values and needs of a diverse community, a whole nation, can be sustained and nourished by an accepted liturgical practice. Some of these practices are "indifferent" so latitude is counseled. In matters of salvation, however, the proper practice should be more strictly observed. The Calvinists, he argued, leap from their liturgical preferences to polity without using reason to think through whether the practice is a matter of indifference or salvation.

It is surprising that children do not occupy a more prominent place in Book V. There is the mention of "children of God" (5.56), but that is largely with reference to God's chosen people as adults. In his comments about marriage (5.73) he noted that the single life is more "angelical and divine" but that women, who are easier to perceive than define, are to be man's helper for having and raising children. His remarks about pregnant women (5.74) are poignant, considering the loss of the two little boys in their family and the pain and danger of childbirth experienced in their household. He defends women against the disapproval of their dress and condition during these significant periods in a family's life.

He had more to say about children (and uneducated adults) in the context of education. The elements of religion must be taught with consideration "to the weak and slender capacity of young beginners." To accomplish this the Christian belief should be "drawn into few and short articles, to the end that the weakness of no man's wit might either hinder altogether the knowledge, or excuse the utter ignorance of needful things" (5.18.3).

Teaching might take place in schools or families, but it is a mistake to leave it to preaching, because preaching turns it into a "public performance thereof in the open hearing of men, because things are preached not in that they are taught, but in that they are published" (5.18.3).

The sacraments also teach. They "teach the mind, by other senses, that which the Word doth teach by hearing," but they also affect "infants which are not capable of instruction." This means that for Hooker the sacraments are not just to be used to teach doctrinal abstractions as illustrations, but they always make possible "some other more excellent and heavenly use" (5.57.1). God is invisible, so sacraments are a way to "take notice of his glorious presence" (5.57.3). Baptism for example, is embraced "not only as a sign or token of what we receive, but also as an instrument or means whereby we receive grace, because baptism is a sacrament." It enables us to be "incorporated into Christ by the "Holy Ghost, which giveth the powers of the soul their first disposition towards future newness of life" (5.60.2). Infants "may contact and covenant with God, the law is plain," he wrote, but they lack the ability to speak for themselves. This is why we have not only parents but also godparents, who can perform this function. They are "Fathers and Mothers in God" (5.64.3).

Books VI–VIII were about the kinds of authority found in elders, bishops, kings, and popes and how they are to be used to govern. In these books the references to children are very sparse and mostly limited to illustrations, such as the church needing a rod to keep her "children" (adults) in line, or that things need to be made plain so that even "a child" (an obtuse adult) could understand the point.

In general Hooker's optimistic view of natural law, the usefulness of reason, and the importance of civil law to govern both the church and state provide ways for children, who are born sinful without hope of salvation except by God's grace, to grow up and live a good life. On the other hand, he emphasized God's gift of reason and natural law as a means to cope with sin by steering one's way between Geneva and Rome to achieve the best life possible for all with God's help in the Christian commonwealth of England.

Conclusion

We have now come over half-way in our story. It is time to look back to where we have come from and look forward to where we are going. When we look back, two points in particular deserve further comment before we

move on. One has already been mentioned more than once. There are not
women in this story until modern times. The second point is about the
pervasive and complicated influence of Augustine of Hippo that continues to this day.

It would have been possible to include women such as Mechthild of
Magdeburg (c.1212–c.1282), Julian of Norwich (c.1342 to after 1416) and
perhaps others during the Middle Ages, but that would have distorted the
general picture of how the scriptural, philosophical, and scientific texts
were used to support the ascendant norm of maleness, which is a part of
our heritage that needs to be felt as well as thought about. It is hoped that
the absence of women will continue to make the reader uneasy.

The remarkable women who did write books in the Middle Ages usually wrote in their vernacular and were closer to their own cultures and
more innovative than the more narrowly formed monks, friars, and university students who lived in a male world and communicated with each
other professionally in Latin. The women were mystics by temperament
but also because their relationship with God had to be direct, since the
church usually excluded them from the normal ways in which leadership
could be developed. They also had to weigh the richness of their own experience of God against what the church said they ought to feel and think.
If their writing was tinged with depreciation, it was because they usually
worked with a male confessor, and this was the only way their voice could
be heard to affirm what they knew to be true. All this is really another story
for another time.

The second point, as we look back, is the pervasive and complex
influence of Augustine of Hippo on future theology. For example, in the
first two volumes of Blackwell's *The Great Theologians* series Augustine
appears briefly at the end of the first volume about the early church
and then he appears in full force at the beginning of the second volume.
The first sentence of the first chapter of the second volume says, "The
Writing of Bishop Augustine, a man predestinate, as his first biographer put it . . . set the Western theological tone for more than a thousand
years" (Rist 2001, 3).

At the end of the second volume we find Paul Rorem reminding us
of Princeton Seminary's Benjamin B. Warfield's (1851–1921) famous
epitaph, "The Reformation, inwardly considered, was just the ultimate
triumph of Augustine's doctrine of grace over Augustine's doctrine of the
church" (Rorem 2001, 365). Augustine was and still is found quoted on
many sides in the same theological discussion.

Luther and Calvin relied heavily on Augustine's doctrine of grace and, though tempered by a confidence in natural law, so did Hooker. To put this in a negative way the doctrine of original sin for Luther and Calvin found children to be deformed unless redeemed by God's grace or election. Hooker agreed, except with more optimism and less interest.

What is most important about the sixteenth century, it seems to me, is that a gap began to appear between an interest in the education and care of children and their fate already being determined before birth. Luther enjoyed children and learned from them. Calvin cared for them and saw their promise. Both did this despite their commitment to Augustine's original sin. Hooker, on the other hand, saw children more in terms of natural law and an ability to grow through reason, although he did nod toward original sin. His inconsistency was different from that of Luther and Calvin and more ironic. He was more confident that children could participate in their own growth but he did not promote such growth as much as Luther and Calvin in his writings, although his daily rounds as a parish priest must have involved him in much that supported the children in his home and parish.

Hooker hoped to lay a broad and reasonable foundation for the church that would free people from the ill will and gall of theological controversy, which finally swept England into a bloody, religious, civil war. After this paroxysm the church was better able to nourish and educate her children and care for all her members, but this hope is seldom perfectly realized and part of the reason is because the *de facto* doctrine of children that the church lives by, is flawed.

When we look ahead to the next chapter, the seventeenth and eighteenth centuries, the church's struggles will continue and become more complex. Still, the reality of grace continues to play an important role in the survival of the church. The fractured and fracturing church will not only survive by God's grace but it will became more creative and diverse as the centuries go by so it can learn to more adequately meet the needs of all kinds of Christians in all kinds of situations, including children. There is something sacramental about the part children have played to bridge the centuries.

CHAPTER

5

REFORMING THE REFORMATION AND THE NEW SCIENCE: 1600–1800

Caravaggio's life (1573–1610) was as full of conflict as the period in which he lived. He contrasted his Madonna and Child with those of the Middle Ages and the devotional images his patrons expected him to paint. A full-blooded young mother is leaning against her doorway, rising lightly up on her toes. She is a combination of weariness as a mother and boredom with being objectified by the pilgrims. Still, as she holds her large and heavy baby, she remains almost weightless as her bare, white feet demonstrate. She is no stone statue in a niche.

The baby is making a vague sign of a blessing over the pilgrims, who are poorly dressed in contrast to most religious paintings of the period. The man's bare feet are thrust into the viewer's face. They are dirty and calloused from walking the pilgrim's path and the poverty of the pilgrims.

The Council of Trent in the middle of the sixteenth century had ordered no innovation in church art be allowed and that no sexuality or attractive beauty should be shown (Robb 1998, 268, 270), but this new age was one of science and realism, as well as political and religious struggle. Not only is this painting realistic, but the Madonna was real. She was easily recognized as the courtesan Maddalena Antognetti or Lena.

The child of the early church was symbolic, like a lamb being carried. In the Middle Ages the child was the Logos, an ageless image of the Holy Trinity blessing the viewer. In the sixteenth century real children and their games flooded the painting of Bruegal. Now the Incarnation is presented with a dramatic emphasis on the humanity of Jesus and his Mother, with the light of the afternoon sun playing on their faces in the shadows of a Roman doorway.

Notice that in this image Mary has the only halo.

◀ *Madonna di Loreto*, Caravaggio (1603–06)
Sant'Agostino, Rome
(Scala / Art Resource, NY, S. Agostino, Rome, Italy)

The breakup of Catholic unity in Europe and the British Isles continued in the seventeenth century. The Protestants and Catholics
reformed themselves over against each other while Protestant
splinter groups also found new identities by contrasting themselves to
other Protestants. In the eighteenth century reason and science become
more established, so all the various parts of Christianity began to sense
that they had something in common again. It was the challenge to their
way of understanding the world presented by an emphasis on the use of
reason and the scientific method. In this chapter we will look at both the
seventeenth and eighteenth centuries to see how theologians wrote about
children in this new environment when the reformation of the sixteenth
century was being reformed once again.

The Seventeenth Century:
Theological Indifference about Children
Except As Pawns

Compromise or reconciliation among political-religious groups seemed
impossible in the seventeenth century. Each new religious group had its
own specific political interests and culture, demanded conformity in education, and required a single kind of worship for each occupied territory.
Today the religious differences of this period may seem to be a re-trenching
and an endless elaboration of minutia, but these doctrinal details aroused
great passion and much bloodshed. The story of this period concerning
the theological views of children was one of conflict among adults on all
fronts—the political-religious conflict, science versus religion, and even
conflict within each religious group. There was little energy or interest in
trying to understand the place of children in the church except as weapons
in these conflicts.

Political-Religious Conflict

The political-religious conflict in Northern Europe stimulated the Thirty
Years' War, which raged from 1618–1648. Fields, lives, fortunes, govern-

ments, and learning were wasted. The population on the Continent fell from sixteen million to less than six million people (Walker 1959, 396). The children must have looked on with wide eyes as the adults slaughtered each other and families and homes fell into ruins around them.

Across the channel in England the century began with great optimism. The crowning of James I seemed to signify that the Elizabethan troubles were over. England and Scotland would soon become one country, people thought, and there would be peace in Europe. The children no doubt enjoyed the pageantry of the celebrations that marked these days. The King James Bible is perhaps all that is left of that glorious vision. Adam Nicolson wrote that "Nothing in our culture can match its breadth, depth and universality, unless curiously enough, it is something that was written at exactly the same time and in almost exactly the same place: the great tragedies of Shakespeare" (Nicolson 2003, 239).

While the beginning of the century began with hope it continued with civil war. This conflict was one in which "a higher proportion of the British population was killed than in any war before or since" (Nicolson 2003, 62). The children, like the children on the Continent, learned to hide and knew the bitter taste of fear on their tongues.

The bloodshed ended under William and Mary with the Toleration Act of 1689, but that toleration was extended only to various kinds of Protestants. Roman Catholics did not begin their journey toward complete freedom until 1778 and it did not end until 1829.

In France the Protestants, known as Huguenots, grew in number during the sixteenth century despite savage wars with short truces in between. For example, in 1572 on St. Bartholomew's Day in Paris some eight thousand Huguenots were massacred. By the end of the century, however, the Edict of Nantes was declared, which allowed Huguenots to hold public office again and their children were no longer required to receive Roman Catholic instruction.

In the seventeenth century, however, the persecutions began again. In 1624 Cardinal Richelieu became the king's first minister under Louis XIII. *Une foi, un loi, un roi*—one faith, one law, one king—became the cry! The Huguenots struggled for a measure of independence, but Rochelle, the last major fortified Huguenot city, fell in 1628, which marked the end of their resistance. Louis XIV was crowned at Rheims in 1654 and hoped to make France entirely Catholic once again; so the Edict of Nantes was revoked in 1685, which reduced the Huguenots once again to terrible persecution destroying homes and driving thousands into exile.

The Conflict between Science and Religion

The second kind of conflict during this century was between science and religion. Much of this controversy centered around Galileo, who died in 1642, the same year that Isaac Newton was born in England. Two illustrations will show how threatening this was to the church.

First, the new science disrupted the satisfying correlation of space and destiny that most people pictured in their minds. Hell was at the center of the earth, far from God who was in the heavens. The whole drama of sin and salvation was shattered when the new science described the earth as only one of many planets circling around the enormous sun. The perfect realm of the heavens, considered so near God, now could be seen to be imperfect by looking through one of the new telescopes at the pockmarked moon if you had the courage!

Second, the physics used in Galileo's book *The Assayer* challenged the reality of the way the Roman Catholic mass was considered. The old physics from Aristotle allowed for both an essence and accidents to make up matter; so the accidents might remain the same on the surface of the bread and wine when the essence was changed by the Holy Spirit into Christ's body and blood. The new physics held that what is sensed is what is real, which was declared an error by the Council of Trent. A concern about protecting the mass caused the doctrine of transubstantiation to be protected at all costs, as Redondi has argued (Redondi 1987, 162–165).

The conflict spread from cosmology and the understanding of matter to all the sciences, because the change of method from theology to science changed how all knowledge was understood. Authority no longer resided in texts alone but in careful observation, experimentation, and mathematical detail. The authority of science was pitted against the authority of the Bible, the church, and revelation. The conflict was so severe that the only way of coping by the church seemed to be by force, as in the case of Galileo, who was imprisoned in his house, and before him Giordano Bruno, who was burned at the stake.

The rise of the new science brought greater concern about children's health and the care taken in their upbringing, but the conflict between the church and science must have left children amazed if they were interested at all. What they knew was known with their senses and their method was wonder, which led both to a greater understanding of the world around them and of the mystery of religion.

The Struggle between Inner Piety and the Official Church

The third major conflict of this century that will be highlighted here was the struggle between inner piety and the dominating, official churches that controlled various regions of Europe and the British Isles. Three examples will be given—one each from Lutheran Germany, Anglican England, and Catholic France. They are Jacob Boehme, John Bunyan, and Blaise Pascal. Their views of children will be examined as well as those held by missionaries to New France, which today is the Quebec region of Canada.

Boehme, Bunyan and Pascal were all lay theologians, which was a new phenomenon. None of them were university-trained in theology or any other field of learning. Boehme and Bunyan coped with the challenge of science by ignoring it, but Pascal, who was taught at home by his father, embraced the conflict and with great brilliance discovered the limits of science. All three confronted the confessional abstractions and power of the established church where they lived. The missionaries of the Jesuit and Ursuline orders who worked directly with children show another side to this struggle. They were faithful to their orders and the Roman Church but their experience in the New World raised questions that must have troubled them as they sought to save the souls of the children around them. We will now examine these four examples of personal theological conflict in more detail to see what these theologians wrote about children and the experience they based it on.

Jacob Boehme (1575–1624)
Children Are "Legitimate," "Historical," or "Whore-brats"

Jacob was born into a prosperous farming family. They lived in Alt Seidenberg near Gorlitz, which today is along the Polish-German border. His family was strongly Lutheran and Jacob's father held offices in the local church. Jacob was not strong as a child, so following elementary school in his village, he was apprenticed to a shoemaker. Almost nothing is known about his first twenty-four years except for stories about his visions, some of which may be pious legends.

In 1599 he became a citizen of Gorlitz, which became a city in the thirteenth century, where he entered business as a shoemaker. In May of that same year he married a local butcher's daughter, Catharina Kuntzschmann. Between 1600 and 1611 Catharina gave birth to four sons. Boehme was active in the shoe-making business during that time, but later in life he entered the linen trade.

In 1600 Martin Moller arrived in Gorlitz as the senior Lutheran pastor. He had read widely in medieval mystical literature and was part of a group within the Lutheran church, which was uneasy with the dry, testy, hair-splitting theology of orthodox Lutheranism that at the time was defining itself in detail against the Catholics and Calvinists. Moller developed a practice of warm, personal piety in his parish and organized the "Conventicle of God's Real Servants" to support people who wanted to live together in this redeeming way. Boehme became part of this group and was shaped spiritually by Moller's example and authority.

It was also in 1600 that Boehme had an important vision. Perhaps it was related to his meditations on the reflection of his eye in a pewter dish as if it were his soul (Boehme 1978, 6). In any case he began to write. His essays were copied and passed around, but after Moller died in 1606 the new Lutheran pastor, Gregory Richter, arrived. He was a devoted defender of orthodoxy, who prohibited Jacob from writing any more. This caused what Boehme called his "sabbath of years." He did not write again for seven years.

The last years of his life were a struggle. In the background to everything was the bloody and dangerous Thirty Years' War. He was also at war with his pastor. In the midst of all this he was struggling to write a description of the spiritual journey, which culminated in his *The Way to Christ*. The book was immediately attacked by Richter, who got Jacob exiled from the city. He moved to Dresden, but late in 1624 he returned, sick and weary. By that time Pastor Richter was dead. The new pastor was called to Boehme's home to hear his confession. He accepted Jacob's confession as orthodox and he was able to receive the Lord's Supper. Jacob Boehme died several days later on November 17.

His masterpiece, *The Way to Christ*, is divided into nine "treatises." There are at least 25 direct uses of the term "child" or "children" in the book (Boehme 1978—34, 40, 41, 66, 68, 70, 77, 82, 83 100, 119, 121, 130, 132, 134, 140, 156, 158, 159, 165, 166, 168, 170, 173, 227), but this topic was not included in the index of "The Classics of Western Spirituality" edition of *The Way of Christ* .

He used the term "children" mostly as a metaphor for the adult spiritual maturity in *The Way To Christ*. For example "becoming like a child" was thought of as spiritual sinlessness and being born again. He wrote about "the child who knows nothing of sin" (Boehme 1978, 132) and Nicodemus' encounter with Jesus in John 3:5–6, when Jesus told Nicodemus that he must be born again. Adults "must become as a child that knows nothing and groans only for the mother who bore it" (Boehme

1978, 140). Boehme's model of spiritual maturity is adult dependence on God that results in being sinless. The child is also used to illustrate the positive use of the will, which "should hang on to grace as a child to its mother's breast" (Boehme 1978, 77).

The play of the child is also mentioned. There is a negative use of the term "play" that indicates how everything is a plaything to the sinner by which he spends his time in restlessness" (Boehme 1978, 30), but there is a positive use as well. He prays to God to "Play on me in Your reborn image and lead my harmony into Your divine kingdom of joy." Being born again is when one's spirit becomes a stringed instrument on which the Holy Spirit plays (Boehme 1978, 53). He also invites the reader to join in the writer's journey "to tread the paths where one plays with Sophia" (Boehme 1978, 57) and he prays in an evening prayer to God: "Let my mind only play in Your temple in You and let Your good angel remain with me so that I may rest with certainty in Your power. Amen" (Boehme 1978, 64). He also referred to how "My spirit plays in Your power and rejoices in Your truth" (Boehme 1978, 84).

Boehme speaks of three kinds of children, but this is a typology of adults. There are "legitimate children." They are born anew (Boehme 1978, 156, 136), as the "true child" (Boehme 1978, 158), with the "child-like essence" (Boehme 1978, 159). Second, there is the "historical child," who remains only human instead of purely spiritual. Finally, there is the "whore-brat" of the "stone church" (Boehme 1978, 163). "The saint . . . has his church with him and in him at all places," but the "whore-brat" is the hypocritical "whore of Babylon," who uses the "stone church" for her purposes.

Boehme's way to Christ appears to begin after childhood when one is an adult. The goal of this great journey is called the *Mysterium Magnum*. The path begins with repentance (treatises 1 and 2), moves on to learning how to pray well (treatise 3), then resigning one's self completely to God (treatise 4), then experiencing new birth (treatise 5), and finally growth in the contemplation of God (treatises 6 and 7). He then summarized this journey by a dialogue between the enlightened and unenlightened soul (treatise 8), and offered practical advice for pilgrims of various personality types (treatise 9).

After his death in 1624, Boehme's work was spread across Europe by his disciples. One of the most intriguing of these followers was Johann Scheffler (1624–1677), or Angelus Silesius, as he is better known. He was influenced by many German mystics such as Meister Eckhart and *The Theologia Germanica*, which Luther reissued in 1516/1517, but also by Boehme (Angelus Silesius 1986, 24).

The Cherubinic Wanderer (Angelus Silesius 1986) was re-discovered by one the greatest philosophers of the twentieth century, Martin Heidegger (1889–1976), who wrote in *The Principle of Ground* that "What is unsaid in the saying, and everything depends on this, is rather that man, in the most hidden ground of his essence, first truly is, when he is in his own way like the rose, without why" (quoted in Caputo 1986, 189). What he probably was referring to was one of Angelus Silesius' many succinct and poetic summaries of Boehme's theology which translates something like this: "My heart could receive God if only it chose/ To turn toward the Light as does the rose." The jubilant rhythm of Alexandrine verse does not always translate perfectly, but this carries the gist of one of his many rose meditations (Angelus Silesius 1986, 44, 54, 76).

Children are natural mystics and naturally turn toward God, like the rose, but children were not Boehme's emphasis. Instead, he seems rather indifferent to them in his writing except as symbols of adult perfection. Actual children don't seem to have much to teach adults for Boehme. This indifference was also true in the account of the spiritual life created by John Bunyan in England.

John Bunyan (1628–1688)
Children Are To Be Fled From For The Spiritual Journey

John Bunyan (1628–1688) was born in a small village about a mile south of Bedford, a major city in Bedfordshire, England. The southern border of Bedfordshire, the smallest of the "shires," is only some thirty miles north of London. His father was a tinker, but not the vagrant kind of tinker who was often of gypsy origin. He was permanently settled in Elstow and his son, John, learned that trade as well. Little is known about John's early life, but he did have some schooling, perhaps two to four years. He really learned to read and write, however, from his first wife after they were married.

During the English Civil War, the sixteen-year-old John Bunyan joined the Parliamentary Army and served for three years until a religious experience turned him to religious matters. He lived sixty years and wrote some sixty works—debating theological issues of the time, explaining scripture and theology, and providing practical help for the spiritual life. In 1678 he published *The Pilgrim's Progress*, for which he is best known.

Bunyan spent a good bit of time in jail off and on during his life because he refused to stop preaching without a license. He could have left jail at any time, merely by saying that he would not preach, but he refused. He also had no interest in university training or becoming an Anglican priest.

His famous quip about the *Book of Common Prayer* was that he could find no place in scripture where it said he should read from it when he worshipped.

Bunyan was married at age twenty-one. He and his first wife had four children. During this time he was baptized by immersion in the River Ouse at Bedford and began to worship with the Baptists. After his first wife died he remarried in 1659. Two more children were born to this union. Three children survived his death. Blind Mary, about whom he famously wrote in jail, did not.

In 1660, almost immediately after his second marriage, he was jailed again at Bedford for preaching without a license. He made "long tagged laces" to help support his family while in jail and was sometimes allowed to sleep at home. While in jail he also preached to the some fifty other non-conformist clergy and lay people. This "congregation" was large because one could be jailed for listening to an illegal sermon as well as for preaching one. While in jail he did a great amount of reading and writing. His spiritual autobiography, *Grace Abounding to the Chief of Sinners*, was published in 1666. He may also have written *The Pilgrims's Progress* during this period. When he was released in 1672 he became pastor of the Bedford Church.

Finally, he was released from jail for good in 1675 and continued on as pastor at the Bedford Church. *The Pilgrim's Progress* was published in 1678. Bunyan died ten years later while on a trip to London from Bedford.

The Pilgrim's Progress is an allegorical story about a man named Christian who followed the Puritan's eight steps to salvation: election, calling, faith, repentance, justification, forgiveness, sanctification, and perseverance in the story of his life (Greaves 1969, 50). The view of children in this work is dramatically portrayed when Christian fled his wife and children with his fingers in his ears to seek his own personal salvation (Bunyan 2003, 13).

The family of Christian was left out of his allegory of salvation until six years later in 1684. Bunyan, with his long hair parted in the middle and swooping mustache, finally added a sequel that included Christian's family and their journey to salvation. This was, perhaps, prompted as much by a spurious continuation of the allegory by Thomas Sherman published in 1682 as a concern for or interest in Christian's fictional family, or children and families in general.

His own family had been taught to take care of itself and to help support him while he was in jail, reading and writing. He chose his right to preach without a license over the care of his family, since he could have left jail at any time to care for them by continuing his trade as a tinker like his father. He did, however, write about his suffering and worry when he thought about his family while he was in jail. This may have been in part motivated by a plea for public sympathy to be freed and to make his point about the freedom to preach.

The contrast between Bunyan and Boethius, who each wrote a masterpiece in jail, is dramatic. The sixth-century *Consolation of Philosophy* and the seventeenth-century *The Pilgrim's Progress* are so different that it is hard to realize that they are both about the salvation of the soul. Neither has much to say about children, however, so we will move on, only to smile about what it would have been like if the bombastic, uneducated tinker and the cultured, intellectual politician had been in the same jail cell!

Bunyan had no use for bishops or the rest of the Anglican establishment's theology or liturgy. His temperament was vastly different from the Anglican Richard Hooker. He used a calm, learned analysis of scripture, the traditions of the church, and the careful use of reason to reach his theological conclusions while Bunyan preferred emotion and drama. Hooker's university training, so important to him, was irrelevant to Bunyan who approached theology in much the same way that an inventive tinker might fix things that were broken in the home. What Bunyan knew above all was people, and he understood the struggle of the spiritual journey. That is what made his *The Pilgrim's Progress* so powerful and popular. It has not been out of print since it was first published in English and, as W. R. Owens tells us, it has been translated into two hundred languages (Bunyan 2003, xiii).

We can conclude, then, that Bunyan was generally indifferent to children in his writing and his journey toward salvation. They had little to teach him about his main theological concerns. He probably did miss his children while in jail and worried about them, especially blind Mary, but his focus was on adults, their foibles, and their progress as pilgrims toward the Celestial City.

Blaise Pascal (1623–1662)
Children Are Unchangeable by Natural Means

While the people in Germany and England were mostly Protestant in France they were mostly Roman Catholic. We have described the troubles of the Huguenots in France, but among Roman Catholics there were also disagreements about how the church defined the religious life. The Roman Catholic bishop of Geneva, Francis de Sales (1567–1622), who lived in Catholic France rather than Reformed Geneva, promoted the spiritual life of lay people outside the walls of the monastery while the theologians at the University of Paris attempted to control what they considered theological truth in France. Pascal, as a lay person, pushed both the limits of the spiritual life and the theological dictates of the church, as he struggled with the limitations of his own vocation as a scientist.

Blaise Pascal (1623–1662) was a mathematical and scientific genius. This was recognized early by his father, who found him working out the geometry of Euclid on his own as a child, developing his own terminology, because of his interest in shapes. He knew Rene Descartes (1596–1650) through his father's circle of scientist friends and was about fourteen when Descartes published his *Discourse on Method* in 1637.

Descartes, like Pascal, was a Roman Catholic. He argued that all knowledge begins with doubt, that mind and matter are opposites, and that proof must have the certainty of a mathematical demonstration to be correct. Pascal, on the other hand, placed more emphasis on faith as a means of knowing, as he grew older, and drew a major distinction between science, which used the knowing of the body by the senses and the knowing of the mind by reason, and what Pascal considered the knowing of "the heart" by faith. These ways of knowing could not be added together any more than x, the square of x, and the cube of x could be. Each had to be understood in terms of its own dimensions.

Pascal was austere and often in ill health. He experienced the presence of God in 1646 and again in an even more decisive way in 1654, but he never spoke about this. What he did do, however, was challenge the Catholic establishment with his reason and scorn in the *Provincial Letters*, which he began to publish in 1656. During the last four years of his life, he began to collect notes to write a substantial statement of the Christian faith. This resulted in his *Pensees* (*Thoughts*) published for the first time in 1670, eight years after his death.

His scientific interests included mathematics and physics. He invented a calculating machine called the Pascaline, performed dramatic experiments related to contemporary questions and prejudices about vacuums and barometric pressure, wrote on the theory of conic sections, began to think in terms of what we call today probability and decision theory in relation to the gambling that was so fashionable during his time, and speculated on other scientific matters. As a scientist, he had learned to trust his observations, so what he learned from observing his experiences of God was that the heart has "reasons" of its own.

He wrote in the *Pensees*:

   ↻ We know the truth not only through our reason but also through our heart. It is through the latter that we know first principles, and reason, which has nothing to do with it, tries in vain to refute them . . . . For knowledge of first principles, like space, time, motion, number, is as solid as any derived through reason, and it is on such knowledge, coming from the heart and instinct, that reason has to depend and base all its argument . . . . Principles are felt, propositions proved, and both with certainty though by different means. It is just as pointless and absurd for reason to demand proof of first principles from the heart before agreeing to accept them as it would be absurd for the heart to demand an intuition of all the propositions demonstrated by reason before agreeing to accept them. (Pascal 1995, 28, #110) ↺

Blaise Pascal lived in his father's home until his father, Etienne, died in 1651. In January of the next year his younger sister, Jacqueline, moved to the Port Royal convent in Paris. His older sister, Gilberte, had already married Florin Perier in 1641 and was raising her own family. Blaise was alone for the first time without family around him for support at the age of about thirty. Jacqueline took her vows in 1653.

When he experienced God on November 23, 1654, Pascal knew what his heart was telling him, but never told anyone. Nine years later, just after he died, his nephew was going through his clothing and found a memorial pinned inside his coat near his heart. On further examination he found a piece of crumpled parchment with a faded paper wrapped inside. His "night of fire" had been recorded in his own handwriting. When he wrote about the heart having its own reasons, he knew what he was talking about and he committed himself to "Complete submission to Jesus Christ and to my director" (Connor 2006, 148). He placed himself under the direction of a succession of spiritual directors and took up the cause of Jansenism. Nothing else seemed changed outwardly, however, which worried his sister, the nun at Port Royal, who wrote that he seemed "so jolly a penitent" (quoted in O'Connell 1997, 105). He did not even give up his association with the notorious gamblers, whose company he enjoyed.

Children did not appear on his horizon in any significant way. His emphasis was on the feelings and intuition as the means to know God. This, of course, leaves room to discuss how children might know God the same way, even if they cannot articulate what they know by their hearts, but he did not develop this theme. In the *Pensees*, however, he did mention children many times (Pascal 1995, 12, 18, 22, 32, 36, 41, 42,, 72, 151, 155,

159, 236, 244, 278, 279, 294, 303, and 308). These instances are mostly in phrases such as "false impressions of childhood," "these poor children," "religion taught its children" (12, 18, and 72). He did note that "Wisdom leads us back to childhood. *Except ye become as little children*" (22). This single sentence in the *Pensees* is not developed.

Another sentence is especially intriguing. He wrote, "These children are amazed to see respect paid to their fellows" (151). Who paid respect to them? Jesus? Other children? Adults? This is the problem with many of the random notes he jotted down. One does not always have an adequate context for their interpretation.

Pascal's view of child development was touched on in a section about children being frightened by a face (seen in a mirror?) that has been "daubed" (perhaps with some kind of dark paint?). He mentions this twice in the *Pensees* (41, 236) and the second time he draws this conclusion:

> ◡ Children, who are scared of the face they have daubed, are just children, but how can someone who is so weak as a child become really strong when grown up? Only our imagination changes. Everything that grows progressively better also declines progressively. Nothing that was once weak can ever be absolutely strong. It is no good saying: "He has grown, he has changed"; he is still the same. (Pascal 1995, 236) ◡

In other words, not much changes in human development. We might expect such a view from a mathematical prodigy. His younger sister was also precocious but in a literary way rather than in science. His sisters were the only children he really knew. The Pascal children did not go to school with other children and were taught at home by their father, who introduced them to adult groups of scientists, the political elite, and literary figures rather than people their own age.

In one case he spoke of faith being like a child who is pulled two ways. A thief who has stolen a child pulls the child his way and the child's mother pulls in the other direction, trying to pull the child back. This shows, he argued, how "our natural vice resists supernatural grace" and "our heart feels torn between these contrary forces." The point is that the child loves "the loving and lawful violence of its rescuer," and it hates "the injurious and tyrannical violence of those who wrongfully hold on to it" (Pascal 1995, 294). This metaphor does not make the mother very nourishing but she is strong and determined to take the child back. Pascal's own mother died when Gilberte was six, Blaise was three, and Jacqueline was only about a year old. His father never remarried. At one level, perhaps, he longed for his own mother to come to his rescue as well as "supernatural grace."

The conflict Pascal had with the established church grew out of his association with Jansenism, a movement named after Bishop Cornelius Jansen (1585–1638), the author of *Augustinus*, published in 1640, two years after his death when Pascal was about seventeen. The movement grew largely through the efforts of Jansen's colleague, Abbe Saint-Cyran, an absentee abbot who enjoyed the revenues of his monastery without residing there (O'Connell 1997, 65) and Mere Angelique, the abbess of the Port-Royal convent, who was part of the vast and influential Arnauld family.

This movement advocated for an Augustinianism of moral rigor to combat the more relaxed, semi-Pelagian views of sin and grace held by the Jesuits. It was said that Jansen "had read the whole of the vast Augustinian corpus ten times and the anti-Pelagian material thirty times" (O'Connell 1997, 41).

Most Jesuits followed the theology of St. Thomas Aquinas with its optimistic balance between faith and reason, but in 1588 a Spanish Jesuit, Luis de Molina, got specific. He published his *De concordia liberi arbitrii cum donis divinae gratiae (On the Harmony of Free Will with the Gifts of Divine Grace)* and the theological debate exploded!

Molina argued that grace and free will worked jointly and simultaneously to bring about the justification of the individual. This view was completely rejected at the Port-Royal Convent in Paris, where Pascal was often present and his younger sister Jacqueline lived as a nun. Pascal took up the cause and attacked the traditional sources of theological power— pope, king, bishops, and the university—with scorn and humor as they circled around the Jansenists to extinguish their movement (O'Connell 1997, 129). His weapon was the *Provincial Letters*, which were published anonymously between January 27, 1656 and March 24, 1657. They did not work, brilliant as they may have been, and by 1660 it was over.

The king took charge and ended Cardinal Mazarin's policy of tolerance. Sensing which way the wind was blowing the Cardinal attacked Jansenism in an hour-long denunciation which argued that "two popes and the overwhelming majority of the French bishops had condemned and which, since mildness had failed to stem its baneful influence, must now be treated with severity" (O'Connell 1997, 177).

During this time Pascal was also collecting his thoughts (*Pensees*). Perhaps the most famous was about his wager (Pascal 1995, 121–125) that was connected with the heart having reasons of its own (Pascal 1995, 127). God cannot be known by reason so a reasonable wager is needed. Gambling was the rage in France so this metaphor must have resonated with many.

If God exists, we have much more to gain than we have to lose if God does not. This wager does not resonate with children like his idea of the heart having reasons of its own, but the playfulness of the suggestion does.

His quick wit was never far away. He wrote, "The heart has its reasons of which reason knows nothing. We know this in countless ways. I say that it is natural for the heart to love the universal being or itself, according to its allegiance, and it hardens itself against either as it chooses. You have rejected one and kept the other. Is it reason that makes you love yourself" (Pascal 1995, 127)? There is no belly laugh here, but perhaps an ironic smile is in order.

Pascal's health continued to decline and, finally, he moved into his older sister's house in June 1662. He lived only six more weeks, staying mostly in bed. Madame Perier invited Pere Beurrier to visit her brother to hear his confession. The priest came several times and Pascal took much consolation from this. The priest was also edified by the way Pascal endured his sufferings. "He is like a little child," he said to Gilberte, "he is so humble, he is submissive as an infant" (quoted in O'Connell 1997, 189).

We have now taken a brief look at three lay theologians of the seventeenth century. They were not much more inclined to include children in their thought than the clergy, Protestant or Catholic. Boehme struggled in the conflict between inner piety and the official Lutheran orthodoxy. Bunyan struggled with the Anglican establishment. Pascal struggled in the conflict between religion and science as well as between inner piety and the official church, in his case the Roman Catholic Church. We turn now to how Catholic missionaries to New France saw children as they worked there with sincerity and energy to convert the Native Americans.

Jesuit and Ursuline Missionaries in French Canada: Children Are Pawns in Religious Conflicts

During the sixteenth century, South and Central America had been settled by Spain and converted primarily by the Franciscans, Dominicans, and Jesuits to Catholicism. The English colonies in North America were settled by Anglicans and Puritans, except for Maryland, which was Catholic. The French settled in what is now Quebec, which became Catholic mainly through the aggressive work of the first bishop, Francois de Laval (1623–1708).

Clarissa W. Atkinson studied the Jesuit and Ursuline missionaries who helped settle Quebec. She wanted to understand their assumptions about the nature, education, and discipline of the indigenous children they worked with in the 1630s and 40s. She based her study (Atkinson 2001, 227–246) primarily on the reports that Jesuit and Ursuline missionaries sent back to their orders in France. They used children as the primary means to Christianize the "heathens" for the long-term increase of the church to which they were devoted.

The Jesuits had been trained in the humanist tradition to work with older boys while the Ursulines had been pushed back into the cloister in France after being founded in the fifteenth century to teach girls in the towns and cities of southern Europe. In the New World the Jesuits found them-selves teaching little boys their alphabet and the Ursulines taught reading, writing, and needlework to children in their boarding schools to draw the native Hurons toward a kind of Christianity that was mixed with the French culture of a settled middle class marriage (Atkinson 2001, 233).

These missionaries thought that all native people were "childlike," since they did not know French, which meant that they could not reason properly. They focused their energy on the Huron because they were a settled tribe. The Huron, however, did not feel inferior about the way they reasoned. They seemed to think that they were doing the missionaries a favor to give them their children to instruct, feed, and dress.

In addition, the Huron did not think that French ways of rearing children were appropriate. The missionaries admired the love the Huron people had for their children, but they were shocked that they did not use corporal punishment, which was taken for granted in French homes and schools.

These cultural differences compelled the missionaries to set up board-ing schools so they could get more control over the children, to raise them in the way the missionaries were accustomed to. This looked to the Huron like incomprehensible brutality. They were also puzzled as to why the mis-sionaries did not have families of their own. The vow to celibacy seemed ludicrous to the native people.

There was another, more subtle cultural difference between the mis-sionaries and the Huron People. The missionaries had an inner conflict between the love they felt for the children they worked with and their love of God. They felt that they could love the children but they could not love them too much, because that would get in the way of their ultimate love of God. This too was incomprehensible to the Huron.

The Jesuit missionaries of the sixteenth century to Latin America had used a theological anthropology shaped by Aristotle and Thomas Aquinas, which found that human nature, including that of the native people, was basically good and worthy of study in its own right. The Catholic missionaries to North America in the seventeenth century, however, were shaped more by French than Spanish culture and were less warm and optimistic.

Atkinson notes: "Peter Goddard has argued persuasively that French Jesuits departed from the humanist, Thomist, and (according to their enemies) lax traditions of their own order." Instead, they thought in terms of the Augustinian "total corruption of nature" and used the Indians as examples (because of their cultural differences) of what terrible things could happen when evil human nature is "unrestrained by Christian teaching and practice" (Atkinson 2001, 242).

Perhaps the most tragic miscommunication was about baptism. This was commented on often in the reports by the missionaries because it marked the inclusion of adults and children into the Christian Church, which was their reason for being in the New World. To get adults to agree to being baptized the Jesuits used education, money, and the fear of hell. Economic pressure included such incentives as allowing firearms to be sold only to baptized Native Americans.

In the case of children, however, they tried to get parental permission for baptism, but in the terrible epidemics brought by the white people— smallpox in 1634, influenza in 1636, scarlet fever 1637 and a recurrence of smallpox in 1639—there was not always time (Atkinson 2001, 228, 243). The missionaries were desperate to baptize the children to save their souls, but some of the Huron began to think that baptism *caused* death because so many baptized babies died. They also thought that it might be better for a dead child to go to the place where his or her dead relatives might be rather than to a foreign, Christian heaven.

The missionaries tried to explain that children did not have to experience conversion like adults to be baptized and if they were baptized they would go to heaven. They also argued with kindness that if the babies were not baptized they would still go to a kind of limbo described by Aquinas (Atkinson 2001, 243). This was a place where the infants do not suffer the pains of hell. They are nevertheless excluded from those who enjoy God's presence for eternity. This was a logical but chilling compromise, often unfathomable to the Native Americans but sometimes gratefully received. The doctrine of *limbo infantis* was ultimately rejected in 2007 by Rome.

The well-meaning missionaries had come to the New World to save souls. This idealism was merged with incorporating them into the French Catholic culture they brought with them. They were not the first, nor the last, missionaries to merge cultural and Christian ideals. From the missionary point of view the need to make the children French Catholic converts was not only important in the conflict with pagans but also with the Protestants.

As the seventeenth century drew to a close, the heat of the political-religious conflicts cooled and people began to realize that both the Protestants and the Roman Catholics were there to stay. Outside the church the growing intellectual and political freedom allowed confidence in science, reason, and education to develop, and science began to be thought of as a means for progressive reform for all humanity, including children. Finally, at the end of the century the distance between popular and "enlightened" (historically conscious, reasonable, and critical) religion was increasing. Into this new situation stepped two English-speaking theologians—John Wesley and Jonathan Edwards. One was from England and the other from the New England.

The Eighteenth Century's Theological Anxiety: Children Need To Be Converted and Controlled

Some have located the beginning of the modern age during the eighteenth century. This is because reason and science became established as criteria to evaluate the truth of ideas and values. In some areas—such as medicine, physics, and biology—reason and science even prevailed over the authority of church tradition and revelation, mediated by Christian clergy.

This was also a time when Christian people recognized that the divisions of the sixteenth century were permanent. Catholics and Protestants stopped attacking each other and Protestants fought among themselves with less intensity. The major problem in this century was the challenge by secularism, which confronted Protestants and Catholics alike.

The response to this in England took two major forms. One was the development of a highly rational theology that gained some traction among the upper and better educated classes. The other development was a kind of Christianity that was full of feeling and urgency, which brought hope to people in the mills, the mines, and the sprawling, growing cities. This alternative was not tied to the parishes of the countryside or in the great cathedral communities, but worship took place in huge meetings out of doors and in unofficial meeting places indoors.

The emphasis on rational theology can be illustrated by merely noting the titles of three books published near the beginning, middle, and end of the century. John Toland's *Christianity not Mysterious* was published in 1696 and Joseph Butler's *The Analogy of Religion* in 1736. Just after the turn of the century William Paley's *Natural Religion* was published. This approach almost sounds like an effort to think about religion without being religious. It certainly did nothing to touch the lives of the people who struggled to make a living in the cities, mills and mines.

A great division appeared, therefore, in the English-speaking world between the theologians and people going about their daily lives. The attempt to be as scientific and secular as possible lost contact with ordinary people's feelings and gave rise to the major religious movement in the eighteenth century. Two English-speaking theologians, one on each side of the Atlantic, led the way. John Wesley in England and Jonathan Edwards in New England understood the longing for a more personal and emotionally satisfying way to be religious and to live a better life. Their leadership had important consequences for children.

Focusing on two English-speaking theologians does not mean that Europeans were not aware of the same sort of challenge. The Moravians are an illustration of Continental awareness about the need for a more emotionally satisfying way to be religious. Count Nikolaus Ludwig von Zinzendorf allowed the Moravians to found a village on his estate in Germany, which was named *Herrnhut*. Zinzendorf was ultimately banished from Saxony and by 1741 he was in New York. He then traveled to eastern Pennsylvania, north of Philadelphia, to meet with some Moravians there who had come from Georgia. On Christmas Eve of that year he founded a settlement in Pennsylvania and called it Bethlehem. It was not far from where, in the winter of 1777–1778, some twelve thousand soldiers of the Continental Army wintered at Valley Forge.

John and Charles Wesley were greatly influenced by the Moravians, some of whom they met on shipboard when they traveled to Georgia. They remained in contact with the Moravians while they were in Georgia and also after they returned to London. We shall meet the Moravians again in the nineteenth century, because they also influenced the theologian Schleiermacher; but for now let us turn our attention to how John Wesley and Jonathan Edwards thought about children and the experience they based it on.

John Wesley (1703–1791)
Children Need a Method for Perfection

John Wesley was born in the rectory at Epworth in Lincolnshire, England. When he was about six years old the rectory caught on fire. All the family and the nurse escaped only to discover that little John was still inside. When he awoke, his room was on fire and the staircase aflame. He climbed to the window and was pulled out just as the roof fell in (Hattersley 2003, 25–27).

His mother promised God that she would be "more particularly careful of the soul of this child, that Thou hast so mercifully provided for, than ever I have been, that I may do my endeavours to instill into his mind the disciplines of true religion and virtue" (quoted in Hattersley 2003, 27). Being "particularly careful" may have led to John's later ambivalent relations with women (Rack 2002, 78–79, 257–269). He once wrote to his brother, Charles, concerning his relationship with Grace Murray, that he would never marry "because I should never find such a woman as my father had" (quoted in Rack 2002, 261).

Somewhat like the itinerant friars who met the new challenges during the Middle Ages, John Wesley met the challenge of the new age in England, which stood on the brink of the industrial revolution. This revolution would change England from an agricultural to a manufacturing society during the last third of this century. Instead of staying put in a parish, as Anglican priests like his father did, he and his growing movement met people of the lower and middle classes and their children in the city slums and grim industrial towns where the need was greatest.

In 1720 John went up to Christ Church College, Oxford, and his brother, Charles, followed him there six years later. Between 1726 and 1729 John helped his father in his parish and was also chosen as a Fellow of Lincoln College. To be a Fellow he had to be in Holy Orders and was ordained a deacon in 1725, which began the spiritual struggles that lasted the rest of his life.

Meanwhile at Christ Church, Charles had helped start a club for support, study, and the salvation of the students' souls through a sober and ordered life. When John returned to Oxford he took over leadership of the club, which the other students called the "Methodists" to belittle them. The name stuck. George Whitefield was one of the club's first members and he too became a leader in the evangelical revival of the church in both England and New England.

John learned his orderly approach to achieving perfection from his mother. She managed wet nurses, maids, cooks, gardeners, butlers, and other help on the income of a country rector. She also organized her household so that only five or six of ten surviving children were ever at home at the same time. During his days as a tutor at Lincoln College, Oxford, he asked her for a description of the way she reared her children. This was published after her death in his *Armenian Magazine* in 1779.

She wrote, "When turned a year old (and some before), they were taught to fear the rod, and to cry softly; by which means they escaped abundance of correction they might otherwise have had; and that most odious noise of the crying of children was rarely heard in the house; but the family usually lived in as much quietness, as if there had not been a child among them" (Heitzenrater 2001, 284). There were "no first hand accounts to indicate the actual daily practices in the Wesley household" (Heitzenrater 2001, 283–284, note 19), so the severity and frequency of her approach to "fear of the rod" must remain an open question.

Education was important in the Wesley family. It was typical of the times for the mother to be in charge of the children's early education, but Susanna was exceptionally scrupulous. The alphabet was begun on each fifth birthday and reading was learned from the Bible. Susanna made sure that the girls learned to read well before they began to learn their homemaker skills.

It is no surprise that John also valued education. He taught that education needs to begin with awe and respect, hopefully resolving into love, to be successful. He, like his mother, focused on the will. It needed to be broken before age two, he thought. If you wait, it will still need to be done, and each year you wait the more trouble it becomes. In his sermon "On Obedience to Parents" he commented that "The trouble it causes at ten or twelve years of age is what you deserve for waiting" (Heitzenrater 2001, 285).

John Wesley never had a family of his own. He finally married the widow Mary (Molly) Vazeille, whose late husband had been a London merchant. John had had complicated relationships with women and ambivalence about marriage since he and his brother traveled to the new colony of Georgia in 1735. Sophy Hopkey of Savannah was ready to marry John when he backed off, but he would not let her go. She married soon afterward in spite of his ambivalence and her new husband objected to her continuing in her intimate religious discussions with Wesley. Legal action was started against Wesley, which helped him decide to return to England. When he finally did marry about sixteen years later he was forty-eight and his wife was forty-one years old. They never had children of their own.

John, however, read widely about children and was a good observer. Among those he read was Rousseau. In his "A Thought upon the Manner of Educating Children," he wrote that Rousseau's "Emilius, (is) the most empty, silly, injudicious thing that ever a self-conceited infidel wrote." On February 3, 1770, he also wrote privately in his journal: "How was I disappointed. Sure a more consummate coxcomb never saw the sun" (Heitzenrater 2001, 288–289)!

Wesley was not the only one to have doubts about Rousseau's novel about education. The chief censor of books in Paris passed the book *Emile* for publication but then official tolerance suddenly came to an end. "The fourth part of the book, entitled the 'Profession of Faith of the Savoyard Vicar,' caused the work to be condemned and burned for contesting the authority of the church and the rule of dogma. To the question 'What role should the clergy play in a child's training?' Rousseau's answer was simple: none at all" (Edmonds and Eidinow 2006, 34). This would have mattered to John Wesley. It would also have mattered that Rousseau had never actually been involved in education. Wesley had, as we shall see.

Rousseau had trouble in both Paris and Geneva, so he decided to move to England. One of his benefactors was David Hume, the Scottish philosopher, who at first admired Rousseau as an author and a human being. Later that admiration evaporated when he tried to help him get settled in England. Hume's interest in *Emile* had always been limited. He thought that intermingled with genius there was "some degree of extravagance . . . (O)ne would be apt to suspect that he chooses his topics less from persuasion, than from the pleasure of showing his invention, and surprising the reader by his paradoxes" (quoted in Edmonds and Eidinow 2006, 41).

Wesley was not alone then in his frustration with *Emile*, but his impatience went beyond the French censor and the Scottish philosopher, because he had actual experience with schools as well as his inherited and treasured ideals about children. His *Plain Account of Kingswood School* described life in one of the schools he established.

Children rose at four o'clock in the morning and went to bed at eight o'clock. There was no loud talking. They had to always be in the presence of a master, otherwise they might "run up and down the wood." Children ought never to play. They would be ruined, he thought, if allowed such free rein. Proper recreation was walking, working, or singing. Wesley thought that learning and piety work together for self-knowledge and salvation, but "without love, all learning is but splendid ignorance."

His goal for education was the same as his goal for religion. It was to achieve "perfection," the complete love of God and neighbor. The earlier instruction begins the better, because corruption begins early. His journal included descriptions of children as early as three years of age who had what he considered a proper conversion experience.

Wesley, much like Luther, held that each child was "justified and yet a sinner," but he did "not have a consistently clear position on this matter" (Heitzenrater 2001, 294). His general goal, however, was clear. It was to "promote, so far as I am able, vital, practical religion; and by the grace of God, beget, preserve, and increase the life of God in the soul of men" (Dowley 2002, 454). John Wesley was a "reasonable enthusiast" (Rack 2002, xvi), who sometimes used clear and logical thinking and at other times was illogical and deeply emotional. He was always rigorous and he always worked hard.

Our story continues among English-speaking people, but it now moves from England to New England. Jonathan Edwards also combined the apparently contradictory personality traits of deep and emotional piety with a profound respect for reason. He too was a hard worker and worked out his salvation as he worked with his congregations and family in the New World.

Jonathan Edwards (1703–1758)
Children Are Beloved Vipers in Need of Conversion

Oliver Wendell Holmes (1809–1894), the famous American jurist, quipped sarcastically that Jonathan Edwards must have thought that Jesus said, "Suffer the little *vipers* to come unto me, and forbid them not" (Brekus 2001, 325 and note 73).

This dry humor juxtaposes Jesus' high view of children as teachers of mature spirituality with Edwards' ambivalent view. He defined children theologically as sinful and attempted to cure their depravity by manipulating them into dramatic conversion experiences to save their serpentine souls, and yet he cared for children, especially his own.

It is an irony of the larger story of children and theology that John Calvin, in contrast to many of his followers, "always emphasized the gradualness rather than the suddenness of conversion and the difficulty of making progress in the Christian life." He "was inclined to minimize the importance even of the conversion of Paul" (Bouwsma 1988, 11). Calvin especially had reservations about the most famous conversion experience of his day, that of Martin Luther. Despite Calvin's view that the truth would emerge "little by little" by the eighteenth century, the evangelical revival of religion had pinned its hope on a sudden, dramatic, and emotional conversion. Ironically, this seemed to prove in some objective and reasonable way that people were truly one of God's elect.

Edwards was born in the same year as John Wesley, but lived only a little past mid-century (1758). Both were engaged in the spiritual renewal that was called the Great Awakening in the Colonies and the Evangelical or Methodist Revival in England.

Jonathan had been taught by his father what Marsden has called "the hermeneutics of self-suspicion" concerning salvation, so Edwards had anxieties about his own election until a decisive conversion experience in 1727. This restored "his ability to find the spiritual intensity he had lost for three years" (Marsden 2003, 111).

On July 28, 1727, he and Sarah Pierrepont, the daughter of one of the founders of Yale, were married. They settled in Northhampton where Edwards began to work for his grandfather, the legendary Solomon Stoddard. In 1728 Sarah bore their first child and the next year grandfather Stoddard died. "At the age of twenty-six Edwards was now a man of authority" (Marsden 2003, 132).

Jonathan Edwards usually rose at four or five in the morning and spent thirteen hours in his study each day. He interrupted his theological work only for private and family prayers, family meals, solitary rides to reflect on God and nature, and the leadership of his congregation. This meant that he turned over the management of the house, barn, fields, livestock, and children to Sarah. In addition to these responsibilities during the 1730s, she was pregnant with great regularity so that by the end of the decade they had six girls and a boy. Her only help was "an African woman slave" (Marsden 2003, 135).

When Edwards began his pastorate in Northampton, he included sermons to children and youth because he thought that the adults were already hardened in their "dispositions to evil." He was also disturbed by the failure of "family government" and worried that the youth had become addicted to "frolicking," the frequenting of taverns, and "lewd practices." In a sermon about avoiding the stirring up of lusts, he did not mince words and spoke directly about the "shameful custom of fondling women's breasts" (Brekus 2001, 308). His solution was that parents should keep their children home in the safety of their Puritan upbringing and that proper family government be restored.

By the end of his first decade in Northhampton, the Great Awakening was at its peak. His oldest daughter was about twelve by that time. Parts of one of his most famous sermons, "The Wrath of God," has been included in Louis Untermeyer's *Library of Great American Writing*. It was preached on July 8, 1741, in Enfield, Connecticut. Edwards did not try to persuade this congregation to be saved, but tried to literally scare the hell out of them. He vividly pictured a "dreadfully provoked" God holding each member of the congregation "over the pit of hell much as one holds a spider or some loathsome insect over the fire." He did not overlook the children in his preaching and stressed that God was angry with every unconverted child in the congregation "every day and every night" (Untermeyer 1960, 90–95).

Edwards published *A Faithful Narrative of the Surprising Work of God* to report on the Great Awakening. It included his analysis of the conversion of Phebe Bartlet, who was four. She disappeared into her "closet" to pray and weep for salvation. Finally all fell quiet. She turned to her mother, who had apparently joined her in the closet, and smiled. She said, "Mother, the kingdom of heaven is come to me!" She then carefully recited her catechism and wept at the thought that her unconverted sisters might "go to hell." She even, like Augustine, "repented for stealing some fruit—a handful of plums—from a neighbor's tree" (Brekus 2001, 300–301). For reasons unknown, however, Phebe was not admitted to the Northampton church until 1754, four years after Edwards had been dismissed from its pulpit. She joined the church shortly before her marriage, as many others did in her time (Brekus 2001, 300–301, note 1).

Edwards was dismissed by his congregation at Northampton in 1750 at the age of forty-six by a vote of 230-23 after twenty-three years of leadership. Marsden devotes a chapter to this incident and asked whether this was the tragedy of a great man following his principles or an "impractical intellectual whose prudery and zeal for control brought out the latent pettiness of a small town." His conclusion was that "it was a mixture of both the exalted and the pathetic" (Marsden 2003, 369).

After awkwardly remaining in Northhampton for a year, Edwards moved his large family to the village of Stockbridge that was gathered around a mission church at the western edge of the frontier of Massachusetts in the Berkshire hills, where he preached to Native Americans and settlers. In January 1758 he became president of the College of New Jersey at Princeton (later Princeton University) when his son-in-law, the previous president, died. Edwards died himself just two months later from smallpox at about the age of fifty-five.

According to his contemporary the Reverend Samuel Hopkins, Edwards was a loving parent. He prayed with his children. He quizzed them on the Bible and the Westminster Shorter Catechism. Out of his concern for them, he discouraged "frolicking," and, to his relief, several of his children experienced conversion. His oldest daughter, Sarah, was "born again" at age seven (Brekus 2001, 311). The family was held together, however, by his wife, Sarah. One cannot help being utterly amazed at the apparent warmth, energy, and organizational skills she brought this household and how she nourished her family so beautifully and gracefully and met the many responsibilities that her long days must have brought.

Most Puritans held to infant damnation and that God chose some for salvation and some for hell, but they believed that their own children, the children of the "new Israel," were part of a special covenant that provided unique favor with God. Cotton Mather (1663–1728), for example, reassured parents that grace, like original sin, was hereditary. Edwards had no

such gloss of kindness in his public sermons. Privately, however, he seemed
to share Cotton Mather's assumption that "the infants of the godly that die
in infancy are saved." His public position was that parents should not be
misled by infant baptism. It is only a sign and not salvation itself. You must
be born again regardless of your age to be saved.

Many eighteenth-century philosophers disagreed. John Locke, Lord
Shaftesbury, David Hume, and Frances Hutcheson challenged the idea
of original sin and Edwards responded prolifically with such books as
Freedom of the Will, The Nature of True Virtue, and *Doctrine of Original Sin
Defended.* For him all humans were metaphysically present with Adam in
the Garden of Eden because sin is like a tree with many branches. While
he defended Puritan orthodoxy assiduously, his "underlying views were
far more complicated—and far more ambivalent" (Brekus 2001, 312). In
his personal devotions he meditated on the ideal child and wanted to cling
to Christ as a little child. He may have had his doubts about older children
and adolescents, but he thought that young children were capable of salvation, like four-year-old Phebe, and they could be saved unconsciously as
infants and would learn "to exercise grace gradually as they exercise their
reason" (Brekus 2001, 312).

On balance, however, there is a frightening ambivalence about children that reverberates with Edwards' ambivalence about Christ. Brekus
noted that Edwards may have a reputation as a hellfire preacher, but he
also wrote lyrical descriptions of Christ's "sweetness," "beauty," and
"excellence." His terrifying images of divine wrath were combined with a
"sweet sense" of Christ's beauty. This "holy gentleness" of Christ that he
spoke of was at odds with the vengeful and angry God he also preached. He
saw children as sinful serpents and yet he saw himself as a child, clinging to
Christ, as babies cling to their mothers for succor and safety.

Conclusion

This chapter has covered two centuries of enormous change. It began after
the century when Protestant theologians began to live with children in
their own homes. It continued as the theological conversation broadened
to include people who were not theologically trained in the university or
monastery. This included non-Latin-speaking participants like Boehme,
Bunyan, and Pascal.

Boehme and Bunyan were married but seldom mentioned children.
Bunyan lamented not being with his children while in jail, but placed his

calling to preach above their needs. Pascal neither married nor attended school with other children when he was young. He also has little to say about children. The Catholic missionaries to New France were not married, but they spent more time with children than most theologians discussed in this history. Their vocation and theology shaped the way they related to the Native American children under their care and they failed to learn much from them about family life or the care of children because they were so urgent to save the children's souls, according to their cultureal limitations.

In the eighteenth century Wesley was married with no children while Edwards kept his fatherly distance from his family, as many did in those days. Still he participated in the richness of family life with children around him, largely mediated by his wife, Sarah. Wesley placed more emphasis on a child's ability to be trained for salvation than Edwards but both found the conversion experience to be ultimately important. Edwards emphasized the conversion experience as a sign of election, so he worked hard and somewhat illogically to induce it, since he knew that only God chose which children were saved or damned. We have seen all of these attitudes already—the high and low views, the ambiguity about children being symbols versus real living creatures, the indifference of busy people, and grace—and we will see them in later centuries as well.

Grace remained a powerful theme in these two centuries despite all the controversy and confusion about how to define it and how it actually works. Grace was present when the children carried the church to the next generations again, regardless of what theologians said or did not say about them.

Perhaps the really new feature of this period is the example of a single theologian who was emotionally ambivalent within himself about children. In the story so far we have seen theologians with high views and others with low views of children, so the story *as a whole* has been ambivalent. In this case, however, there is ambivalence located in a single theologian when we consider Edward's books, his sermons, and his family life all together. The father at home with his family, despite being stern and distant as custom dictated, was still warmly present to his own children, but the children around him also attended church regularly and heard their father's sermons with their ringing good/bad child and mild/angry Jesus ambivalence in them. That powerful language and the emotions that burned in his dramatic preaching—despite this rhetoric being chosen for laudable reasons or not—may have also induced ambivalence about themselves, even when they believed it was for their own good. Perhaps this was his intent as well as his inclination, because of what he experienced in his own child-hood as "the hermeneutics of self-suspicion" inherited from his father for *his* own good.

In the next chapter, which covers 1800–2000, will begin with another Congregational minister, but one unlike Jonathan Edwards. Horace Bushnell in Connecticut inherited the conversion theology of Edwards, but reframed it as Christian nurture to the dismay of some and the delight of others. A high view of children was also articulated in Europe by Friedrich Schleiermacher, a German theologian and pastor in the Reformed Tradition. Schleiermacher came from the theological tradition begun by Calvin in Geneva some three hundred years before. As you can see, this story continues to add layers of complexity to the *de facto* doctrine of chil-dren held by the church.

CHAPTER

6

MODERN THEOLOGY: 1800–2000

The idealization of some well-born children in the Victorian era hid the brutal exploitation of children in the mills and the mines. Starving and weary children were as suffused with toil as heaven and they came to their parents with their wages as much as they came "trailing clouds of glory," as Wordsworth spoke of them in his poetry.

Hugh Cunningham noted that the romantic view of childhood was especially strong from 1860–1930 (Cunningham 1994, 74). Children in literature were portrayed as saving the souls of adults, as Eppie did in George Eliot's *Silas Marner*. In fact childhood became a kind of genderless force so children were dressed accordingly.

When Thomas Gotch's painting, which is displayed at the head of this chapter, was seen at the Royal Academy in 1894 some thought it was a picture of Jesus, but it is childhood itself that it worships. In the Middle Ages the enthroned Madonna held the infant Logos to be worshipped and to bless the viewer, but no mother or father was needed in Gotch's idealization of children. The *child* is enthroned.

◀ *The Child Enthroned*, T.C. Gotch (c. 1894)
Private Collection, The Bridgeman Art Library, London

W e have come a long way in our story, some eighteen hundred years. This chapter is the prelude to our own time and covers the nineteenth and twentieth centuries. It looks back over an extraordinary variety of times, places, and people and looks forward in the next chapter to the contemporary theological discussion about children in the United States. Chapter 7 will then sum up this brief history by describing the *de facto* doctrine of children it embodies and then the final chapter will propose a formal doctrine as an alternative to the informal one that has shaped the church's view of children for so long. With this larger context in mind let us now return to this chapter and the nineteenth century.

The Nineteenth Century's Quiet Revolution Concerning Children and Theology

The nineteenth century saw the spread of trade and industry from Europe to the rest of the world. By about 1870, however, this interest in trade developed into one of empire. For example, in Africa in 1880 there were a handful of isolated European colonies and trading forts. By 1900 almost the whole continent was under European control. This was accompanied by a broad missionary expansion, which for the most part followed the flag.

During this century the Roman Catholic Church also discovered its new role in European politics. The Papal States were annexed by Napoleon in 1809 and Pope Pius VII was exiled. This actually increased the prestige of the papacy and resulted in the papal title "His Holiness," which named the pope's new role. It was one of persuasion and spiritual leadership rather than political and military power.

In 1848 some fifty revolutions, many of them bloody, took place in Europe and were quickly suppressed, yet the seeds of democracy had been sown. Other seeds also took root that year. Marx and Engels published their *Communist Manifesto* in 1848. The revolution in theology took place in 1859 when Charles Darwin's *On the Origin of Species by Means of Natural Selection* was published. In 1871 *The Descent of Man* added to

Darwin's challenge of long-held theological assumptions. The metaphor of "development" began to dominate most areas of thinking, including theology.

It is against this background that we will discuss the quiet revolution in theology concerning children. It was quiet, because evolution and political events, not children, dominated the headlines. The two leaders selected to demonstrate the change in theological thinking about children are Friedrich Schleiermacher in Germany and Horace Bushnell in the United States. Schleiermacher was a Reformed Pastor in Berlin who came from the tradition of John Calvin, and Bushnell was a Congregational Minister who served his whole career in Hartford, Connecticut, and came from the tradition of Calvin and Jonathan Edwards. We turn to Schleiermacher first.

Friedrich Schleiermacher (1768–1834)
Children Are a Kind of Consciousness

Schleiermacher was the greatest Reformed pastor and systematic theologian between Calvin (1509–1564) and Karl Barth (1886–1968). He was born into an extended family of clergy and academics and received his early education among Moravian Pietists, whose warmth had also influenced John Wesley.

The Moravians thought that religious indoctrination by church and state was so cold and formal that it was as likely "to produce a dead legalism as living Christian faith." They thought it was better for children to experience religion first in the warmth of the family, a church within the church, before being instructed how to *think* about their experience in doctrinal terms (DeVries 2001, 333).

Schleiermacher's mother wrote in a letter to her brother, "I think you will agree with us . . . that children must not be compelled to learn by punishment, but we should seek to teach them through play and through their striving for recognition" (DeVries 2001, 343, note 40). This valuing of play was shared by Count Nikolaus Ludwig von Zinzendorf (1700–1760), the leader of the Moravian Pietists in the eighteenth century. He emphasized play in the education of young children in contrast to Wesley's prohibition of play in his schools.

As a boy, Friedrich attended a Moravian boarding school with his sister and brother. This shaped his thinking about education. He defined play in his 1813/14 "Aphorisms on Pedagogy" as "being entirely in the present, the absolute negation of the future." Another aphorism noted play's significance: "Being a child should not prevent becoming an adult; becoming

148

Children and the Theologians

an adult should not prevent being a child" (quoted from DeVries 2001, 343, note 40).

Some of the context for this theological interest in play was the larger romantic movement that began at the end of the eighteenth century and is usually understood as a reaction against rampant industrialism and urbanity. The romantics glorified freedom, originality, genius, the arts, and a view of childhood as innocent and uncorrupted. Sutton-Smith drew on the work of Mihail Spariosu—a classicist interested in play, power, and literature—to say that "For two thousand years, since Plato and Aristotle, art and play had been confined to roles as secondary sources of knowledge. By making play essential to the aesthetic, and by attributing moral power to the aesthetic, play was potentially dignified for the first time in Western civilization" (Sutton-Smith 1997, 129). It should be noted in passing that Spariosu also provided in 1989 a much-needed interdisciplinary survey of play since the Greeks (Spariosu 1989).

Two examples of the German romantic interest in play are Friedrich Schiller (1759–1805), the philosopher and poet, and the German educator Friedrich Froebel (1782–1852), who were both contemporaries of Schleiermacher. Schiller is famous for saying that "Man plays only when he is in the full sense of the word a Man, and he is only wholly a Man when he is playing" (quoted in Sutton-Smith 1997, 131). Froebel "developed the view that play was the highest phase of a child's development, the function of the imagination being the peak of the child's self-active inner representation" (Sutton-Smith 1997, 131).

During Schleiermacher's first period in Berlin, as a young theologian, he was deeply involved in the artistic life of the city, which resulted in 1799 in the publication of his *On Religion: Speeches Addressed to its Cultured Despisers*. The "despisers" were the artists and other educated people he knew who thought religion had been eclipsed and surpassed by modern learning, art, and culture. In 1800, when he was thirty-two, he followed up *Speeches* with a book about his own religious experience entitled *Soliloquies*.

In *Soliloquies* Schleiermacher argued against dividing life into two stages, childhood and adulthood. Rather than two stages following each other, these periods are "a two-fold activity of the spirit that should exist in its entirety at every time of life, and it is the perfection of human development ever to become more intimately and more clearly conscious of both its aspects, assigning to each its own peculiar and proper functions" (Schleiermacher 2002, 98).

In *Speeches*, and later in his systematic theology *The Christian Faith*

(1821–22), he defined religion as a particular kind of consciousness or feeling to distinguish it from artistic or moral knowing on the one hand, and scientific or metaphysical knowing on the other. Religion cannot function apart from the arts, the moral life, science, or philosophy, but neither can it be reduced to any of these other activities.

He argued that religious consciousness is *the* fundamental human characteristic and that Christianity, among the religious of the world, has especially understood and appreciated the importance of redemption, as found in Jesus' life, death, and resurrection. The experience of God is a sense of dependence, but it is "never entirely self-awareness, for the self can never be extracted from the realm of otherness" as Clements has argued, following Schleiermacher (Schleiermacher 1991, 37).

Children, Schleiermacher thought, share religious feeling with all of its nuances as the fundamental quality of the religious life on an equal basis with adults. Religion is not about a quantity of academic knowledge, accumulated adult experience, or cognitive development. It is about the redemptive quality in relationships to which children are, perhaps, more open than adults and which they can initiate in adults, even when they are unaware that they are doing this.

An example of the child as a means of grace is Schleiermacher's 1806 novella, probably best translated as *The Celebration of Christmas: A Conversation* (Schleiermacher 1990). It tells a respectful, sensitive, and multi-faceted story about a child's intuitive wisdom concerning the mystery of Christmas. In the story the child, Sophie, revealed the depths of Christmas by her singing and the diorama she had made, which she showed to the guests with deep feeling. As the party continued, however, the discussion turned to the meaning of Christmas in adult terms. The story ends with Joseph, an older guest who arrived late, demanding that the adult intellectualization of Christmas end and that they invite Sophie back (if she is still awake) to sing for them if they really want to know what Christmas means.

Schleiermacher's view of children was worked out amidst the European crisis of Napoleon's appetite for conquest and a German culture that was moving from an agrarian and feudal one to a view of families as an independent refuge from the turbulent public life of politics and work. Fathers competed outside the home while mothers educated and ruled within. This was the period when the kindergarten was begun by Froebel, mentioned above in connection with play. His view of children's education respected their natural intelligence and sense of aesthetics. It began in Germany and spread to many other countries. This period also saw a dramatic increase

in the publication of children's literature and a wider interest in and avail-
ability of toys in Europe, England, and North America.

Schleiermacher advocated for the new view of children, family, and
education. His library included the volumes of Rousseau, including
Emile—which he read more enthusiastically, no doubt, than John Wesley,
the censor of eighteenth-century Paris, or Hume had. For Schleiermacher,
like Rousseau, children were not considered to be miniature adults who
merely lacked the discipline and orderly habits to be considered mature.
He was concerned with their intuitive wisdom, like Sophie's, and how it
might be developed or distorted by adults.

By 1818 Schleiermacher had been married about a decade. He was
fifty years old. That year he delivered nine sermons called "Sermons on the
Christian Household" at Trinity Church in Berlin, where he was a pastor.
This was his most complete, direct, and formal statement about families.

He thought parents should be as concerned about the manner of play
and whom their children played with as they were about their formal education. Play with all kinds of people broadens tolerance, he thought, so com-
panions need to be chosen primarily for their ability to assist children to
grow in "wholesome self-knowledge." Play stimulates and exercises important abilities in the child, which helps them "learn to use and control all
those powers least called for in their work" (quoted in DeVries 2001, 343).

In 1829 Schleiermacher presided at the burial of his only biological
son, nine-year-old Nathanael, who had died from diphtheria. He was now
about sixty-one years old and only five years away from his own death. He
disagreed with those who tried to comfort him by saying his son had died
before he could be corrupted by the world. He rejected that view because
"he had already seen the love of the Savior at work in his little boy's life"
(DeVries, 2001, 347). This experience mattered and moved him to hold a
high view of children, which included their redemption and the redemption of others. He knew this about children, because he had allowed himself to become deeply involved with his own children and even fictitious
children like Sophie on Christmas Eve.

The high view of children expressed by Schleiermacher also appeared in
the New World during this century. Horace Bushnell was the leading advocate. Robert Bruce Mullin's wonderful biography called him *The Puritan
as Yankee* (Mullin 2002). Instead of being a character in Mark Twain's
Connecticut Yankee in King Arthur's Court, Bushnell was a Connecticut
Yankee tinkering with theology, children, and the kingdom of heaven.

Horace Bushnell (1802–1876)
Children Know a Higher Kind of Play

Horace Bushnell was a Congregational minister, like Jonathan Edwards. He was born in Litchfield, Connecticut, in the northwestern corner of the state, while Edwards was born closer to Hartford, which is in the northern central part on the Connecticut River. Both were educated at Yale. A descendent of Jonathan Edwards was one of Bushnell's biographers (Edwards 1992) and served Immanuel Congregational Church in Hartford, which was an offshoot from old North Congregational Church, where Bushnell served his entire ministry, 1833–1859, resigning after twenty-six years due to poor health.

Jonathan Edwards had focused on the conversion experience to ensure the salvation of children, but Bushnell thought there should never be a time when children were not sure they were Christian. He did not disregard sin, but argued for the power of nurture as a means to salvation. He called the family a "little church" and used the metaphor of children and a kitten playing at home on the floor to suggest "another and higher kind of play, which is the noblest exercise and last end of man himself" (Bushnell 1979, 10).

Bushnell spent time with and enjoyed children. Mary Bushnell Cheney, one of the Bushnell's three children, published *Life and Letters of Horace Bushnell* in 1880, four years after his death. She recounted the warmth and laughter of the family she grew up in. She wrote, "First among my recollections of my father are the daily, after-dinner romps, not lasting long, but most vigorous and hearty at the moment" (Cheney 1880, 452). The impromptu picnics and astonishing antics like "my father would occasionally electrify the children by taking a flying leap over their heads" (Cheney 1880, 453) made for a splendid and stimulating childhood. His friend C. A. Bartol wrote in a letter to Mrs. Bushnell that playfulness was one of his most significant traits. "The boy never quite left the man" (Cheney 1880, 186-187).

One summer while staying with a friend, the custom was established, to spend Sunday evenings out on the lawn to discuss religious subjects. Written questions were dropped into Bushnell's hat. He would pick out a few and use them to start a discussion. Everyone had their say and when he summed up at the end his words were few and "were generally meant, not to settle the questions, but to help us to do so, if that were possible, or, at least, to think them out as far as we could. The whole household took part in these talks, and enjoyed them heartily" (Cheney 1880, 461).

In 1847 he published *Christian Nurture* to say as clearly as he could
that the exclusive focus of his colleagues on a single emotional experience
to validate children's salvation left most families engaged in "ostrich nurture." One whole chapter was devoted to attacking "nature's type of all
unmotherhood" (Bushnell 1979, 65). Lamentations 4:3 ("but my people
has become cruel, like the ostriches in the wilderness.") was quoted at the
head of the chapter and referred to the legend that ostriches buried their
eggs and left them to hatch on their own. These words must have been
intended also to echo that burying your head in the sand about nurture
won't make its need go away. In other words "ostrich nurture" abandons
children and considers a conversion experience all that a child needs to
become a Christian. This amounted to theologically organized cruelty, he
thought.

Bushnell argued that natural actions like feeding, bathing, and play
hold potential religious significance for children. This means that mothers are especially important for the spiritual journey because they are the
ones who spend the most time with their children. They have more oppor-
tunities for nurture than fathers or others do. It is especially important,
therefore, that mothers master their impatience, anger, and anxiety about
their children, because the most significant period for religious nurture
ends at about three years of age. This is when free will and choice begin
to function. Language also begins during this period, which adds to the
child's reasoning ability in the service of choices and the willing of action.
Margaret Bendroth called this emphasis in Bushnell's theology the "near
salvific power of a godly mother" (Bendroth 2001, 358).

Bushnell seemed to be controversial in spite of his deep loyalty to
the church in general and his own parish in particular. The mutual love
between him and the congregation at old North Church was deep and
steady. Perhaps this was because if you knew him well his piety and integrity became obvious. Unfortunately his integrity was sometimes incau-
tious. No volume he published shows this better than *Christ in Theology*.
Mullin wrote concerning this book:

> We see here the ultimate tinkerer—little concerned with
> theory, but greatly interested with results. In his introductory
> comments he admitted that only after publishing *God in Christ*
> did he begin to engage in a systematic study of the history of
> doctrine, and that he was amazed at what he had discovered.
> "I am so much nearer to real orthodoxy than I supposed," he
> proclaimed, "and . . . the New England theology, so called, is so
> much farther off." (Mullin 2002, 171)

He sometimes wrote first and thought later, letting the chips fall where they may. The conservative and cautious advocates of "the New England theology" were not amused or patient with this trait in their colleague.

Bennet Tyler, also a Congregationalist from Connecticut, rushed to refute *Christian Nurture* the year after it was published. He wrote in 1848 that children should not be encouraged in the delusion of their own righteousness, but be given a realistic view of their depravity so that they can look forward to their salvation. Bushnell was naïve, Tyler argued with scorn, because scripture is full of faithful parents with disappointing children (Bendroth 2001, 360). Nurture is, therefore, not enough, Tyler concluded.

Another early critic was Charles Hodge, professor of theology at Princeton Theological Seminary (Hodge 1847) and an Old School Presbyterian. He found much to admire in Bushnell's techniques, but found him to be in grave error on original sin. Since his positive and naturalistic assumption about human nature was false, all that followed from that premise was, too. Children needed to be "quickened" by the power that raised Jesus Christ, he argued, rather than be gradually nurtured by human beings.

Bushnell was not systematic about his views, but he also was not as blind to sin in children as his critics thought. He thought that sin was neither chosen nor inherited but something in between. He had a "stronger understanding of human fallenness than either revivalism or liberal rationalism could offer." This was because of his use of the "federal" theory of the Puritan divines with its emphasis on "the corporate experience of human sin" (Bendroth 2001, 361).

Bushnell had a high view of children, which was not supported by his Calvinistic colleagues. Perhaps they could not even hear what he had to say about children because they were so offended by his literary style, his optimism about human nature despite sin, and his view of scripture as symbolic rather than literal, to deeply appreciate the place of children in his theology. Their concern was that he was not "progressive" in any positive sense but merely another Unitarian and/or Pelagian heretic. Karl Barth, a Swiss Reformed theologian in the next century, might have had the same concerns about Bushnell's writing. He was certainly very worried about Schleiermacher's influence in Germany. We turn to the twentieth century now.

The Twentieth Century's Cautious Connection Between Children and Theology

The twentieth century was marked by enormous technological progress, the devastating destruction of two "world wars" and other "conflicts," such as Korea and Viet Nam. During this century it began to be understood that all politics and economics had a world-wide significance. The three theologians selected to represent this part of the story are Barth, Rahner, and Williams.

Karl Barth (1886–1968)
Childhood Is a Time of Preparation

Karl Barth is one of the few theologians in this story that I have actually met. He and his assistant Charlotte von Kirschbaum visited Princeton Theological Seminary for several days in 1962 when I was a student there.

Meeting Barth was very different from reading him. I had read him for several years before we met, mostly for his long historical asides and to prepare for courses about his theology, but as he moved around the campus informally and lectured formally in the Princeton University chapel it became clear why so many students from Princeton had gone to Basel to study with him. Here was a theologian who not only had much to say, but he had a twinkle in his eye and a rich sense of humor!

Barth was born in Basel, Switzerland, into a clergy family. His father, Johann Friedrich (Fritz) Barth, began to teach New Testament and early church history at Bern when Karl was two years old. Werpehowski, a leading Barthian scholar, tells us that Karl's relationship with his parents was "strained" (Werpehowski 2001, 387–388, note 7), but on the eve of his confirmation, when he was fifteen, he decided to become a theologian, like many of the men in his family, to better understand for himself the creed he had just been studying and had committed himself to.

He continued to study theology as an undergraduate in Bern, Berlin, Tubingen ,and Marburg between 1904 and 1909 and by 1911 had graduated and was a pastor in Safenwil, Switzerland, where he remained for ten years. He was married in 1913 to Nelly von Hoffman, a talented violinist, and they began to raise their family, which ultimately included four boys and a girl.

It was during his days in the parish that he became aware of his difficulty relating to children and youth. He tended to lecture to young people and later wrote that he often stood "awkwardly in front of bored faces," and that he often "simply ran out of steam, even in the most well-known things" (Werpehowski 2001, 387–388, note 7). It sounds like he was bored without the sharp debate he enjoyed with well-prepared older students and colleagues.

The theological debate going on in his mind during those days soon found its way into print. In the summer of 1916 he began to work on a commentary about Paul's letter to the Romans. He worked on this in the context of the daily round of parish life that also involved him in the active support of the workers in Safenwil, where the leading industry was textiles.

His commentary was first published in 1918, as World War I was coming to an end, and revised in 1920 and in 1921. Its publication opened the way to a teaching career in Germany, which lasted until he refused to give an unqualified oath to Hitler. This was the culmination of his resistance to the Nazi regime, which had included being a major author of the Barmen Declaration in May of 1934. After his dismissal from Bonn, he returned to Basel where he taught at the university until he retired in 1962.

While teaching in Germany, he began to write his *Church Dogmatics*, which occupied him the rest of his life. It was also where he wrote *Anselm: Fides Quarens Intellectum* (Barth 1960). This little book affirmed Anselm's proposition that one must believe in order to understand. Barth himself had stepped into the circle of belief to understand and it was from within this circle that he often ignored and sometimes defamed the "important results of modern exegesis, history and theology," as Hans Kung respectfully argued (Kung 2002, 203). It was Barth's view, however, that without the radical centrality of Christ as the object of knowledge through faith, we are really only talking about ourselves, although perhaps "with a loud voice."

One might think that a major implication of Christ's centrality and believing to understand would be that children are as qualified to know God as adults are. Barth, however, was suspicious of an experience-based knowledge of God like Schleiermacher described in the previous century. Misleading feelings and misplaced enthusiasm, after all, had been the major weakness of the German Christians who had followed Hitler. Belief was more cognitive than mystical in Barth's scheme and children were no more equipped without training and maturity to know the truth than the Hitler Youth were equipped to criticize Hitler's use of them for political reasons.

If belief is a kind of rational choice for which a person can take responsibility, then children's naive belief seems to be of low value. Even if belief is the beginning of understanding it must be guarded by a proper doctrinal fence to be valid, so children seem to stand on the outside of the fence looking into the circle, where Barth stood to declare the Christian faith. A child's time in life, he thought, is one of preparation for understanding theology before assuming a legitimate role in the church.

The church for Barth was not a social movement based on religious experience or the moral example of Jesus. It is a community in which God's Word stands over against the church members and judges them. After achieving this clarity personally, to his own satisfaction, he said that he had recovered from "the children's disease of being ashamed of theology" (Casalis, 1964, 17). Perhaps this "disease" he had overcome came from confusing *lectures* on doctrine with knowing God at an early age. There is a distinction between faith as awareness and faith as cognitive assent. Children don't need to be "ashamed of theology" because they don't understand its propositional statements if their experience of God is rich and authentic. The words of doctrine refer to God's presence, not to other words. Besides, if God is beyond the ability of God's creatures to put into words, then children's lack of this cognitive ability need not keep them outside the circle of faith in the church.

Barth's blurring of God's self-communication with children and the need for them to understand doctrinal statements about God can be clarified by considering Schleiermacher's and Barth's vision of Christmas. When Barth reviewed Schleiermacher's *The Celebration of Christmas* in 1924, he did not mention what the *child* taught the adults in the story or that the adults were cautioned to keep their *childhood* alive to be fully mature in their understanding of the mystery of Christmas. His interpretation reduced the book to showing how music and women were the "royal road to the divine" (DeVries 2001, 339, note 23).

For Schleiermacher it was Sophie who revealed the meaning of Christmas by her spirit and unselfconscious actions. Barth's approach to this mystery in his book *Christmas* (Barth 1959) was to collect his doctrinal essays about the Incarnation. This approach also differed from Luther's telling of the Christmas story. Luther's empathy and wonder concerning the *people* in the narrative is how he expressed the meaning of the Christmas mystery, beautifully shown in the collection of Luther's Christmas sermons made by the historian Roland H. Bainton (Luther 1948).

Children were seldom mentioned in Barth's *Church Dogmatics*, a work of some nine thousand pages in English. William Werpehowski, however, has found three Bartian ideas about "being a child," drawn from the *Church Dogmatics* and Barth's other writings (Werpehowski 2001, 386–405).

The first idea is that children are "needy beginners" in the sense that they realize that they have much to learn. The second idea is that children live, as Mozart played music. He "sounds and sings," Barth wrote, without self-preoccupation. This was in contrast to Beethoven, who focused on personal confession, and Bach, who was busy communicating doctrine or some other message. The third idea was that children inhabit a "freedom in limitation." (Werpehowski, 2001, 392–393). This is a kind of "freedom" that comes from having few options. For Barth, then, children are aware of their ignorance, lack self-awareness (except for their ignorance), and participate in a kind of freedom governed by their limitations.

Barth also thought that children set out on their religious quest wholeheartedly. The mature adult, however, takes this up with greater seriousness with an awareness that the time is now for bold ventures and good work to be done, "following the preparations of youth." Despite this seriousness, Barth argued, the adult still needs to be "a 'child at play,' a 'student,' or an 'explorer,' keeping a humble good humor" (Werpehowski 2001, 393). Children and youth are, thus, relegated to a time of "preparations," in contrast to adulthood, which is more serious although not entirely without play and exploration.

There is an inconsistency in Barth's conclusion about children, however. He wrote in *Anselm: Fides Quaerens Intellectum* (*Anselm: Faith Seeking Understanding*) that "he could not emphasize too strongly that prior to any desire or ability to find theological answers is the question of dedication on the part of the theologian himself. What is required is a pure heart, eyes that have been opened, child-like obedience, a life in the Spirit, and rich nourishment from Holy Scripture to make him capable of finding these answers" (Barth 1960, 34). The inconsistency is that he considers childhood as only a time of preparation but that the "dedication" needed by a mature theologian, according to Barth, is child-like. He only acknowledges "child-like obedience," but the other characteristics he lists that mark the "dedication" needed to be an authentic theologian are possible for children. Children could even teach such "dedication" to adults if one has the ears to hear and the eyes to see what they teach by merely being themselves.

Perhaps, Barth overlooked children because of his affirmation that they are bearers of original sin. How could they teach what a theologian needs to be a theologian with this disability? He rejected the hereditary transmission of sin that Augustine and others had proposed but he was uneasy with the idea that original sin ruled out individual responsibility for sin. Still, it may be that he did not see children as a means of grace, despite the emphasis on grace throughout his theology, because of this doctrine.

Ethical issues concerning children also did not play much of a role in his theology. In general Barth did not consider ethical issues as central to his theology. This was in part because, as Werpehowski has said, he considered moral problems to be outside his province as a systematic theologian (Werpehowski 2001, 404, note 58). When this view of ethics is combined with his doctrinal stance about original sin and election, however, there is really little to say about parenting, assuming this part of the Christian life has moral implications. Much of what he did have to say about parenting was in Volume III, Part 4 of *Church Dogmatics*. It is there that he laid out the theological basis for parental authority.

Parents are to represent God to the child, but God alone is the real parent, so we should see children from God's standpoint and remember that adults are also the children of their own parents and of God. On the other hand, children have their own relationship with God, as Jesus did, which was demonstrated when he was twelve years old and went to the temple without his parents' knowledge or permission. This, Barth says, is a relationship that needs to be respected.

In summary, then, Barth is largely indifferent to children in his theological work. His mention of Mozart's play, the innocence of "child-like obedience," and children's responsibility for their own relationship with God are glimmers of interest, but when compared to the vast ocean of words in his collected works these few moments are almost completely submerged.

Barth's distance from children in his writing may have been paralleled in his household. In his own home he and his secretary of thirty-five years, Charlotte von Kirschbaum, tended to theology while his wife, Nelly, tended to the house and the five children. In 1933 he even wrote to his wife to suggest they divorce, but she declined (Selinger 1998, 8). He continued on with theology and his secretary, whom the children called "Tante Lollo." She lived with the family and appeared in at least one family picture, standing next to Barth while his wife stood at the edge of the group. Tante Lollo was buried in the family tomb (Selinger 1998, 10).

We turn now to Karl Rahner, another towering figure in twentieth-century theology. He too wrote an ocean of words about theology but little about children. What he did write about them, however, was very focused, deep, creative, and influential.

Karl Rahner (1904–1984)
Children Are Open To Eternity

Karl Rahner was born 730 years after the death of St. Thomas Aquinas. He is the first Roman Catholic priest to step into our story's vignettes since Thomas in the thirteenth century. Instead of being a Dominican, as Thomas was, Rahner was a Jesuit, but his interest in Thomas' theology was profound.

From about 1850–1950 Roman Catholic theology attempted to return to the scholastic tradition of the Middle Ages. The comprehensive and systematic work of Thomas was chosen to give Catholics a unified view of the compatibility of faith and reason and the positive authority of the Roman Catholic Church. This was done to combat the attacks of secularism and science that began during the seventeenth and eighteenth centuries.

Unfortunately, by the nineteenth century the teaching of Aquinas had become simplified and tightly organized into a static and superficial (safe) version of his creative work. This tendency began under Pius IX (d.1878) and reached its peak under Pius XII (d.1958). Rahner argued against this modern, stultifying view of Thomas as "that potted version" (Hinsdale 2001, 416). Instead he wanted to center theology around pastoral concerns and the experience of God in everyday things.

Karl Rahner was born in Freiburg, Germany, the middle of seven children. He described his childhood as being "ordinary, unremarkable, and typical of the German middle class at the turn of the twentieth century" (Hinsdale 2001, 415, note 36).

When he joined the Jesuits at the age of eighteen he followed his older brother Hugo (1900–1968), although his vocation was independent. He studied philosophy at the University of Freiburg, where Martin Honegger, who held the chair for Catholic philosophy, turned down his doctoral thesis. In *I Remember: An Autobiographical Interview*, which includes a photograph of him with his one hundred-year-old mother toasting her on her birthday, he noted with some irony that he "was flunked by the Catholic Honecker for being too inspired by Heidegger" (Rahner 1985, 42), who has already been mentioned in connection with Angelus Silesius in chapter 5. His rejected thesis was later published as *Spirit in the World* in 1939 and was translated into many languages. Despite his rejection by Honegger at Freiburg, he earned a doctorate in theology from the University of Innsbruck and began teaching there.

Robert Kress tells us that Rahner enjoyed "a glass of wine, a mouth-watering Schnitzel, a good cup of coffee—frequent metaphors in the

Rahnerian vocabulary" (Kress 1982, 1). When he lectured he was like "a
preoccupied bear tracing and retracing his steps" as he "paced back and
forth on the elevated room-wide platform before 250 and more students,
thinking his theological thought aloud in a deep, rumbling voice" (Kress
1982, 7).

What Rahner wanted to do was to create a theology that is a "mystagogy of the mysticism of everyday life" (quoted in Kress 1982, 67). He
wanted to nourish an initiation (mystagogy) into the experience of God in
ordinary events, because faith originates within one's own existence and
cannot come from the outside by indoctrination. He wanted to find the
fundamental condition for the possibility of experiencing God, which he
found to be openness (self-transcendence) to God's self-communication.
This involves "even the most humble aspects of our daily routine, such as
our working, sleeping, eating, drinking, laughing, seeing, sitting, and getting about" (Egan 1998, 58). This shows how natural it was for Rahner to
respect children in his theology.

Karl Rahner's "Ideas for a Theology of Childhood" (Rahner 1971) is
the concise summary of his thinking about children. Mary Ann Hinsdale
traced the origin of this important essay, which will be referred to by every
theologian reviewed in the next chapter, as examples of the contemporary
theological discussion in the United States about children. Rahner's article
was first a lecture given in 1962 and then was published in 1963 in the
pastoral journal *Geist und Leben* before it found its way into his collected
works in Volume 8. He was about sixty when the article achieved its final
form (Hinsdale 2001, 421, note 64). Given the value of the article to theologians writing about children today, it is interesting that in the "Subject
Index" to Volume 8 there was no entry under "children."

This article began by observing that Jesus did not define the child,
nor is there any definition of children in the whole Bible! We, therefore,
must supplement scriptural studies by understanding the children around
us and remembering our own childhoods to know what Jesus was talking
about. Rahner also worked backward from references in scripture to adult
"children of God" to actual children and then worked forward again from
children to adults to conclude that life ought to be lived in a child-like way.

To think theologically about children was not "petty sentimentality"
and goes "beyond pedagogy," the field of Christian education to which the
subject of children is usually dismissed by theologians. The question his
essay asked was: "In the intention of the Creator and Redeemer of children
what meaning does childhood have, and what task does it lay upon us for
the perfecting and saving of humanity?" (Rahner 1971, 33).

His answer, much like that of Schleiermacher, was that children are open to God in a way that does not assume childhood is a prelude to later stages of development. This is because at every stage one can grasp oneself as a whole. Eternity is not a final stage either, because the whole of existence is always redeemed. We, therefore, do not move away from childhood toward eternity but we move toward the eternity of childhood.

When he wrote about baptism, Hinsdale suggested, "Rahner lamented the atrophy of the doctrine of original sin. He felt that the doctrine had largely become 'a catechism truth' for modern people, a topic mentioned at its proper place in religious instruction and then forgotten in daily life and average preaching" (Hinsdale 2001, 429). Original sin for Rahner is the "state of what ought not to be," but what is most important is that "original sin" is not more powerful than "original redemption" (Hinsdale 2001, 429).

A good summary of Rahner's view of children is to say that what children and child-like adults have in common is " . . . a state in which we are open to expect the unexpected, to commit ourselves to the incalculable, a state which endows us with the power still to be able to play, to recognize that the powers presiding over existence are greater than our own designs, and to submit to their control as our deepest good" (Rahner 1971, 42). Rahner has a high view of children, even though most of his writing seems indifferent to them. Perhaps we can say that his general interest in the theology of everyday things brings children implicitly into the center of this thought.

Rahner does not dissolve the differences between adults and children or suggest that these differences do not matter. The power differential between children and adults, for example, matters greatly and can lead to abuse as well as to responsible parenting. The differences in life experience and cognitive development between children and adults can also lead to children's lack of judgment but also to the loss of child-likeness for adults. The point Rahner is making, however, is that with regard to the experience *of God* there is nothing inherently different between the nonverbal appreciation of children and adults, even though adults might talk about the mystery of God's presence in a very different way than children do.

Rowan Williams (1950–)
Children Are Lost Icons

As the second millennium of Christian theology drew to a close, Rowan Williams wrote what he called "a sort of journal of the 1990s" (Williams 2000, ix). It was a book that attempted to articulate his anger about the "apathy and narcissism of our imaginative world" (Williams 2000, 9). He was concerned that language in the closing decade of the millennium had decayed to the point that we were losing the ability to speak about our life together in a mutually regarding, deeply human way. He wanted to call attention to the "lost icons," which he thought of as "clusters of convention and imagination, images of possible lives or modes of life, possible positions to occupy in a world that is inexorably one of time and loss" (Williams 2000, 186). These icons, which are going out of existence, he argued, are childhood, charity, remorse, and souls. We will return to his book *Lost Icons: Reflections on Cultural Bereavement* as this vignette concludes, but first we must ask what sort of person would write such a book and include children in his theological thought.

Rowan Williams was born in Swansea, the birthplace of Dylan Thomas, and Williams, too, has published some volumes of poetry. His birth took place in June of 1950. He was precocious as a young scholar and went on to Christ's College, Cambridge. His BA was completed in 1971 in theology and he earned his MA in 1975. He shifted to Oxford at Wadham College for his DPhil, entitled *The Theology of Vladimir Nikolaevich Lossky: An Exposition and Critique*, which he earned also in 1975. His interest in the Russian Orthodox experience had, perhaps, much to do with his appropriating of the image of icons for his critique of culture in the 1990s.

Williams became a deacon in 1977 and a priest in 1978 while he served as Tutor at Westcott House in Cambridge from 1977–1980 and then lecturer in divinity at Cambridge University from 1980–1986. He married Jane Paul, also a lecturer in theology, whom he met while living and working in Cambridge. They have a daughter, Rhiannon, born in 1987 and a son, Pip, born in 1996. Williams' academic career was crowned when he was called to be Lady Margaret Professor of Divinity at Oxford, a position he held from 1986–1992. It was from there that he was called to become one of the scholar bishops in the British Isles, when he was elected bishop of Monmouth in 1991 and then archbishop of Wales in 1999. It was during this period that he worked on the chapters of *Lost Icons*.

In July of 2002 he was elected the 104th archbishop of Canterbury, which made him the leader of the Anglican churches around the world. The official website of the archbishop of Canterbury calls the archbishop a "Focus of Unity" for the Anglican Communion, which involves over 80 million members in 160 countries.

Rowan Williams is the second theologian in this book that I have met. I was invited to be part of a small group at Trinity Episcopal Church, Wall Street, in New York, that was called together to discuss theology with

Williams on the morning of September 11, 2001. As we were having our coffee, the first plane hit. By the time the second plane hit the Twin Towers, our nearby building was filling up with smoke so that it was difficult to see or breathe. We moved out into the streets, which by that time were covered with wreckage, running people, and that terrible, unforgettable gray dust. I lost contact with most of the group as I made my way to the southern tip of Manhattan and then up the East Side. A few years later we had a reunion at Trinity, and subsequently I was present in Cambridge at Little Saint Mary's when Williams lectured a few years later. He reflected on the experience of September 11 in his book *Writing in the Dust* (Williams 2002) of which I have an inscribed copy.

Rupert Shortt's *Rowan Williams: An Introduction* (Shortt 2003) observes that when Williams was at Oxford he worked with disadvantaged children in south London (Shortt 2003, 24) and elsewhere. We also read that when he was at Cambridge he served in the city's northern suburbs and for three years lived in the curate's house on the Arbury council estate, a housing development. It may be surprising to some, who may even know that Williams ran a large and successful Sunday school in those days, that he also developed a talent for preaching "beautiful, chiselled little homilies" to children, even though his adult sermons were sometimes very difficult for adult parishioners to understand (Shortt 2003, 39).

As bishop of Monmouth he was involved in finances, national politics (in which he has always been involved), counseling, schools, and church politics. What is important to notice for our purposes is that, as Shortt writes, "No one who worked alongside him thinks that his zeal was muted by family ties—including the unexpected blessing of his son Pip's birth in 1996—or that his workload led to strains at home. His friends repeatedly highlight his devotion to family; one told me that she knows of 'no one else who has learned more from their children'" (Shortt 2003, 58).

Mike Higton wrote an introduction to Williams' theology in 2004 (Higton 2004). It was organized into seven parts, an introduction and six chapters, presenting six primary topics that Williams is interested in. This list includes (1) the "difficult gospel" of God's "disarming acceptance," which disarms our selfishness; (2) that God is the "source of life," which is the love we need for living as much as oxygen is needed for breathing; (3) how the church, when it is the church, shows adults how to reject being infantile in their desires and accept their finitude and weakness to bear a concern for the wholeness of Jesus' relationship with God as their own; (4) so that children can be taught to be more than infantile adults; which results in (5) a life together of informed politics concerned with other people and what is good for all and (6) as a case illustrating fundamental ethics, sex is discussed as "the self-giving vulnerability of love, which mirrors the life of God rather than being reduced to what goes where" (Higton 2004, 142). It is *unusual*, and we can say this with confidence by this point in the larger story, for a theologian's concern for and interest in children to be about one-sixth of the total theological picture.

Williams is also a historian, which his *Arius: Heresy and Tradition* (Williams 2001) shows along with other books, articles, and book chapters. In *Arius* he wrote:

> ☜ There is a sense in which Nicaea and its aftermath represent a recognition by the Church at large that *theology* is not only legitimate but necessary. The loyal and uncritical repetition of formulae is seen to be inadequate as a means of securing continuity at anything more than a formal level; Scripture and tradition require to be read in a way that brings out their strangeness, their non-obvious and non-contemporary qualities, in order that they may be read both freshly and truthfully from one generation to another. They need to be made more *difficult* before we can accurately grasp their simplicities. Otherwise, we read with eyes not our own and think them through with minds not our own; the "deposit of faith" does not really come into contact with *ourselves*. And this "making difficult," this confession that what the gospel says in Scripture and tradition does not instantly and effortlessly make sense, is perhaps one of the most fundamental tasks for theology. (Williams 2001, 236) ☞

In some ways this book about children and the theologians has attempted to make things "strange" so we can really come to grips with the *de facto* doctrine of children that has shaped the church's thinking about them. Once this informal doctrine is better understood then a more adequate formal doctrine can be proposed.

In his *Why Study the Past: The Quest for the Historical Church* Williams also wrote that the Reformation was a time when the reformers made the Church "strange" to itself! They did this in a way that both revived and radically changed the historic and vitalizing question of the Church's true identity. They changed the question, as well as the answers to the question: "What is the church" (Williams 2005, 87). The book before you also wants to change the question. We need to ask what the doctrine of children is that we are operating with and to move forward to a more adequate doctrine that can be put into action as a spiritual practice in the church.

Williams wrote many things about children that have not been widely published. This informal writing appeared in reports concerning schools and the church. He has also talked with teachers and parents about education and religious education in many settings. Much of his thinking concerning children, however, is crystallized in the chapter "Childhood and Choice" in his book *Lost Icons*, to which we now return.

His thought about the lost icon of the child begins by taking the long view. The young of our species have a long period of biological vulnerability. It is needed to develop the language and creativity we need for survival. This development takes place through play, so children's development needs to be protected and respected. Children need a pressure-free space in which to learn playfully how to make real choices.

This pressure-free space is being damaged in the culture of North America and Europe, and to an increasing degree around the world, by a definition of the child as a consuming creature. The language of *things* is being taught by the advertising media to parents, who have become co-opted by the advertising establishment, so that children are imagined in economic terms by adults and have been taught to think of themselves in the same way. Children are beginning to assume that the purchase of things will provide meaning for their lives. They are also learning that things should be desired to make one desirable.

The culture also teaches us all that decisions can be made in a vacuum without cost, as if one were a kind of abstracted will, freely picking things off a supermarket shelf without reference to anyone or anything else. Adults often revert to the fantasy that choices have neither cost nor risk under the tutelage of business and advertising people. The far-reaching economic downturn of 2009 has helped to call all of this into question but much of Williams' critique from the 1990s still pertains, because a choice for something always means a choice against something else, and all choices impinge on others. To be blind to this fact produces an adult who cannot understand or speak about children except in self-deceptive ways, because they are unaware of time and change. They also do not have the ability to remember their own childhood and recognize the boundary between adults and children. When this critical boundary is blurred, children are prevented from growing up to be more than infantile adults, which endangers our life together as human beings with other creatures and the life of planet earth itself.

Williams has made a persuasive critique of how close we are to losing the icon of childhood as a way of speaking about and understanding human beings. This is a danger that not only affects children, but the adults they will become, who in turn will raise the next generation.

A possible winding-down of the species is at hand. In Christian terms, holy communion is at risk. With these thoughts in mind we turn now to a summary of this chapter.

Conclusion

Williams is a transition into the twenty-first century, but the period covered by this chapter began in the nineteenth century with Schleiermacher and Bushnell, who both held a high view of children and made children an explicit part of their theological reflection. Rahner did not talk as much about children in the many volumes of his theological writing as Schleiermacher and Bushnell did, but he had a high view of them that was articulated when his writing did focus on them. As a Jesuit, his life did not include children in a family of his own, but he still wrote about them with deep perception. His brother, Hugo Rahner, SJ, also did this indirectly in a little book about theology and play, *Man at Play*, first published in English in 1965 (Rahner 1965), which includes not only theologians at play but also God and the church as well!

When we turn to Barth we find someone who was usually indifferent to children, although he did have some important insights that might be said to fall somewhere between a low and high view. Mostly he was indifferent, however. Williams has a high view of children and is concerned about how they are understood by today's culture and how they see themselves. He has included them in both his theological thinking and practice of ministry.

In the next chapter we will take a look at the contemporary conversation. It will involve six authors, four women and two men. At last, the gender gap has been closed and all of these authors have a high view of children.

CHAPTER

7

TODAY'S CONVERSATION: 2000–present

Emil Nolde (1867–1956) was a German expressionist painter and a member of die Bruke (Bridge) artists' group. They saw themselves as a bridge to the future. In 1913 Nolde visited New Guinea, which stimulated the distortions and bold colors of his style. By 1937 his graphics and oils were displayed in many important German museums, but they were confiscated by the Nazis, even though he was sympathetic to them, and some sold at auction in Switzerland.

This painting is very similar in composition to Lucas Cranach the Elder's *Let the Children Come Unto Me* (1538), which is in the Kunsthalle in Hamburg, Germany. In both paintings, the men on the left are angry and distant. On the right are the joyous and warm women and children. Cranach showed Jesus holding and blessing children, but Nolde turned Jesus' back to the viewer. Perhaps Christ's face is too overwhelming for most to see, but the women and children rejoice in his presence and embody his powerful light for the onlooker.

▲ *Christus und die Kinder* (Christ and the Children), Emil Nolde (1910) Museum of Modern Art, New York City
(Digital Image © The Museum of Modern Art/Licensed by SCALA / Art Resource, NY)

Let the Children Come Unto Me, ▶
Lucas Cranach the Elder (1538)
Kunsthalle, Hamburg, Germany
(Bildarchiv Preuissischer Kulturbesitz / Art Resource, NY)

This chapter covers the shortest span of time in this long story. The third millennium's first decade will be represented by six authors: Marcia J. Bunge, Bonnie J. Miller-McLemore, Joyce Ann Mercer, David H. Jensen, Kristin Herzog, and Martin E. Marty. As you can see, the voices of women have, at last, joined the discussion in a major way. I, too, am involved, so we will begin with a personal story to say how.

In 1960 if you had walked down a corridor in Stuart Hall at Princeton Theological Seminary you might have seen something quite bizarre. The mildly interesting but absolutely required class in Christian education was being destroyed by the antics of one of the students! I was the disruptive student and Professor D. Campbell Wyckoff (1918–2005) was the insightful professor. He realized that the cause of my frustration was buried so deeply that it would need some care, and certainly another setting, to become clear and be examined. He required me to take a tutorial with him instead of the class and to write my own theory of Christian education.

During the half-century since then, I have slowly realized that the acting out for unconscious reasons in the class had something to do with the lack of reality in the class about children's experiences of God and how to help children understand and develop that. In the background was the lack of interest generally about children in my theological training, which offended me at the deepest level, since my own childhood experiences were the origin of my own theological journey. I was hurt and confused by this indifference but this awareness remained unavailable to me for many years.

In 2000 I accidentally found the paper, written some forty years before, and sent a copy to Cam, who by then was a colleague, retired, and living in Albuquerque. The paper was awkwardly serious and passionate, but what Cam wrote on it became more significant than either of us could have realized at the time. Before he died we got to laugh together more than once about the class and what had happened since then. He wrote:

> ↩ You have built an interesting and potentially fruitful base for
> a theory of Christian education. You leave me rather convinced
> that the heart of the matter is an epistemology (and this could
> be the base for a theory of learning). From this base you could

> proceed to a theory of learning, then to an educational methodology and plan—a proposal. I hope that in time you will do so. (Berryman, personal papers, 1960)

I have done so. The theory was described in *Godly Play* (Berryman 1991) and the method in *Teaching Godly Play,* which is now in a second edition (Berryman 2009). The publication of eight volumes of *The Complete Guide To Godly Play* (Berryman 2002–2009) provides the curriculum. There are also additional books and many theoretical articles and chapters in books, including an integration of history, theory, and practice in Volume One of *The Complete Guide* (Berryman 2002). Two articles in the *Sewanee Theological Review* provide a preliminary statement of the theological goal, which is "mutual blessing" between children and adults (Berryman 2004) and the means to reach that goal which is "playful orthodoxy" (Berryman 2005). As you have already guessed, this book, *Children and the Theologians,* is also part of this larger project, begun so long ago.

The author of this book, then, is a participant in the current conversation, but in such a different way from the six other authors that I am in a unique position to provide a balanced overview of their contributions. They are theologians with a taste for being with children, while I love working with children and have a taste for theology.

The tone of the contemporary discussion can be found in the emotion-laden brush strokes of Emil Nolde's *Christ Among the Children*—which reverberates with the images of Lucas Cranach the Elder's *Let the Children Come Unto Me,* painted in the sixteenth century. A cropped version of Cranach's painting is on the cover of Bonnie J. Miller-McLemore's book, which has almost the same name, *Let the Children Come.*

The similar design of Nolde's and Cranach's two paintings advocates visually for the high view of children, which dominates the contemporary debate. In Nolde's painting, which is at the beginning of this chapter, Jesus stands between the dark on the left and the light on the right. There are heavy clothes and scowling faces on the left and bright nakedness and open faces on the right. There is anger on the left and joy on the right. On the left there is distance and men talking among themselves while on the right there is the intimate, spontaneous energy and enthusiasm of the children and women. Jesus has his back to us and to the dark figures on the left. Perhaps his face would be too much for either the viewer or the disciples to see directly, but the children are not afraid of it and absorb its brilliance to make it manifest for us. If we look into the faces of the children we can see Christ's presence. This is like what Jesus said about when we welcome children. When we welcome them we welcome him.

Children in this painting, then, are a means of grace. They mediate the light of Jesus' presence to the onlooker. This is like Luther's appreciation of God's "little jesters," Schleiermacher's two kinds of consciousness, Bushnell's "higher kind of play," Karl Rahner's "original child," and Williams' lost "icon" that mediate the high view of children that is shared by the six authors reviewed in this chapter.

The authors include a professor of theology and the humanities who is the leading historian of children in Christian theology, two professors of pastoral theology, a systematic theologian, an independent scholar with a global perspective, and a not-very-retired historian who has written over fifty books on a wide range of theological, historical, and social topics. These authors include parents of pre-school children, parents of college-age young adults, grandparents and a great-grandfather. With this introduction to the group it is now time to meet each author individually. We begin with Marcia J. Bunge.

Marcia J. Bunge:
Historical and Scriptural Foundations

Marcia Bunge promotes children's well-being through her scholarship, teaching, advocacy and in her own family as a mother. She lectures regularly to and mentors college students at Christ College, which is the honors college at Valparaiso University in Indiana, as well as lecturing world wide. In addition to her work on children in theology and scripture, which will be reviewed here, she will publish *Children and Childhood in World Religions: Primary Texts and Sources* in 2009. She also serves on the National Task Force on Education for the Evangelical Lutheran Church in America (ELCA). She graduated from St. Olaf College in English and music and earned her MA in divinity and PhD in religion and literature from the University of Chicago.

A sound discussion about the theology of children needs three things: a history of the theme to give it context, the scriptural basis to provide a proper foundation, and a respected place for the debate. Marcia J. Bunge has made it her business to provide all three. With Lilly Endowment's support she has edited and contributed to the history and scriptural basis for a theology of children. She has also led the way to establish children as a recognized subject for scholarly debate at the American Academy of Religion.

Church historians began to take an interest in children around 1994, when a wide-ranging collection of papers was read at meetings of the Ecclesiastical History Society in England. They were edited by Diana Wood and published as *The Church and Childhood*. The overall theme of the volume, as noted by Dr. Wood in her Introduction (Wood 1994, xix), was the ambiguity of how the church thinks about children.

Marcia J. Bunge's *The Child in Christian Thought* then appeared in 2001. It provided the first major collection of secondary sources about the history of children and theology, but it did more. It also contributed to the wider debate about children in our culture by its relevance to "the nature of children and our obligations to them" (Bunge 2001, 3).

The Child in Christian Thought was written by experts on specific theologians and the other topics covered. This division of labor was important, because most theologians' comments about children are often buried in asides, far from the primary themes of systematic theology, except, perhaps, for the doctrine of infant baptism. Experts were needed to discover such clues and to follow up on them. The editing, organization, and authors chosen for this volume made it an instant classic.

This book's some five hundred pages cover about two millennia of theological thought and are divided into seventeen chapters, to inform readers both inside and outside the church in three areas. First, the work has added to the growing number of studies about the history of childhood. Second, it has contributed a theological point of view to the cross-disciplinary discussion about the nature of children in our time. Third, it has provided the basis for a theological rationale to support Christian advocacy to meet children's needs. It has succeeded in its goal to "combine historical integrity, theological insight, and resonance with contemporary issues" (Bunge 2001, 8) and by inference, to awaken readers to the possibility, as well as the complexity, of placing children more toward the center of theological reflection.

The interest of scripture scholars in children began during the Year of the Child in 1979 with Hans Ruedi Weber's *Jesus and the Children: Biblical Resources for Study and Preaching* (Weber 1979). This initiative continued in 1992 when Peter Müller published his major (447 pages in German) study about children in the midst of the community in the New Testament. His *In der Mitte der Gemeinde: Kinder im Neuen Testament* (Müller 1992) has unfortunately not yet been translated into English.

Marcia J. Bunge then published *The Child in the Bible* with herself, Terence E. Fretheim, and Beverly Roberts Gaventa as editors. This book, like *The Child in Christian Thought* is about five hundred pages long

(Bunge 2008). It includes chapters about Genesis, Exodus, Proverbs, the Prophets, and other texts in the Hebrew Scriptures in its first section. The second section includes chapters about the place of children in each of the Christian gospels and in Paul's letters. The third section includes scriptural themes such as a chapter on adoption and one about the image of God. Leading biblical scholars such as Patrick Miller, Walter Brueggeman, Judith M. Gundry, and Beverly Roberts Gaventa were selected to write the individual chapters.

When the theological and scriptural resources Bunge has provided are combined with social histories such as *Families in Ancient Israel* (Perdue, Blenkinsopp, Collins, Meyers 1997) and *Families in the New Testament World* (Osiek, Balch 1997), the foundation for the theological discussion about children becomes more solid with the passing of each year. The addition of her new book about children in the world's religions now places this Christian foundation for thinking theologically about children within the context of the rest of the world's religions.

We turn now to the contributions of the other five authors. Most of them, as well as myself, have drawn liberally from Bunge's rich resources. We continue the contemporary discussion with two pastoral theology professors, then a systematic theologian, an expert on children in world religions and finally Martin Marty, who will address the fundamental mystery of children.

Bonnie J. Miller-McLemore: An Integrated Theological, Psychological and Feminist View of Children in the Church

Bonnie J. Miller-McLemore is Professor of Pastoral Theology and Counseling at Vanderbilt Divinity School. Like Bunge she earned her MA and PhD at the University of Chicago, but her field of study was religion and psychology. She also trained at the Center for Religion and Psychotherapy in psychoanalytic self-psychological therapy. She and her husband have three sons 18, 20, 23 and they have figured in her books since her first one—*Also a Mother: Work and Family as Theological Dilemma*, in 1994. As a mother, wife, and scholar, she is deeply interested in the cultural influences on children and families and the role of the church in nourishing a deep and creative spirituality among them despite the dark side of our society's influence.

Miller-McLemore's 2003 *Let the Children Come* explicitly draws on theology, psychology, and feminist theory to answer the question "Can Christianity make any difference in how people understand and seek to empower girls and boys today?" (Miller-McLemore 2003, 45). All three sources are needed, she argues, to correct each other, so she devotes two chapters to each resource in her book.

When Miller-McLemore began to write this book she thought it was going to be about child-rearing. She soon realized, however, that the church's whole understanding of children had to change, so it became about "how adults think about children," which is a descriptive task, and about "how adults should think about children," which is a prescriptive and normative task (Miller-McLemore 2003, xxv). When this preliminary volume was done she published her child-rearing book in 2007, to which we will return at the conclusion of this chapter, because it shows how the contemporary discussion has changed over the last few years.

Miller-McLemore analyzed six adult views of children that need better understanding and correction. In each case she addressed not only how adults think about children but how they *ought* to think about them. The six topics covered are: the changing concept of childhood, children as victims, children as sinful, children as gifts, children as a labor of love, and children as moral agents. A complete re-thinking of the whole field of theology needs to be considered, she argues, to more adequately treat these subjects.

The reason the field of theology needs changing is because of its general dismissal of children to the so-called "practical application" fields of religious education and pastoral care. This implies that systematic theology decides what subject matter to present to children and the educators decide when and how to do it, while the counselors decide when families need additional pastoral care. The reason this method needs changing is because it does not account for the feedback that children and families contribute to theological reflection and how pastoral care, counseling, and Christian education, when combined with the social sciences and biological studies, can enrich theological ideas about the fundamental nature of human beings. Many seminaries team-teach across departmental lines today to help remedy this, but real progress is slow and Miller-McLemore's point is as relevant now as it was when she made it in 2003.

The view of children changes over time and theologians have interpreted them in very different ways from being locked in sin to being gifts of God. Miller-McLemore carefully moved through these conflicting views and arrived at Menno Simons's theology to provide an "intermediary position between views of children as innocent or guilty of sin" (Miller-McLemore 2003, 70). Simons (1496–1561) was an anabaptist leader in what is now The Netherlands and his followers are called Mennonites today.

This "foray into classic texts" provides her with the theory to accompany her personal experience as a mother and professional experience in counseling to make "concluding observations" about how children are involved in the sin of the world. Her conclusion is that children are neither completely innocent nor completely sinful, but a combination of both. This makes them *responsible* for their actions. Since they are responsible it follows that they can be forgiven—rather than merely being thought of as victims, who can only protest. This is, perhaps, the most important argument in her book.

Joyce Ann Mercer:
Healing the Disconnects between What
the Church Says and Does with Children

The second pastoral theologian selected to represent this part of the conversation is Joyce Ann Mercer. Her training began at the University of Virginia with a BA and then moved to Yale University School of Divinity for an MDiv. She then earned her MSW from the University of Connecticut, a DMin from McCormick Theological Seminary and finally her PhD from Emory University. When she wrote *Welcoming Children* she was Associate Professor of Practical Theology and Christian Education at the Graduate Theological Union and at San Francisco Theological Seminary in the Berkeley area of California. She moved to Virginia Theological Seminary in Alexandria, Virginia, in 2006 to continue her teaching, writing, and research there and where she is now Professor of Practical Theology.

She and Larry Golelmon, a consultant and researcher with the Alban Institute, have three children from eleven to thirteen years of age. They all enjoy the outdoors from mountain climbing and hiking to beaches, horses and big dogs. Her experience as a mother, a social worker and a resident of the Philippines, where she and her family lived, have informed her scholarly interest about children in the church.

Like Miller-McLemore she has been critical of the tendency in theological education to limit pastoral theology to the practical or applied part of the theological enterprise. This is because, she cautions, most people's motivations do not come primarily from ideas and thinking. While it is true that some personality types are more inclined to be motivated by ideas than other types, theological *thinking*, she writes, "cannot guarantee either more just and loving practices with children or a 'better childhood' in the day-to-day experience of any particular child. Put differently, the content of theology does not alone dictate its effects and meanings at the level of practices" (Mercer 2005, 27). Theology, therefore, needs the feedback from practice not only to adjust the relevance of theology's content but to make it more true.

For example, when a congregation refuses to welcome children fully into its life, it misses something critical for understanding God. There is something "messy, playful, noisy, active, spontaneous, restless and unpredictable" about the Divine that children can teach adults. When this aspect of God is missed by worshippers and theologians, they put the church in peril (Mercer 2005, 262).

Mercer also argues with energy and sharpness that the church ought to liberate children from the culture's educational program, which is designed to sell them an identity. The church's educational program is very weak for children in comparison to what major retailers in the United States do to convince them to be consumers. The church needs to do a better job, she argues, to help children form an alternative identity as Christians to the consumer identity that is so skillfully and widely promoted. This is hard to accomplish, however, because of two primary "disconnects" within the church.

The first disconnect is between thinking and action in the parish. For example, she argues, most congregations think they welcome children while their life together and worship works, mostly unconsciously, to "shun, exclude, or erase children from such an involvement" (Mercer 2005, 213).

This disconnect was evident in two out of the three groups she studied in her Children in Congregations Project. The congregation that included children "assumed the regular presence of children for the whole of worship each week, but it did so at the expense of any structured and intentional process of religious education for children. In the other two congregations, parents were among the most vocal opponents to children's participation in the entirety of worship each week" (Mercer 2005, 185–186). Still, most parishioners in all three parishes saw themselves and their congregation as being open to and accepting of children.

A second disconnect is between the academy and the parish. Mercer writes that theological education encourages " . . . an 'application' model of the relationship between thought and action, akin to the errant notion that practical theology is the 'application' of the thoughts from systematic theology into the realm of human experience . . . . This 'application' model further makes action separate from and subordinate to thought in a way that I find objectionable" (Mercer 2005, 213). Mercer's critical feminist viewpoint seeks to liberate children from this theological confinement and to awaken the church to welcome children by reconnecting these two disconnects.

Disconnects are hard to see, however. There is also a disconnect present in the lives of the two theologians Mercer has chosen to illustrate her theology. She found Karl Rahner to be "particularly insightful" and bases her "liberatory theology of childhood" on his work (Mercer 2005, 149). This is because he saw children as involved in the structures of sin but still, as she puts it, "blanketed on all sides by the grace of God" (Mercer 2005, 151).

As a Jesuit, however, Rahner belonged to a religious tradition that systematically excludes it members from having families of their own. Rahner is clearly one of those people who does not allow their restricted experience with children to limit their views about them, but it would have been interesting to have Mercer comment on the power of systems and how this affects the Roman Catholic theology of children.

Karl Barth is also famous for his disconnect between theology and his family life. This was mentioned in chapter 6. Mercer's comments about Barth, however, seem to have another goal. She seems intent on correcting the misunderstanding of Barth by conservative Christian writers, who sometimes use him to promote the absolute authority of parents over children. She notes that in *Church Dogmatics* (Volume III, Part 4) Barth qualified his call for the subordination of children by declaring that parents need to realize that they, too, are children from the viewpoint of God. Children, therefore, are not property, political subjects, or servants. They are apprentices entrusted to adults, who as elders in the church should lead children as God leads them.

Mercer also argues that in addition to moving children into the center of congregational life we also need to move them into the center of theological thought. This is because regardless of age we are all dependent, in need, and vulnerable like children. This is not a side issue, then, such as discussing a child's moral status or how children relate to a doctrine such as baptism. Furthermore, when children are thought about as "doers of the Word" instead of "receivers of knowledge and as passive learners " they become central to the ministry, worship, and theology of the church. She explains how this might work:

    ∾ Children as learners are participants in social processes, practices, and relationships with others, whose collaboration with children not only "scaffolds" the learning of children, but also engenders clarification and renegotiation of meanings and practices within the larger community of practice for its continual renewal and learning. (Mercer, 2005, 205) ∾

Education through participation in the community and its central worship is education not only for children but also the congregation and the academy, Mercer argues. For example, a focus on providing children with an identity in the church that is not centered around seeking happiness by buying and accumulating the market's goods, will not only affect the church of the present but of the future. It will change the church and the academy when children discover their identity as those who care for others and who are cared for in the church. The disconnects will be healed when they become leaders for the next generation of parishioners and students.

David H. Jensen: Grace and Vulnerability in a Theology of Childhood

David H. Jensen is Professor of Constructive Theology at Austin Presbyterian Theological Seminary. His training began at Carlton College with a BA and then an MAR at Yale. He then earned his PhD from Vanderbilt. He and Molly Jensen have two children who are three and ten years of age. His advocacy for children comes out of his experience as a husband and a father as well as his training as a theologian, as his reference to the birth of Hannah Grace demonstrates in his theology of childhood.

    Like the other authors in this chapter, Jensen has struggled with how to locate his reflections about children in the traditional theological categories. As his book progresses he tries out several alternatives. He is writing a "contextual theology" (Jensen 2005, xvi). It is also an "inductive theology," which is the basis for "an ecclesial ethic of care for all children" (Jensen 2005, xii). The resulting ethic is also based on the Baptismal Covenant (Jensen 2005, 106, 111). He is also engaged in a "critical recovery of the doctrine of sin" (Jensen 2005, 99). The overarching vision of his task, however, is embodied in the book's title: *Graced Vulnerability: A Theology of Childhood*.

    The core of this theology is in chapter 4, "Vulnerability and Violence" (Jensen 2005, 65–100). The argument moves forward in three steps. A description of children as victims (about thirteen pages) is provided, then, the inadequacy of the language about sin (about fourteen pages) is described. Finally a "critical reconstruction" of the doctrine of sin and salvation (about seven pages) is attempted.

To clear the way for the reconstruction he observes that the "church bears no definitive, early statement on sin and salvation" (Jensen 2005, 78) when compared to the completeness of the classical statements about Christology and the Trinity. This might be debated. For example, Bernhard Lohse has written:

> The decrees of the councils of 418, 431, and 529 are, of course, important. A new area of affirmations of the Christian faith had now been clarified dogmatically and took its place alongside the doctrine of God and Christology. From now on a radical concept of sin, consisting in man's lack of freedom insofar as he is related to God, a belief in the necessity of the divine work of grace, and an understanding of the primacy of grace rather than of human merit, are definitely among the basic affirmations of the Christian Faith. (Lohse 1985, 127–128)

Whether these councils did define sin adequately or not, there was no "fist of the empire," as Jensen reminds us, to enforce their actions. There was no one like the Emperor Constantine with the interest, energy, and power to establish doctrines throughout the church as had been done in the fourth century.

As part of the Reformed Church—like Calvin, Schleiermacher, and Barth—Jensen reminds us that the church is called to be "always reforming" (*semper reformanda*) so he does not look back only to Calvin for the final definition of the faith.

As he moves forward, then, he still acknowledges the importance of the history that shaped the doctrine of sin by giving the reader a "Brief Tour" because "harmonization is impossible; yet some broad consistencies emerge" (Jensen 2005, 88). The itinerary goes like this: Paul talked in terms of the Adam/Christ typology, Augustine in terms of original sin and pride, Calvin in terms of disobedience, and Schleiermacher in terms of God-consciousness and relationships (Jensen 2005, 78–87).

The three "broad consistencies" that emerge from Jensen's tour are that sin is pervasive, children possess some power to sin, and children should be held responsible for their actions. Jensen then makes a creative move. He looks at the doctrine from the child's point of view.

The language of judgment and magisterial grace defines the child in terms of flaws they have no control over, and salvation they do not deserve. The actual situation for children is that they are too dependent to be likely to turn away from God or those around them, whom they need to survive. Children are also less likely than adults to assume they have superior power over others, although they can imagine magical powers. Since children are not yet independent thinkers, they are also unlikely to be unfaithful. Children are also deeply relational, even more so than adults, since they have not yet developed an adult capacity to use language for deception. This means that they will be hurt rather than improved by being accused of sin. What becomes apparent when sin is looked at from the child's point of view is that it is more adequately thought about as the context into which children are born rather than some condition they are born with. The classical adult view of children's sin is like blaming victims for the damage already done. This kind of condemnation also tempts adults to evade their responsibility to care for the children in their midst, because they are already condemned by sin.

Jensen concludes that sin be defined as "the aberration of creation" (Jensen 2005, 98). It is a disease that is always present and yet life cannot be reduced to it. This nuanced view of Augustine and Calvin was embodied in the birth of Hannah Grace, Molly and David Jensen's daughter. Her birth "was not epitomized by depravity and doom; rather, it was graced by vulnerability, relationship, and hope. Yet, at the same time that Hannah Grace came into the world with such promise, she became open to the wounded nature of creation itself" (Jensen 2005, 98). She became vulnerable to life's aberration.

Hope remains, however, despite this vulnerability, because salvation is always available when it is thought of as "the restoration of fellowship between creation and the Creator ." When salvation is thought of only as "the removal of a stain that covers humanity," there is less hope and more blame (Jensen 2005, 100). Jensen sounds at times, it seems to me, like a combination of Augustine and Calvin tempered by Irenaeus, but with his own creative voice. This is why it seems strange that Irenaeus (125–200) was left out of his tour of sin's geography. As was noted in chapter 2 Irenaeus (125–200) argued for a developmental model for humankind. Eric Osborn writes:

> While some have doubted whether Irenaeus coordinated (and not merely juxtaposed) his ideas, theocentric optimism pervades all. It matters to man to know that he is a copy of the incarnate Christ, that God's first loving concern after the fall was to put Adam into more comfortable clothes, that life is a sign of God's gift and that the weakness of flesh is the correlate of God's strengthening grace and goodness. (Osborn 2005, 231)

This sounds closer to what Jensen is proposing than what the others on the theological tour had in mind.

What does this reconstructed view of sin mean for congregations? His emphasis on children's vulnerability caused Jensen to take a closer look at the nature of the church. He concluded that it should be a place for baptism, peace-making, and sanctuary so that "graced vulnerability" is more understandable and realizable.

Jensen then shifts our gaze away from reading Calvin's views about children in terms limited to election and predestination and asks us to look at his view of the sacrament of infant baptism instead. Calvin considered baptism to be the sign whereby "the cleansing of sin and the believer's participation in the death and resurrection of Christ are made visible" (Jensen 2005, 104). Jensen sums this up, as a Presbyterian, by saying that "Infant baptism is not an elixir for original sin, but a token of God's promise to children of the covenant" (Jensen 2005, 105). This shift of emphasis brings into the foreground of Calvin's theology God's adoption of children and promise to them that they are saved, although other Calvin scholars might still read Calvin as being more committed to the model of election than adoption.

In any case, Jesus' challenge to become like children is not a comfortable escape into sweet romanticism. "To become like a child is to open one's eyes again to the violence that surrounds us, but also to fall into the arms of God's grace, the God who experiences the violence that scars the earth and announces the final word of peace" (Jensen 2005, 128).

He concludes by quoting Karl Rahner, to say that childhood is "a state in which we are open to expect the unexpected, to commit ourselves to the incalculable, a state which endows us with the power still to be able to play, to recognize that the powers presiding over existence are greater than our own designs, and to submit to their control as our deepest good" (Rahner, quoted in Jensen 2005, 128).

Jensen's great contribution in this book, it seems to me, is to argue along side of Rahner for the doctrine of "original childhood" to temper the adult-isms of the original sin doctrine. This is realistic because adults cannot outgrow their dependency on God even when they are all grown up.

Kirstin Herzog:
Christianity and Children in the
Context of the World's Religions

Kristin Herzog is an independent scholar and writer who lives part of the year in Durham, North Carolina, part of the year in Germany, and part of the year in Peru, where she works with children and families. Her PhD is from the University of North Carolina in Chapel Hill. She is nearly eighty, and is a grandmother and has godchildren in Peru. She is presently organizing her husband's papers for the library at the Divinity School of the University of North Carolina. The late Frederick Herzog was Professor of Systematic Theology at Duke and pioneered the work in Peru to support the clergy and parishioners there and to expand the horizons of the seminarians at Duke. Kirstin Herzog's book is enhanced not only by her global experience but by her creative use of fourteen pictures of children to evoke the images of how the major world religions imagine them. This gives the reader a feeling base as well as a conceptual one for understanding the religions the children of the world are involved in. This book is also available in a German translation.

Children and our Global Future urges that theological meaning about the earth's future cannot be made without including children. This idea was prompted by the suggestion that Jesus considered children to be teachers of spiritual maturity, a view purported to be unique in the history of world religions (Herzog 2005, 51). Though initially skeptical, Herzog's research led her to conclude that this is true, which led her to study children in all the major religions as a matter of the earth's survival.

Herzog grew up as a Lutheran but for the last forty years has been a member of the United Church of Christ. Her life in Germany, the United States, and especially the work she and her late husband did in Peru with women and children has demonstrated to her that people in all religions need to seek a "common ground" for cooperation. Children, she argues, should be this common ground. The question is not *whether* a child will lead us. The question is whether children will lead the world toward peace or greater violence, a violence that can destroy the earth!

The question of whether the child is a savior or destroyer has been masked by the image of children as victims. The truly awful global plight of children is usually described in such large numbers and horrific abstractions that they leave one numb. These facts and figures have been copiously provided in all the books reviewed in this chapter, but I found myself

turning these pages quickly, already convinced, and not finding any new
emotional resources or insights in the statistics and lists. Herzog, however,
has provided the reader with a simple compass that points irrefutably to
the enormity of the global suffering of children. She wrote, "While theologians have tried hard to wrest some meaning from the events of September
11, 2001, in which almost three thousand people were killed in a day, few
pay any attention to the estimated thirty thousand children under age five
who die every day around this globe from preventable causes, according to
UNICEF statistics" (Herzog 2005, 1). She then asks, "Should that not be
of concern to theologians?"

I do not know how this earth could sustain adding those thirty thousand
children a day to the world's population if they did survive, but clearly the
suffering of children is too easily overlooked. How we think about children
shapes how we care for them and how we care for them shapes the future.
Are they victims, saviors, or destroyers? Even this seemingly simple question becomes complex when asked in a global setting. For example, children who are suicide bombers are seen by some as saviors and by others as
destroyers who have no respect for the lives of others or themselves.

The argument of Herzog's book begins by noticing that Christian
theologians are not open to seeing children in their own scriptures, much
less in the other scriptures of the world. To stimulate more openness toward
children one needs to be in touch with both the words and the images of the
world's religions since how we treat children is not only a matter of reason
but also of emotional understanding.

Being open does not mean being mindless or boiling down the concept
of "children" to a single essence or even to simmer the fourteen images she
provides to make a stew. The diversity of the world's religions and *each*
religion's complex understanding of children both need to be honored to
inform us well. This means that people need to know their own traditions
deeply (Herzog 2005, 136) while at the same time being open to others.
Many Christians fail on both counts, she notes.

The remedy for this failure is for Christians to realize that our global
future is in danger. This danger compels us to help adults "mature into
childhood," which includes both learning from and teaching Christian
children about "justice and peace, but also the integrity of creation"
(Herzog 2005, 120).

Herzog uses her personal experiences in Peru as case studies to show
how learning *from* children about the "web of life" can help one in the
struggle to overcome the reduction of children to the dichotomy of savior/
victim. Thinking about children as "agents of liberation" without losing
sight of their uniqueness is the way forward for the church.

This way forward requires that we do three things, according to Herzog. First, the challenge of one's particular scriptural heritage concerning children needs to be fully appreciated. Second, one needs to be open to other cultures and religions concerning the meaning of children and how to care for them from each religion's point of view. Third, the web of relationships with all people and the natural environment needs to be more fully understood and appreciated (Herzog 2005, 174).

"Learning from children to become like children will mean becoming more curious, frank, hopeful, trusting, and eager to relate and communicate, and being full of vitality and imagination" (Herzog 2005, 177). Adults who can experience this change of heart will help create a global future that is constructive rather than destructive. This is worth paying attention to today, because the stakes are so high.

With this global perspective in mind we now turn to the fundamental mystery of children. They resist an easy definition, so how to think about them, to care for them, and to be like them is not as easy to figure out as some might think.

Martin E. Marty: Balancing Mystery and Control in the Care of Children

Martin Marty is the Fairfax M. Cone Distinguished Service Professor Emeritus at the University of Chicago, where he also taught, at the Divinity School, since 1963. He is author of some fifty books including *Righteous Empire*, which earned him the National Book Award, and his three-volume *Modern American Religion*. *The Mystery of the Child* was written for many personal reasons but was commissioned by The Child in Law, Religion, and Society Project at the Center for the Study of Law and Religion at Emory University's School of Law.

Martin Marty was born in West Point, Nebraska and was ordained as a Lutheran pastor in 1952. His extended family today includes his wife, Harriet, seven children (including two foster children), nine grandchildren, and three great-grandchildren. His broad professional interests, accomplishments, and rigorous schedule are integrated with the life of this extended family with enthusiasm and a rich sense of humor.

All the authors in this chapter have directly or indirectly acknowledged the mystery of the child, but Martin Marty has made this the explicit center of his focus in two fundamental ways. First, he brings the perspective and experience of a great-grandfather, and second, he applies his wide-ranging interests as a historian, theologian, and interpreter of culture to this theme.

A great-grandfather's perspective is important. It includes the experience of one's own children and their children as well as the children of grandchildren. In the midst of births and growing families, however, death also crowds into so many years, such as the death of his first wife, and adds to one's wisdom in profound ways. This is why Joan M. Erikson added a ninth stage of development to her husband Erik's eight stages in a revised edition of *The Life Cycle Completed.*

She told about picking blueberries with a grandchild on a sunny day at the Cape. He came up to her and said, "Nama, you are old and I am new." She wrote that this was "an unchallengeable pronouncement" (Erikson 1997, 115), but what she wanted to know was how to be new despite being old. The vision of Joan Erikson staying new each day was beautifully captured in Joan Anderson's *A Walk on the Beach* (Anderson 2004) as she charmed the younger Joan into becoming like a child again. Crispation can creep into life at any age, but one need not automatically become "elderly," a word that Joan and Erik Erikson steadfastly reframed as "elders." The seasoning that Martin Marty brings to this discussion is that childhood is not about birthdays. It truly is a mystery.

The second way that Martin Marty broadens this discussion is by his wide-ranging reading. For example, one of the many striking resources he turns up is that of the French novelist Georges Bernanos, who wrote in his *The Diary of a Country Priest*:

> ℧ You hear the hypocrites, the sensualists, the Scrooges, the rotten rich—with their thick lips and gleaming eyes—cooing over (Jesus' invitation) *Sinite parvulos*, "Let the little children come to me," without any indication that they're taking note of the words that follow—some of the most terrible ever heard by human ears, "If you are not like one of these little ones, you will not enter the Kingdom of God." (Quoted in Marty 2007, 75) ℧

Marty notes that this paragraph (and a number of others) are omitted in the English translation. There is no explanation provided by the translators. Perhaps it was too disturbing, Marty theorized, because the words are truly terrible, but he also writes toward the end of his book:

> ℧ It is not creative, however, for anyone to hear these words about change as causes for regret or envy . . . . "If only I had let those terrifying words soak in sooner, I would not now have the terror of concern about whether I am too late to follow this course

> . . . (and) have failed to be swept up in the kingdom (or humanis-
> tic equivalents of the fulfilling life)." (Marty 2007, 232)

People may ask, he writes, "Why was I not told to change and become like a child?" and the answer is that you *were* told. You just failed to notice how terrible these words really are and did not appreciate them until your later years when you realized that your imagination, confidence, and wonder had decayed with your body and that you are now dependent and over-looked, like children, but without a child's exuberance and resilience to respond.

To understand the mystery of the child is important for both adults and children because to miss this reduces children to the problems of the problem child, which diminishes both children and adults. He draws on Gabriel Marcel, the French-Catholic existentialist philosopher to enliven the idea of mystery.

Mystery is something that cannot be known unless one is involved in it. If you turn children into objective problems for analysis, the mystery evaporates. Being with children, however, places one in a relationship that includes the edges of their being and knowing, which in turn arouses the anxiety these limits stimulate in one's own life. David Tracy mapped this existential territory as a triangle of limits: finitude, contingency, and tran-sience (Marty 2007, 20). Marty argues that to truly know children is to know that they can die, that they are vulnerable to good and bad accidents, and that they will not stay put, no matter how urgently adults need perma-nent solutions to their boundless energy and growth.

How then should we approach children to be aware of their mystery? To answer this, Marty draws on the work of Sam Keen, author of *Apology for Wonder* (Keen 1969). Keen's defense of wonder began when he was a graduate student at Princeton University. His thesis and first book were about Gabriel Marcel and he finished his book about wonder while a young professor at Louisville Presbyterian Seminary. This part of Marty's book is like meeting old friends. I met Gabriel Marcel when he visited Princeton Seminary when I was a student there and Sam Keen taught an evening seminar on existentialist philosophy, which I took part in. Later he, James W. Fowler, and I published a book together called *Life Maps* (Berryman 1978).

The core question of Marty's book is how to balance mystery and con-trol in the care of children. Control is important for rearing children, but the urging of mystery is to refine this control. How? Marty cites Margaret Donaldson, professor emerita of psychology at the University of Edinburgh to emphasize the balance needed:

⅘ All of this leads to a central dilemma for those who want to
teach the young. There is a compelling case for control. The
young child is not capable of deciding for himself what he should
learn: he is quite simply too ignorant. And he needs our help to
sustain him through the actual process of learning . . . I can see
only one way out of this dilemma: it is to exercise such control
as is needful with a light touch and never to relish the need. It is
possible after all for control to be more or less obtrusive, more
or less paraded . . . . If the ultimate aim of the control is to render
itself unnecessary, if the teacher obviously wants the children
to become competent, self-determining, responsible beings and
believes them capable of it, then I am convinced that the risk of
rejection of learning will be much diminished. (quoted in Marty
2007, 33) ⅙

To further explore the proper balance between control and mystery
Marty carries on a "staged literary conversation which is the centerpiece
of this book" with Karl Rahner's often-mentioned article "Ideas for a
Theology of Childhood" (Marty 2007, 107–116). He isolates fifteen ideas
to which he poses the statement "If this is true, then the provider of care
will recognize that . . ."

First, the provider of care needs to keep in mind that it is important to
include the Hebrew Scriptures and the New Testament views of mystery
in one's understanding of the child as moving aside one veil after another
to find that there is no final veil. The child may be "effable"—measurable
and explainable in terms of weight, temperature, appearance, health, and
"other visible and palpable aspects of her being"—but the child is also inef-
fable. The provider of care also needs to be free from the impulse to control
all aspects of the child's life since that will only lead to a bland normality.

Rahner's article also implies that only considering short-term plan-
ning for the caregiver is short-sighted because the child always exists at
the threshold of the eternal. "Original childhood" is about forever and not
just today. This is part of why naming is important. It gives an identity
to the child, as a child of God with whom mystery is shared. Nurturing
the love of God is realistic as part of care, because God's accepting love is
present in the child's life, whether the child can speak about it or not, and
making room for this kind of love gives the child access to infinite openness
to growth. The child is both dependent and independent, so the caregiver
needs to attend to relational demands by the dependent child in a way that
encourages independence.

Caregivers also need to keep in mind that the child is open to expecting
the unexpected and that they can awaken in the caregiver "the power still

to be able to play." This means that providers of care need to be ready to be surprised themselves and find "age-appropriate ways to express this readiness." Play then is fundamental to "childness," which Marty prefers over "childlikeness," (Marty 2007, 237–244) and needs to be valued, encouraged, and enjoyed with the child for the benefit of both. The child's ending is revealed in the immense potential of his or her beginning.

Finally, the child is best revealed, after all, as a child of God, which brings us back to the first observation. The more one understands children with the wonder of their mystery, where there is no final veil, the more one can be open to one's own mystery.

In 1908 G.K. Chesterton wrote in "The Ethics of Elfland," a chapter in his book *Orthodoxy* what he had "learnt in the nursery":

> This elementary wonder, however, is not a mere fancy derived from the fairy tales; on the contrary, all the fire of the fairy tales is derived from this. Just as we all like love tales because there is an instinct of sex, we all like astonishing tales because they touch the nerve of the ancient instinct of astonishment. This is proved by the fact that when we are very young children we do not need fairy tales: we only need tales. Mere life is interesting enough. A child of seven is excited by being told that Tommy opened a door and saw a dragon. But a child of three is excited by being told that Tommy opened a door. (Chesterton 1959, 53–54)

Today children are so wired into their music, television, and video games and hurried by adult scheduling in and out of doors from car doors to school doors that the wonder of just opening the door is overwhelmed with hurry and the sound and fury of the "virtual world," which is neither real nor wonderful. In the midst of all this Martin Marty has asked us to slow down and appreciate the mystery of children to counteract their reduction to the problems of the problem child and the technology of care. In fact the wonder of the wondering child is something that cannot be overlooked if one aspires to provide children with responsible care or to become a wise adult.

Conclusion

The conversation of these six authors is remarkable when placed against the centuries of theology portrayed in this book. In contrast to the majority view they share a high view of children and see both story and play as vital connections between children and the theologians. They would all like to see children moved toward the center of theological reflection and have a more prominent place in theological education. Finally, they all understand and respect the history of the church that has produced the *de facto* doctrine of children, which still shapes us today.

Learning from history is not currently in fashion, but our age is not new in this regard. George Macaulay Trevelyan, a historian at the turn of the twentieth century, wrote:

> ↻ Of recent years the thought and feeling of the rising gen-
> eration is but little affected by historians. History was, by her
> own friends, proclaimed a "science" for specialists, not "lit-
> erature" for the common reader of books. And the common
> reader of books has accepted his discharge. (Quoted in Stern
> 1966, 228) ↺

About two-thirds of the way through the last century Christopher Lasch commented in his *The Culture of Narcissism* that today's loss of historical interest is related to the narcissism in the culture of the United States. It is not so much that people have fallen in love with a reflection of themselves but that they cannot love or be loved because they don't know where the self ends and the other begins. There is no need for history in such a self-centered world. "For all these reasons, the devaluation of the past has become one of the most important symptoms of the cultural crisis to which this book addresses itself" (Lasch 1991, xviii). That is true for Lasch's book as well as the one you are reading at this moment.

The lack of interest in history during the twentieth century continues today. This creates two problems. The past continues to shape us unconsciously and interest in the future has atrophied. This double danger became especially evident to me when I worked on a treatment and research team at Houston Child Guidance during the early 1980s. We were concerned with families that included suicidal children. A common factor in the families we worked with was that they did not tell stories. The treatment was by and large to get them to tell family stories; when they did, the suicidal children got better. Human beings need their stories about the past to give them meaning and to stimulate their interest in the future.

The theologians discussed here are all interested in history, story, and play, but they also tread lightly when history is discussed. This is because most readers lose interest when too much historical nuance or context is provided. An interest in story has remained stable during the last decade but the interest in play has increased . In a moment we will comment on this author by author, but first a few general comments about play are in order.

The modern interest in play began in the nineteenth century, as mentioned in the last chapter, but it was the publication of Johan Huizinga's *Homo Ludens* in Dutch in 1938 that established a scholarly interest in play. He argued with classical wit and energy that play is fundamental to being human. It is not one of a number of "the other manifestations of culture," but it is culture itself (Huizinga 1955, Foreword), a point often missed by translators and interpreters.

Play entered the English-speaking theological conversation about 1965 when two of Hugo Rahner's German articles were collected and translated to create the little book *Man at Play* (Rahner 1965). Interest peaked about 1970 and declined almost at once. David Miller's *Gods and Games: Towards a Theology of Play* (Miller 1970) provided a detailed literature review and introduction to the subject, but by about 1972 interest had evaporated.

The end was signaled by Jurgen Moltmann's book *Theology of Play*. It supposedly put him in dialogue with leaders in the play theology movement in the United States—Sam Keen, David L. Miller, and Robert E. Neale. When Moltman looked back on this supposed dialogue, he wrote, "We are perhaps not even talking about the same thing." He also noted: "The Puritan of work easily changes into the Puritan of play and remains a Puritan." Perhaps his most trenchant remark was that "If on earth everything turns into play, nothing will be play" (Moltmann 1972, 111–112).

The discussion about play outside of theology, however, did not decline. In 1997 one of the classics about play, though little read by theologians, was published by Brian Sutton-Smith, who had spent a lifetime studying play. He argued in *The Ambiguity of Play* (Sutton-Smith 1997) that play is ambiguous, because it is looked at from seven major points of view, each involving a different technical language or "rhetoric."

Sutton-Smith's summing-up moved a step beyond ambiguity to say, "Clearly the primary motive of players is the stylized performance of existential themes that mimic or mock the uncertainties and risks of survival and, in so doing, engage the propensities of mind, body, and cells in exciting forms of arousal" (Sutton-Smith 1997, 231). Sutton-Smith did not mention the Christian language system but he could have. The teasing and playful aspect of parables, the deep play of liturgy, the identity establishing sacred stories and the awareness of the Creator in contemplative silence are all a kind of "stylized performance of existential themes."

David Elkind's recent book *The Power of Play* is symptomatic of the continuing interest in play among psychologists and the public (Elkind 2007). This book—which echoes the title of a book written by the founders of Creative Playthings, Inc., Frank and Theresa Caplan, a little over thirty years before (Caplan 1973)—is a plea for people to understand that play is integral to children's health. Among the many facets of play discussed outside of theological circles is a developing interest in the neuroscience of play (Panksepp 1998, 280–299).

The existential relevance of play in Sutton-Smith's conclusion, Elkind's demonstration that play is integral to children's health, and the biological importance of play, all suggest together that theologians need to be more open to play's importance in their reflections on the nature of human beings. The year 2000 may have been a significant turning point for theology, because an article on "play" was included in *The Oxford Companion To Christian Thought* (Hastings 2000, 544–545).

Let us now turn to the role of play in the books discussed in this chapter. Bunge's book was published in 2001 and Miller-McLemore published in 2003 and 2007. The year 2005 was also a good year for children. Mercer, Jensen, and Herzog all published their books that year. Marty's came out in 2007. This is to say that during the first decade of this millennium the theological interest in children was blossoming, which drew with it a continuing interest in story and an increasing interest in play.

Bunge's book makes many references to play in the Index. They include a broad range of historical viewpoints from Schleiermacher's and Bushnell's positive views to negative references such as Wesley's. Mostly, however, the theologians reviewed in her book make no reference to play. They were as indifferent to play as they were to children.

Miller-McLemore's *Let the Children Come* did not include the category of "play" in its Index. In addition, she mentions the concept of "unproductive play" in passing (Miller-McLemore 2003, 8). This concept is puzzling, because all play is "unproductive." It is voluntary, pleasurable, and involves deep concentration on the matter at hand so people playing pay little mind to any resulting product. In her next book, four years later, however, both play and story have moved into a more important role. We shall come to that in a moment.

Mercer does not include play in her Index, but play is evident in her book as well. It is mostly implicit in her descriptions of positive family experiences, liturgy, and children's involvement in constructive religious education. There is one especially important moment, however, when play breaks into the discussion in a major way but with an economy of words. In a discussion about the "work" of the Holy Spirit she writes, "Christian education in a liberatory theological framework, however, necessarily involves the work—or play, if you will—of the Spirit of God in the forming and reforming of children's identities as people who walk in the way of Jesus" (Mercer 2005, 178). This association of play with the Holy Spirit deserves follow-up by Mercer.

In Jensen's book there is no Index, but play is discussed in the context of children's vulnerability, imagination, and attention. He even mentions the value of play as a strategy children use to cope with terrible experiences, such as the holocaust (Jensen 2005, 54–63, note 32 144).

In a section called "Children at Play" (Jensen 2005, 54–58), Jensen discusses Bushnell's incorporation of play into his theology of children, which included advising parents to play with their children as a sacred act. Jensen connects adult maturity with becoming open to the same kind of vulnerability that children experience when they are at play.

Play is dignified and differentiated in the Index of Herzog's book with references to play in general, to games, and to play as a symbol of life. These few references, however, do not exhaust how integral play is to her book. It seems to be everywhere, including in her wry writing style.

In Martin Marty's book the Index includes some thirty-three references to various kinds of play and in various contexts in the book. There is a whole section devoted to "Wonder-full Art, Stories, Play, and Imagination" (Marty 2007, 118–122) in addition to the many other references. Clearly play is associated in this book with its more central topics of mystery and wonder.

Now let us return to Miller-McLemore's 2007 book *In the Midst of Chaos* (Miller-McLemore 2007). Her earlier book was for academic colleagues with those who care for children in mind, while this one is primarily for those who care for children with academic colleagues in mind. Both books try to communicate with this broad audience to challenge us all in the church to re-think the nature of the child. In 2003 there was little mention of play but by 2007 the themes of play and narrative are both expanded into chapters of their own (chapters 7 and 8). This suggests the rising importance, at least in her mind, of these two themes related to children and the theologians.

We already mentioned the rise and fall of theological interest in play from 1965–1972. The theological interest in narrative began to rise in interest about 1975. It was, perhaps, John Dominic Crossan's *The Dark*

Interval: Towards a Theology of Story (Crossan 1975) that led the way, as well as symbolized this change. Terrence W. Tilley SJ (Tilley 1990), who draws on Crossan, and Kevin Bradt, SJ (Bradt 1997) provided important surveys of the expanding field of narrative theology as the century drew to a close.

For most of human history, oral story telling was the primary means for making meaning. By the seventeenth and eighteenth centuries in the West, however, people became reluctant to consider stories as bearers of truth. The language of science with its objective method and mathematical demonstrations of truth began to be considered the ascendant carrier of this precious cargo.

Slowly over the last few centuries narrative truth has become more clearly understood and appreciated. Serious narrative is not merely an "attention grabber" or an illustration to make a non-story point. It involves the storyteller, the listener, and the situation of the telling as well as the story itself in the creation of a kind of truth that is respectful of "all the multiple meanings, alternative possibilities, and unconfined diversity of human experience." Scientific truth, on the other hand, attempts to "reduce reality into clear, precise, definable categories that can be tested for their 'objective truth' and normativeness" (Bradt 1997, 102). What is now better understood is that narrative and science complement each other. We need both to understand ourselves and our world.

Stories are not all the same. Terrence W. Tilley, SJ followed Crossan's *The Dark Interval: Towards a Theology of Story* (Crossan 1975, 56) to divide stories into three "shapes" (Tilley 1990, 39–54). Instead of thinking of myth as a lie, as the scholars of the Enlightenment did, myths are now understood to have their own kind of truth. It works more indirectly than scientific demonstrations and works within the assumptions of those who live the myth. An example is the myth of the American dream. It cannot be validated objectively nor is it true from all perspectives, but if one dreams from within this myth, there is a power available to make it come true. Such dreams can be beneficial for this reason but also dangerous if the myth is destructive. Myths, therefore, need to be called into question and it is the task of parables to do this.

Parables question myth indirectly by setting up paradoxical worlds. Science can confront myth with the facts but parables invite one to wonder about the limits of the myth's meaning.

The third kind of story is an action story, which explores myth while still assuming its truth. The variety of ways the myth of the West in the

United States has been explored is an example. Myths comfort, parables outrage, and action stories seem to be "realistic" as helpful guides for living in the myth.

Both play and stories reduce the power differential between adults and children to reasonable proportions. By "reasonable proportions" it is meant that adults do not give up their ethical responsibility to care for and teach children and at the same time children do not need to acquiesce completely to the control of the adults when they share stories and play with them.

The contemporary discussion not only challenges the *de facto* doctrine by its high view of children and celebrates play and story but it also pushes the question forward about whether the theme of children can draw together the other themes of systematic theology in a way that can reorient the shape of the classical doctrines. This question will not be answered here, but it is being pressed both implicitly and explicitly. It will be interesting to see if there is enough energy in this question to sustain the hard work it will take to show how this could be done, if it should be done. This book will say more about this in the next two chapters.

Finally, let us return to 1960 when this chapter began with the disruptive seminarian. If you were to walk down the corridor of any theological seminary today, you would be much more likely to hear children being talked about with respect and perhaps even wonder than you would have some fifty years ago. The six authors reviewed in this chapter have had a lot to do with this change of perception and the re-awakening in our time of Jesus' parabolic challenge from the first century to welcome children to know God and to become like children to enter God's kingdom.

In the next chapter we will discuss more fully the informal or *de facto* doctrine of children that has been developed over the centuries. Its ambivalence, ambiguity, indifference, and hints of grace will then become more conscious so our inheritance can be handled with greater awareness and intelligence. It is now time to play the four levels of the game promised at the beginning of the book, when we left Hermann Hesse burning leaves.

CHAPTER

8

THE *DE FACTO* DOCTRINE OF CHILDREN:
Ambivalence, Ambiguity, Indifference, and Grace

This is a painting of the seated statue of the theologian Richard Hooker (1554–1600) at the Cathedral Church of Saint Peter in Exeter, England. Hooker was born in the village of Heavitree just a few miles from Exeter and attended school in Exeter until the age of fifteen, when he went to Corpus Christi College, Oxford.

John Harris's painting shows today's choristers having a snowball fight around Hooker's statue. At other times they sing in some three hundred services a year. The boys and girls are educated in the cathedral school and come from all walks of life and all parts of England. The painting reminds us that the indifference of theologians toward children is often matched by the indifference of children toward theologians, but when Christian communication between the generations becomes as playful as it is serious, then indifference will pass away and the church will be as much fun as playing in the snow!

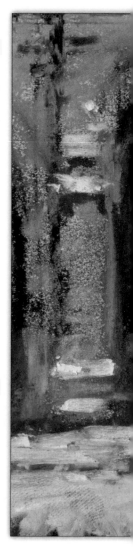

▲ *Richard Hooker and the Snow Ball Fight*,
John Harris (contemporary)
Contributed in Aid of the Exeter Cathedral Choristers

The *de facto* doctrine of children involves ambivalence, ambiguity, indifference, and grace. In this chapter we will take a more systematic look at these themes that weigh heavily but informally on the church to clear the way to make a proposal in the next chapter for a formal doctrine of children.

Let's play our way into the informal doctrine by returning to Hermann Hesse in his garden. The smoke billows up as he burns his leaves and grass once again. His sharp profile is visible and his glasses shine beneath the broad brim of his straw hat. As the ashes fall through the grate and the smoke rises, he dreams. His poem "Hours in the Garden" tells how he hears music as the leaves burn and he sees people from the past and future—the wise, harmoniously building "a hundred-gated cathedral of the spirit," sifting down and rising up with meaning. This chapter is meant to be a reverie like that of Hesse burning leaves. The *de facto* doctrine of children is the hundred-gated cathedral of the spirit.

Each theologian in this history is a gateway, but each gate has a different shape when it comes to children. Some are broken and some are shut, but all gates are meant to be entry points into the search for God. No single gate is for all, so all are needed. This is not the Blame Game. It is the Gateway Game. The main door, under the soaring towers of the cathedral, is where the children freely enter. Perhaps we adults can too, but first we need to clear the way for such grace by reflecting on the history that has encumbered our view of children in the church.

The game metaphor does not mean that this chapter is not serious. Play is always serious and sometimes even dangerous. It lives where "innovation intersects convention," or as T.S. Eliot said about the play of poetry, it is most alive at the point of tension between tradition and individual talent (Ziolkowski 1972, vii).

If our play is dominated by too much tradition, then the game descends into pedantry—cataloguing names, dates, periods, summary statements, and themes—and becomes work. If our play is limited to innovation then the game is reduced to private thoughts and feelings and loses its connection with the church's community of language, time, and space. One needs to be comfortable with both tradition and innovation to reflect on this history in a manner that will truly clear the way for grace. Both extremes are necessary but neither can rule if the game is going to be alive. To be alive it needs to dwell where physicists locate complexity, the place between rigidity and chaos where living systems are found. When the game is alive it can renew itself and those who play it well.

As this book progressed a preliminary set of "game pieces" was collected. These pieces are the vignettes of the theologians. The game, inspired by Hesse's Glass Bead Game, has four levels:

Level 1. The History Level is played to enjoy the story of the theologians. This is what the preceding chapters were intended to provide and the summary below is to remind one of the whole story.

Level 2. The Meaning Level is played to discover the larger meaning of the story, using the themes that have emerged. That is what this chapter is concerned with.

Level 3. The Existential Level is played to find personal meaning about how the *de facto* doctrine of children has influenced one's own views of children in the church.

Level 4. The Action Level is played by taking action, based on what has been discovered from playing at the previous three levels of the game. One moves beyond reflection to act in the church to serve children in ways that are open to grace. This final Level is much like what Joseph Knecht, the Game Master (*Magister Ludi*), did as Hesse's *The Glass Bead Game* drew to a close.

As with any game, one finally needs to stop discussing it and begin. Let's lay out the pieces and play away!

The Story of Children and the Theologians

The story told by this book will now be summarized by laying out the vignettes, like a deck of cards, to get an overview of the game's first level. As we do this, the most fragile moment in the game begins. This summarizing is when the play is most likely to descend into pedantry. The way to overcome the stodgy facts and dry lists is to dream again of faces, times, and places. The summaries of the theologians are starting points for reflection, not endpoints. When all the vignettes are laid out in their periods, they look like this:

From Presence To Texts

Jesus   (?–c.30 CE)   Children reveal God and the kingdom.

From Texts To Theology

The Apostle Paul (c. 6BCE–c. 65CE)   Children are less than adults.

Irenaeus   (c.125–c.200)   Children are developing creatures.

Origen   (186–251)   Children are symbolic of something else.

Chrysostom   (349–407)   Children are like wax for forming
                                                  proto-monks.

Pelagius   (c. 350–c. 418)   Children have strengths for spiritual
                                                  growth.

Augustine   (354–430)   Children are sinful without God's grace.

Latin Theology and the Schools

Anselm   (1033–1109)   Children are gifts to the monastery.

Abelard   (1079–1142)   Children are a bother.

Aquinas   (1224–1274)   Children have a natural potential to
                                                  develop.

Nicholas   (1401–1464)   Children can influence adults with
of Cusa   their spirit.

The Reformation of the Experience Base

Luther   (1483–1546)   Children are God's little jesters, a mix
                                                  of law and gospel.

Calvin   (1509–1564)   Children are sinful but need care and
                                                  education.

Hooker   (1554–1600)   Children are part of God's natural law.

Reforming the Reformation and the New Science

Boehme   (1575–1624)   Children are "legitimate," "historical,"
                                                  or "whore brats."

Bunyan   (1628–1688)   Children need to be left behind for the
                                                  adult's spiritual journey.

Pascal   (1623–1662)   Children are unchangeable by natural
                                                  means.

Catholic   (1600–1700)   Children are pawns in religious conflicts.
Missionaries

Wesley   (1703–1791)   Children need a method for perfection.

Edwards   (1703–1758)   Children are like vipers in need of
                                                  conversion.

Modern Theology

Schleiermacher	(1768–1834)	Children are a kind of consciousness.
Bushnell	(1802–1876)	Children know a higher kind of play.
Barth	(1886–1968)	Children are preparing to be adults.
Rahner	(1904–1984)	Children are open to eternity.
Williams	(1950–)	Children are in danger of becoming "lost icons."

There are no enemies here. There are disagreements to be sure, and there should be, but there is something to be learned from each theologian. For example, the controversy between Augustine and Pelagius was heated but helpful to sharpen thinking about the fundamental nature of children. If we only identify with the theologians in the past who sound like us today or support our personal views, then we will miss much of the basis for the grace that has carried this story forward to today.

The *de facto* doctrine's "cathedral of the spirit" has many additional gates. History overflows the limitations of this book, so readers are invited to add more "game pieces" as the years of play go by. After ruminating among the vignettes and examining the many doors to the cathedral, we move now to the second level of the game, which is the main subject matter of this chapter.

What Does this History Mean: Four Emerging Themes

The second level of the game examines the pattern of meaning that has emerged from the history of children and the theologians. It involves four themes. They are ambivalence, ambiguity, indifference, and grace. We will now look at each theme in more detail.

Ambivalence

"Ambivalence" refers to holding two mutually conflicting feelings about a person, place, thing, or action at the same time. Ambivalence toward children combines delight and aversion, attraction and repulsion, and a movement toward and away from them. This ambivalence confuses and sometimes paralyzes our best thinking about children in the church and frustrates the consistent support and attuned warmth that children need from their parents and mother church. Only a few theologians, such as Jonathan Edwards, might have been personally ambivalent toward children, Others more clearly either moved toward or away from them. Our theological inheritance, however, taken as a whole, is clearly ambivalent since it includes both representatives of the high and low views of children.

The high view is respectful to, moves toward, and is open to learning from children. The low view is dismissing of, moves away from, and only sees children in a narrow, closed way, as objects to be taught and purified. An extreme example of the low view is Fideus, who was a bishop present at an African council in 253. Cyprian reported that Fideus argued against infant baptism on the grounds, among other things, that newborn babies were impure and too disgusting to kiss. The thought of doing this, he said, made one shudder. The council, however, continued to support infant baptism (Bakke 2005, 70). A high view can be seen when Jesus invited children to come to him so he could lay his hands on them and bless them. He also urged that children teach adults how to enter the kingdom and when we welcome them we welcome him and the One who sent him.

The high/low dichotomy, however, is misleading because *both* alternatives have some truth in them. Children *do* lack the general life experience and the cognitive, developmental abilities that adults have, so they need to be taught by those who are more experienced and knowledgeable. On the other hand, children can teach adults by their very being about mature spirituality, although adults need to be open to children, be respectful of them, and move toward them to realize this.

Luther, Schleiermacher, Bushnell, Rahner (though without much opportunity), and Williams are examples of those theologians who enjoyed the company of children; there may have been a few others. The rest did not seem to go out of their way to be with them.

If children give pleasure, one tends to move toward them. If contact causes pain, as with Fideus, one moves away. Why is this important? One needs to be able to genuinely move toward children emotionally and be open to them to know them, because when adults radiate antipathy children go into hiding psychologically and sometimes even physically, under chairs and around corners. Aversive adults constrict children's ability to be open, to play, and to show their wonder. This excludes such adults from learning or re-learning these life-giving traits from them. Negative adults can write about children, based on what they read from texts or talk about them with other adults, but they miss the critique in fact that *actual* children can provide for their theories. Abstractions are profoundly tested and generalizations hard to maintain when the little ones are tumbling about your writing desk or climb into your lap, no matter what century we are talking about.

Sometimes adults can conceal their negative feelings toward children from other adults by putting on a *childishness* mask. Few are fooled, however, except those foolish enough to try this. The condescending, sing-song voice, the manic showing of teeth, and the whipping of children into a frenzy, usually coupled with complaints about how out of control they become, are signs of contempt. The "smiles" of contemptuous adults look like the fangs of wolves dressed up like people in fairy tales and whipping children into self-destructive frenzies reminds one more of the spells of witches with tall black hats than responsible adult leadership. It is no wonder that children become suspicious of loud, unpredictable "giants" in life as well as in stories.

A low view of children, therefore, creates a self-fulfilling prophecy. When children are under threat they cannot be or teach what is best about them. This means that adults with a distaste for children find that their view of children, as learners rather than teachers of spiritual maturity, is "confirmed," though erroneously, by their personal but uninformed experience.

Ambivalence often feeds ambiguity about children and joins with it to frustrate our ability to understand and do what is best for them. People don't mean to prevent good communication about children, but the net result of ambivalence and ambiguity builds barriers of understanding. We turn now to the ambiguity that clouds communication about children in the church.

Ambiguity

"Ambiguity" refers to the possibility that a word might be understood in two or more ways when the context does not make the meaning clear. Psychological and social issues overlap to create such misunderstandings, but logical ambiguity will be emphasized here to narrowly focus on the language problem itself as it relates to certain assumptions people make during conversations about children.

Seven kinds of ordinary ambiguity will be specified. In addition a second–level of ambiguity will be identified. It involves the misunderstandings that bounce back and forth among the first seven. These two levels of ambiguity are powerful and deep, because the opposing meanings all have some truth to them, so it is no wonder that we often talk past each other in the church when we talk about children. An "Ambiguity Check-List" follows for handy reference to help clarify how we use the term "children."

Ambiguity Check-list:

1. Developmental Ambiguity—specifying early, middle, late childhood vs. generalizing about the whole period?
2. Sinfulness Ambiguity—sinful vs. sinless?
3. Contingency Ambiguity—permanence vs. change?
4. Pedagogical Ambiguity—learning vs. teaching?
5. Spiritual Ambiguity—immaturity vs. maturity?
6. Relationship Ambiguity—trouble vs. blessing?
7. Reference Ambiguity—general vs. specific?
8. Meta-Ambiguity—ambiguity conflicts among the above seven ambiguities vs. a single unified meaning?

First, let us look at *developmental ambiguity*. This is a modern phenomenon. It involves misunderstandings about whether the reference is to early, middle, or late childhood. When the developmental period is not specified, confusion intrudes because these three periods have different characteristics, which have been described by child psychology, pediatric medicine, and other such modern specializations. Adult conversation partners may assume different stages and even hold specific faces of children in mind while talking about children in general. This problem is complicated further when one includes both infants and adolescents within the range of meaning for the term "children."

An example of the broader meaning for "children" is the UNICEF definition that includes adolescents used by Kristin Herzog in *Children and Our Global Future* (Herzog 2005, 5), noted in the last chapter. This may be in theory the most "global" definition, but still most people consider childhood as the period between the acquisition of language at about two years of age and puberty, which is about twelve or thirteen years, when "children" can begin to produce their own children. There may be a political advantage for not using these biological markers but usage and common sense resist including adolescents and infants among "children." Most adolescents would certainly resist being thought of as children, whatever the adult reasons for doing this might be.

An example of five-stage developmental ambiguity may be found in the title of O. M. Bakke's *When Children Became People*. This book defines "children" as "human beings from birth to the age of about twenty (Bakke 2005,1)." This may clarify how "children" is used in the context of the book, but the title remains clearly misleading. It appears to mean that during the early church people began to take children seriously. What Bakke actually means is that this happened during a developmental period that includes adolescence, which is not as dramatic or surprising as the title suggests.

Bakke's reason for using the broader definition of "children" is that the Greek physician Hippocrates' (c. 460–c. 377 BCE) did this and his view was most likely assumed during the period investigated by Bakke's book. Hippocrates' developmental periods are birth to age seven, seven to fourteen, and fourteen to twenty, with different Greek words for each one—*paidion, pais,* and *meirakion.* Since these distinctions are made in Greek it is not really necessary to blur all three periods within the single English term "children," which the English translation of Bakke's original Norwegian text does not. It uses the words "small child," the child," and "young person" when referring to Hippocrates' stages.

The bottom line for this and the other kinds of ambiguity is that it is good to take the time to clarify what is meant by the term "children" at the *beginning* of a conversation. This is because there is usually more ambiguity in the term than one might expect, as the ambiguity checklist has already illustrated.

Second, let us consider *sinfulness ambiguity.* It involves opposing assumptions about the fundamental nature of children. Are they born sinful or not? The majority view in the history of theology is that children are born sinful. Only God's grace can redeem and restore a child to God. Augustine is the leading example of this view while Irenaeus is an example of a theologian who understood human beings in terms of development from their fallen beginning to perfection at the end of time. Richard Hooker, who associated children with God's natural law, found them to be contaminated by the fall but also a "blank page" to be written on by the child's experience, reason, and learning about scripture and tradition. These three examples show how complex this kind of inherited ambiguity can be.

Assumptions about the fundamental nature of children are hard to clarify because they are sometimes held unconsciously. It takes patience, effort, and openness to avoid needless misunderstandings about the fundamental nature of children when talking about them.

Third, there is *contingency ambiguity.* Do children change or stay the same? Most people today assume change, although ironically adults often act as if children ought to be always consistent, stable, and under control. Children, however, like change. They enjoy feeling their growth and love to celebrate birthdays while adults long for stability, permanence, and a

lack of birthdays as a defense against declining energy and the other losses
of growing older. The problem is that children change in some ways, such
as size, while in other ways, such as their character traits, they remain
much the same, so this kind of ambiguity is also deeply rooted in reality.
From a purely theological perspective children may change in relation to
each other and by comparison with adults, but children and adults remain
children in relation to God. The phrase, "children of God," almost always
includes adults.

The ambiguity of change versus permanence was, perhaps, more powerful and unacknowledged in the past than it is today. In the past there
was a strong tendency for adults to flee from finitude toward infinity and
from the body toward the soul to find permanence. Augustine in the fifth
century longed to rest from his restlessness, so absolute states appealed to
him. He argued that the absolute of original sin could only be cancelled
by the absolute of God's grace. Irenaeus in the second century, however,
had already acknowledged change as the norm, and in the thirteenth century Thomas Aquinas spoke about children more in terms of a potential
for growth than a fixed state they were born with. Today we probably go
too far exposing children to change and choice, as Rowan Williams argued
in *Lost Icons*, mentioned in the last chapter, because we all need stability as
well as change, and safety as well as sometimes dangerous exploration to be
healthy human beings.

A final cause for this kind of ambiguity is that growth can be understood to include *both* change and stability. We grow in stages. There is
change and then a period of permanence prevails while consolidation takes
place before growing again. Growth and stability, then, can be considered
a constant rhythm of life as well as logical opposites, which also adds power
and plausibility to this kind of misunderstanding.

A fourth kind of miscommunication is *pedagogical ambiguity*. It
involves a set of assumptions about teaching and the direction it moves.
Do children teach adults about spiritual maturity or can they only be
taught? Jesus introduced this ambiguity into the Christian language system when he said that adults must become like children to enter the kingdom or one needs to welcome children to know God. Such statements
imply a kind of teaching by children when we usually think of them as
needing to be taught.

Children can sometimes teach adults about things in addition to spiritual maturity. This is because they have less to *unlearn* when they confront
new ideas and technologies. A common illustration is when children—
usually in middle or late childhood—teach their grandparents and parents

computer skills or how to use the many functions of a cell phone. The distinction between this kind of teaching and teaching about spiritual maturity is that when children teach about spirituality they do not realize they are teaching. Their unconscious teaching is a by-product of their being, so it is not "teaching" in an ordinary sense, which adds to the confusion, needing to be sorted out.

Examples of theologians who understand that children have something to teach as well as learn about the presence of God are Luther, Schleiermacher, Bushnell, Rahner, Williams, and perhaps a few others. It is easy, however, for all theologians to overlook and underestimate children in their adult-dominated and extremely verbal world, because one must be quiet and patient to learn what children have to teach, which is mostly non-verbal.

Spiritual ambiguity is a fifth kind of confusion that needs to be untangled for good communication. When Jesus said that we need to be childlike to enter the kingdom and welcome children to know God, he inferred a kind of spiritual maturity that children have naturally and adults need to re-learn. This upsets the usual correlation between maturity and age.

The key to clarifying this kind of ambiguity is to distinguish spiritual knowing from the knowing of everyday. An example of someone who understood this distinction is Richard of St. Victor in the twelfth century. The knowing of the senses by the body, the knowing of the mind by reason, and the knowing of God by contemplation all need to be distinguished. In the knowing of everyday one can use the senses and reason to understand things, such as a table, from the "outside," an ability enhanced by technology from microscopes to telescopes. When the mind and reason are emphasized, then the knowing of adults, developed during the decades of their lives, has a clear advantage over what children know. The knowing of the spirit by contemplation is different.

When one knows God there is no place "to stand" outside the Creator-creature relationship to sense and think about it from the outside. God can only be known from within the relationship, so the perception of presence is what matters most. Children are by nature better than adults at this because they are not distracted by language. Although language begins to develop about the age of two, children do not rely on it as firmly as adults do until sometime after they get comfortable with reading, during middle childhood or perhaps later.

A second problem with adult analysis and the knowledge of God is that the relationship with God is broken when one objectifies God for study. Inattention can also break relationships, but our focus here is on language, which needs to be stilled to know God's presence. Besides, language is inadequate to express the knowledge of God, as adult mystics eloquently claim, so better language skills will not equate with better knowledge in this case. This means that contemplative knowing is possible for children as well as adults, which adds to the depth of spiritual ambiguity.

Some theologians, such as Schleiermacher and Rahner, have said that children and adults stand in much the same position in their knowing of God but others, such as Barth, have seen childhood as a time of preparation for such knowledge. Both of these views are partially correct, which again intensifies the ambiguity. Children's relationships with God need to be protected from misuse and distortions, so the doctrinal thinking that Barth advocates is important. On the other hand, if God is no more than a concept to be worshipped then theology becomes idolatry, which both the Jewish and Christian scriptures are quick to identify as a very dangerous misunderstanding. In the case of spiritual ambiguity, then, it is good to ask what one means by "knowing God" and how that differs from everyday knowing to clear up this kind of misunderstanding.

A sixth kind of ambiguity involves the quality of the relationship between adults and children. This is *relationship ambiguity*. Some assume that children are trouble, as Abelard did, and others, such as Bushnell, find them to be a blessing. Children are trouble because they take time and demand adult responsibility. They restrict the range of adult choices. On the other hand, they can give deep meaning to life and death by their nonverbal blessings and survival into the next generation, which stimulate an adult's sense of direction in life.

As with the other ambiguities about children, there is something in both of these alternatives that has a ring of truth to it. Children *are* a bother for the theologian, who is called to pray without ceasing, as Abelard said, or troubling to the pilgrim's progress, as Bunyan implied when his hero Christian fled his family with his fingers in his ears. On the other hand, the influence of children in the home can be positive—as Luther, Schleiermacher, Bushnell and, perhaps, a few others understood—and indispensable for understanding the theological meaning of children, which Rahner articulated so beautifully and succinctly despite not being in daily contact with children.

Reference ambiguity is a seventh kind of potential misunderstanding. Does "children" refer to an abstract reality or is the only reality possible unique to each child? Today we take Abelard's hard-won, twelfth-century compromise between these two views lightly as we blithely build up our information to create abstractions like "children" from the similarities among the members of the class the term identifies. There is both a reality and a lack of reality involved, however, when the uniqueness of each child is generalized. Generalizations are useful and important, at least as long as the limitations of the abstraction are kept in mind, but they can easily become reified and turned into independent "things," which blocks the uniqueness of each individual child in adult minds. This is still true today even though there is usually little consciousness of the Neoplatonic and Aristotelian overtones from the past about what constitutes reality.

Today reference ambiguity is stimulated more forcibly by confusion about whether the term "children" is meant symbolically or not. Children have been known as symbols by theologians as different as Origen and Calvin for centuries. When children are not present to challenge symbolic usage by their uniqueness, adults easily become too romantic and idealistic or too negative and pessimistic about them. Projections can add to the confusion this kind of ambiguity causes.

The bottom line is that children can be considered as symbolic of something else, like spiritual maturity, and can also be thought of as individual and unique at the same time. That is why this kind of ambiguity is so deep. Constant monitoring is needed to be clear about the implications of unexamined assumptions when one is sorting out reference ambiguity.

Finally, second level, or *meta-ambiguity*, is always present in discourse about children, because the seven kinds of ordinary ambiguity—developmental, sinfulness, contingency, pedagogical, spiritual, relational, and referential—are always in conflict with each other. These ambiguities are like static in the communication system. The static can only be silenced by knowing its sources and naming them to make the chaos go away, as naming "Rumpelstiltskin" broke his power in the fairy tale collected by the Grimm Brothers in the early nineteenth century.

Understanding these eight kinds of ambiguity helps avoid misunderstandings, but it also has a second use. This nuanced awareness can prevent unconscious projections onto children by adults. Each child who is sleeping in a crib, toddles up to you with a smile, stands firmly before you defiantly pouting, or is jumping up and down to get your attention, is a unique mixture of all these ambiguities. Once one becomes aware of them it is not so likely that unexamined assumptions will obscure the uniqueness of individual children so they can remain completely themselves in adult eyes.

It is important also to realize that while these ambiguities can be named, they are for the most part un-resolvable. As logical contradictions they are also part of a larger system, the creative process, which can explain their unresolved contradictions. The creative process will be discussed in the next chapter, but for now it is enough to realize that assumptions about children as sinful, permanent, only able to learn and not teach, as immature spiritually, as trouble and as abstractions is more typical of people who prefer the closing phase of the creative process. A preference for assuming that children are sinless, changing, teaching, mature spiritually, a blessing, and uniquely fashioned is more typical of those who prefer the opening phase of the process. To completely understand how these ambiguities are more than merely logical misunderstandings and to cope with them more fully, one needs to be able to use the complete cycle of the creative process to relate them in a more constructive way than only as negative logical problems to be "solved," which, as you can see, is largely impossible.

Given the complexity of speaking about children in the church, it is no wonder that many people walk away from trying to talk carefully about them and practice indifference instead. Too much anxiety is aroused and too much patience is needed to engage in conversations about the meaning of children and what is best for them in the church. It is fitting then that we turn now to a discussion about the historical theme of indifference.

Indifference

"Indifference" does not refer to an objective stance taken to better study something one cares about. The so-called "neutrality" of indifference comes from a lack of interest, enthusiasm or concern. Sometimes it even implies aloofness, a sense of being too superior to care. This blurs easily into disdain, although the shift may be unconscious.

In Greek mythology the figure Narcissus personifies indifference in his relationship with Echo. He fell in love with his reflection in a still pool and was unable to respond to her love. It was not so much Narcissus' self-love that isolated him from Echo but his inability to recognize any reality except his own. He was a solipsistic old soul, who was obsessed but not merry. He died from thirst, not wishing to spoil his reflection, and, some say, he turned into a flower. Only Echo's voice survived her encounter with Narcissus, which robbed her of her self. That voice can still be heard in lonely places today, but only repeating what others say.

When theologians ignore children, then, we must carefully weigh the quality of their indifference. It may seem "neutral" to the theologians, an objective ranking of priorities perhaps, but to those who are ignored this feels like rejection or even annihilation if they care what theologians think. Most children, of course, do not care what theologians think. They are as blissful in their indifference about theologians as theologians are about them. John Harris' wonderful painting of the red-robed choristers having a snowball fight around Richard Hooker's statue at Exeter Cathedral illustrates this. Hooker had little to say about children and they have nothing to say about him, as they play in the snow around the cold stone of his memorial. In cases of indifference Christian language, as a language of grace and secure relationships, has failed. More will be said about this in a moment when attachment theory is discussed.

Indifference to children is one of the most frustrating theological responses for people who care about children to deal with. A low view of children is at least a relationship! It can be worked with in a variety of ways and sometimes become positive or at least better understood. There is hope. When there is no relationship at all, hope is hard to muster, since the child for whom the relationship is hoped for does not exist to the indifferent adult. Children can freeze to death in the winter of such stone cold blindness.

Perhaps, the best way to deal with indifference is to be indifferent to it and move on, passing such people by. The motto for "moving on" might be *mox nox in rem*, a Latin aphorism that can be loosely translated as, "Let's get on with it." You can sense the hurry in its sound. Soon (*mox*) night (*nox*) (The verb "is coming" is implied.), so get the thing (*in rem*) done that needs doing. Step over or around the stumbling blocks. Meeting indifference with indifference, however, is only partially successful since it signals the failure of Christian language and frustrates the laughter and play of grace. This raises the question of what grace means, which will be considered now.

Grace

A cluster of Hebrew words—*hesed, hanan, and raham*—conveys a sense of the faithful maintenance of a relationship and the free gift of affection and mercy, even when the relationship is broken. The manifestation of this experience was the Torah, which gave God's creatures a law to live by and the contextual stories to interpret it. In the Christian Testament it is Jesus who manifests grace. He was "full of grace and truth" (John 1:14). This grace was also known among the apostles because a "great grace was upon them" (Acts 4:33). The Greek word *charis* was translated into Latin as *gratia,* as Christianity spread into the West.

The pre-Christian use of *gratia* referred to charm and loveliness as well as a sense of favor, kindness, friendship, and service to others. When it became a technical term in Latin Christian theology it moved into a punitive context, which emphasized God's mercy toward unworthy, sinful human beings.

Today "grace" still retains a sense of loveliness in everyday use, such as when one moves smoothly and effortlessly across a room without stumbling or falling down. There is also a sense of grace implied in the forming of relationships that might otherwise not develop because of undue social awkwardness. Grace has as much to do with elegance, art, and respect in this book as it does law, punishment, and undeserved favor. The term, as used here, also suggests the hard reality of how the church has walked across the centuries without ever falling completely on its face, despite its awkwardness, and has sometimes even moved with effortless elegance.

No matter what the theologians have said about them, children continue to carry the church from one generation to the next in an unexplained, unnoticed, and graceful way. There is something very objective and real about the biology of this, because the church, despite all its distortions of children, continues to live today because children have led the way, as Isaiah said they would (Isaiah 11:6), by being the bridge of possibility from one generation to the next. In the meantime our task as adults is to help clear the way, as best we can, so this graceful movement across time and space can become enriched with and more evocative of grace.

Most of all, grace is non-verbal. It is present in the secure, warm attunement between Creator and creature that is alive and generates life. It lives where safety and exploration interplay. It is a kind of movement that provides stability, as Nicholas of Cusa suggested by his image of the spinning top's firmness. Of course, it is God's nature to be always spinning while we slow down and tip over without an infusion of energy to set us spinning again. God helps keep us in motion and we help each other by being in communion together and with the universe.

Grace is not always easy to identify within the self or in the world around us. A vivid example of this difficulty took place in New York City on September 11, 2001. I was at Trinity Episcopal Church for a meeting with Rowan Williams, who then was Archbishop of Wales, as mentioned in his vignette in chapter 6. There are many stories to tell, but the one about the ambiguity of grace involves St. Paul's Chapel near Trinity. It remained standing despite the devastation and became a center of ministry to all the brokenness that surrounded it.

Some said grace broke out in St. Paul's Chapel, but others only saw chaos, as a multitude of ministries sprang up to meet the needs that presented themselves. The church was filled with children's art, sent from all over the world. Some saw clutter. Others saw beauty and solidarity. Some saw deep divinity when Holy Communion was celebrated amidst people who were eating, coming and going, massaging aching bodies, treating sore and injured feet, murmuring words of counsel and care, and sleeping in the pews with teddy bears to soften the tragedy and tears. Was this a "desecration" of sacred space and a lack of respect for the holy sacraments? Was this ministry out of control? Can grace be controlled? One is never quite sure, but we are called to try to clear the way for grace and to be alert for its presence so we can recognize it when it does break out, even in the church, and support it. When that happens the grace within connects with the grace in the world around us and we become, at least for a moment, co-creators with God.

Finally, there is something mirthfully paradoxical about grace, which is also frustrating. We can't control it and yet we need grace to tell what is graceful and what is not. This means that all we can do is be alert for its presence, recognize it for what it is and clear the way for cooperation with it, even when we know that it is impossible for everyone to agree that grace is truly present in any given situation.

With these few words about grace our reflection on the historical themes is completed. We turn now to the third level of the game to see how these historical themes relate to us personally at the level of existential meaning.

The Personal Level of the Game: An Existential Coherence

The third level of the game plays with the themes that arose during the church's history to bring coherence to them. The coherence is supplied by attachment theory, which shows the interconnections among the themes and brings this coherence home to each individual's early, formative years. But what is "attachment theory"? A little background is needed to answer that question adequately.

At least since Plato's *Republic* and the *Laws*, some twenty-five centuries ago, the connection between infant care and adult life has been noticed and commented on in the West. This link was given a much broader context recently, during the nineteenth century, by Charles Darwin (1809–1882). He looked at children and their parents from a biological perspective over vast periods of time. The human situation is unique, he said, because we have the longest period of immaturity of any species, which makes our relationship with our parents, or others who provide primary care during infancy, of special importance. This has also made us more vulnerable to predators and other dangers than the rest of the species on this earth. On the other hand, our slow maturation has provided us with the creativity to survive, which has been critical since we are not equipped genetically to be the fastest, strongest, best armored, or the highest flyer among competing species.

During the last half of the twentieth century details began to emerge about how evolution has equipped parenting adults and their children to bond in a way to ensure survival. This attachment process is reciprocal. For example, children need food, warmth, shelter, and protection from harm while parents (or parent substitutes) need physical contact, social stimulation, and have a desire to nurture as well as to feel needed. When this interaction is working well, it provides the infant with a safe base from which to explore the world, which in turn develops the creativity through play that is needed to thrive. Attachment also establishes what John Bowlby called an "inner working model" for relationships across the life span.

The two leading figures involved in the discovery of the attachment process were John Bowlby (1907–1990) and Mary Ainsworth (1913–1999). Bowlby arrived on the London psychoanalytic scene in the late 1930s, the son of a prominent baronet and surgeon to the king. He had studied at Dartmouth Royal Naval College and Trinity College, Cambridge and spent a time in progressive schools working with children. At the age of twenty-two he enrolled at University College Hospital Medical School and at the same time began his analytic training, which included his own analysis. He completed his medical degree four years later. In 1946 Bowlby reentered civilian life after military service during World War II and took a job at the Tavistock Clinic in London. He quickly became the deputy director and was in charge of the children's department.

The direct collaboration of Bowlby and Ainsworth began about 1950 when Ainsworth, who was already a professor at the University of Toronto, moved to England with her husband and aided Bowlby with his research. She then went with her husband to Uganda and finally to Baltimore, where the now famous "Strange Situation" research began. An important review of this literature and the story of attachment theory's development may be found in Robert Karen's *Becoming Attached: First Relationships and How They Shape Our Capacity to Love* (Karen 1998). The theory has been placed more recently in the context of the "new science of human relationships" by Daniel Goleman in *Social Intelligence: The Revolutionary New Science of Human Relationships* (Goleman 2007, 162–166, 189–197).

The question that prompted Bowlby's exploration was why children failed to thrive without their mothers. An answer began to form when he discovered the field of ethology, the study of animals in natural settings.

Ethology was pioneered by three European naturalists— Karl von Frisch, Nikko Tinbergen, and Konrad Lorenz. Perhaps, the best known of the three in the United States was Lorenz (1903–1989) but all three were awarded the Nobel Prize in physiology and medicine in 1973. The bonding mechanism found among animals suggested that human infants also needed "to bond" with their mothers to thrive. Bowlby was also influenced by the research of Harry Harlow (1905–1981) with newborn rhesus monkeys. It showed that bonding involves not only food but also comfort and security.

To picture the power of bonding think of Lorenz walking across a field with orphaned goslings following him in single file. He had become their surrogate mother about ten hours after birth when they bonded with him, because they were programmed to follow the first large moving object they saw after they learned how to walk. This behavior is adaptive, because in nature that figure is most likely their mother. Lorenz continued to parent the goslings and even taught them how to fly, which was recorded in a dramatic, moving, and humorous film that showed him rushing across the grass, flapping his arms as the geese took off, leaving him earth-bound, like the rest of his species. He demonstrated not only the bonding mechanism but also that bonding bears ethical responsibility for those who assume the parenting role, even in cross-species situations.

Bowlby argued that human infants also follow such bonding cues. The inherited reciprocal system of attachment for our species is fostered by such elements as soft warm skin, bright eyes, smiles, and the sound and pace of the human voice, especially female voices. He identified four "hard wired" and universal stages for attachment.

During the first six to eight weeks infants show only a general interest in human voices and faces, but, unlike geese, they do not focus on anyone in particular. The second stage begins at about three to six months when smiles, babbling, cooing, and gurgling begin to be restricted to familiar people, while strangers are met with a stare. Clear-cut attachment takes place in the third stage, which begins at about six months when infants begin to crawl and ends when the toddler can walk. This increased mobility is restricted by separation anxiety. Children keep checking on the whereabouts of their parents to retreat to when they are anxious. Parents, for their part, keep a sharp eye on their children. The fourth step takes place from about two or three years of age and lasts until the end of childhood, as the parent and child work out their conscious understanding of dependence and independence in their relationship.

Mary Ainsworth's greatest contribution to understanding the attachment process was the development of her Strange Situation study. During the first year of a baby's life researchers visited homes to observe the parent-child relationship in its natural surroundings. About the time of their first birthday the babies were taken by their mothers to an unfamiliar playroom. The first one was set up in 1963 at Johns Hopkins University with a one-way mirror for observation (Karen 1998, 144–148). It was in this strange situation, compared to the home, that researchers could observe how the children used their mothers as a base from which to explore the toys in the room and how they reacted to the anxiety of brief separations. In the first separation the mother left the baby with a stranger (a friendly female graduate student) and in the second separation the baby was left alone. Each separation lasted three minutes, but was shortened if there was too much distress. The entire procedure lasted about twenty minutes. Three patterns were observed: those for securely attached infants, insecure-avoidant infants, and insecure-ambivalent infants.

The securely attached infants used their mothers as a base from which to explore, as we have said, but when their mothers left the room the children's exploratory play diminished and the children became upset. When the mothers returned the children went to them and then began to explore once more. Home studies showed these mothers were consistently warm and attuned to their children. In 2005 about 65 percent to 70 percent of one-year-olds in the United States exhibited secure attachment (Crain 2005, 55). A year later Goleman reported that 55 percent of the children were securely attached (Goleman 2007, 194). These statistics are not intended to establish a trend as much as to show that there is a range in these numbers, depending on which studies are used to calculate the average.

When the insecure-avoidant children arrived in the strange situation they rushed off, crawling, to inspect the toys in the playroom. They did not use their mothers as a secure base and they did not check in with them from time to time. They simply ignored their mothers. When the mothers left the room the children did not become visibly upset, although some studies show their heart rate and blood pressure increased. When the mothers came back the children did not move close to them before setting out to explore again. The studies in the home showed that these mothers were insensitive, interfering, and rejecting. Their children realized after suffering many rejections that it was better if they blocked out their feelings for their mothers to avoid further disappointment. In 2005 it was reported that 20 percent of one-year-old children in the U.S. were avoidant (Crain 2005, 56) while Goleman reported that this group was 25 percent (Goleman 2007, 195).

The insecure-ambivalent children were clingy. They were so concerned about their mothers' location in the playroom that they did not explore much at all. When their mothers left, the children became very upset. When their mothers returned, the children would at times reach out for them and at other times push them away, almost like they were punishing them. Perhaps they were mirroring them since home visits showed these mothers to be warm and responsive but only part of the time. This inconsistency left the children uncertain about whether they could count on their mothers or not. This pattern was found in 2005 in about 10–15 percent of one-year-old children in the U.S. (Crain 2005, 57). A year later Goleman found this group to be 20 percent (Goleman 2007, 195).

The relationship patterns established by the end of the first year usually continue through adulthood. There are many factors involved in this, such as genetics and temperament as well as the parenting styles of adults, but in general parenting is a very powerful indicator of future relationships. This conclusion is given credibility because attachment is a mature theory that is well documented in various cultures.

The historical themes that have emerged in this book can be given coherence by reframing them in terms of attachment theory. The high view of children is associated with secure attachment and the possibility of grace. The low view combined with the high view suggests ambivalent attachment. Indifference is related to avoidant attachment. The inner working model of relationships between theologians and their parents probably influenced how they related to and thought about children. What they wrote has shaped how we think about children in the church and since much of what they wrote describes insecure attachment, the *de facto* doctrine of children promotes insecure attachment in the church today. At least some of what we think about children, consciously or unconsciously, influences how we relate to them, so the church continues to foster insecure attachment among its members by its words and actions.

In addition to the connection between the historical themes and attachment theory there is also a connection between attachment theory and how people relate to God. Lee A. Kirkpatrick has studied this connection from an evolutionary psychology point of view. Evolutionary psychology is a major school of psychology—like the psychoanalytic, behaviorist, or cognitive schools—but it is the youngest of these schools, having come into existence in the 1990s. It has been built on the foundations of ethnology, sociobiology (the study of the evolution of behavior), and cognitive science (the study of brain and mental processes).

Kirkpatrick argued that "religion can be understood not as an instinct or adaptation designed by natural selection by virtue of survival or reproduction benefit, but rather as a collection of by-products of numerous specialized psychological systems that evolved over the course of human history for other (i.e. nonreligious) functions" (Kirkpatrick 2005, viii). One of these "nonreligious" functions is attachment.

Kirkpatrick went on to say that "ideas about God activate the cognitive machinery of the attachment system, which processes the ideas in attachment terms" (Kirkpatrick 2005, 236). There are five defining characteristics, he argued following Ainsworth, that distinguish attachment from other close relationships: "(1) the attached person seeks proximity to the caregiver, particularly when frightened or alarmed; (2) the caregiver provides care and protection (the haven of safety function) as well as (3) a sense of security (the secure base function); (4) the threat of separation causes anxiety in the attached person; and (5) loss of the attachment figure would cause grief in the attached person" (Kirkpatrick 2005, 56). These behaviors are also evoked when seeking and maintaining proximity to God, God as a haven of safety, God as a secure base, the response to separation from God, and the loss of God (Kirkpatrick 2005, 56–74).

A few theologians have been interested in attachment theory. Bruce Reed's *The Dynamics of Religion* (Reed 1978), referred to in my book *Godly Play* (Berryman 1991, 103–104), also drew on attachment theory to explain the need to have a safe place to retreat to in order to create meaning. This was the foundation for his sociological "oscillation theory" of religion. Kirkpatrick also mentions Reed in passing, but relies most heavily on Wenegrat's discussion from a sociobiological point of view (Kirkpatrick 2005, 52–53).

The connection between attachment theory and sociology might also be applied to understand the relationship between children and mother church better. Peter Marris has argued, for example, that "attachment theory powerfully links the social and psychological aspects of human behavior" and that Bowlby's contribution will "be seen to be as central to the development of sociology as it has been to psychology" (Marris 1991, 77). This suggests that if children experience the church as an attachment object in a warm, attuned, and consistent way then they are likely to become securely attached to that social institution.

Bruce Reed has argued further that individuals experience "periods of engagement with various tasks, alternating with periods of disengagement which may be creative, defensive, or simply periods of rest" (Reed 1978, 41). The church provides one of the important places where such "oscillation" takes place. It is the place where creative symbolic work can be done to help cope with and understand the everyday world. However, when "religion has become impotent to change the status quo, because the regression to extra-dependence it induces is not a creative regression but a withdrawal which does not allow development or growth," then the church is dysfunctional (Reed 1978, 53). This dysfunction makes the church an unsafe place in which to carry on symbolic work.

How does this dysfunction develop? Since our culture promotes anxious-avoidant and anxious-ambivalent relationships, the church becomes saturated with anxious attachment, which threatens the consistent, warm attunement needed for securely attached relationships. Without awareness of this and the conscious effort to confront anxious attachment, the church has difficulty being a place where secure attachment can prevail.

Our culture's promotion of anxious-avoidant relationships has been studied by Christopher Lasch in terms of narcissism and the promotion of anxious-ambivalent relationships has been studied by Kenneth J. Gergan in terms of postmodernism. To develop this theme we will now discuss each of these authors in turn.

Christopher Lasch (1932–1994) wondered in *The Culture of Narcissism* (1991) why we are so enamored by technology with its hyper-reason and paradoxically the anti-reason of New Age Gnosticism. His answer was that "New Age spirituality, no less than technological utopianism, is rooted in primary narcissism" (Lasch 1991, 245). The details of his argument are beyond the scope of our discussion here except to say that a culture of narcissism clearly falls within the range of anxious-avoidant relationships. As Lasch wrote, "Everything conspires to encourage escapist solutions to the psychological problems of dependence, separation, and individuation, and to discourage the moral realism that makes it possible for human beings to come to terms with existential constraints on their power and freedom" (Lasch 1991, 249).

The anxious, narcissistic approach to life has become "normal" in our time, so it is worth quoting at length from Lasch's book to show how this has come about:

> Narcissism appears realistically to represent the best way of coping with the tensions and anxieties of modern life, and the prevailing social conditions therefore tend to bring out narcissistic traits that are present, in varying degrees, in everyone. These conditions have also transformed the family, which in turn shapes the underlying structure of personality. A society that fears it has no future is not likely to give much attention

to the needs of the next generation, and the ever-present sense
of historical discontinuity—the blight of our society—falls with
particularly devastating effect on the family. The modern parent's attempt to make children feel loved and wanted does not
conceal an underlying coolness—the remoteness of those who
have little to pass on to the next generation and who in any case
give priority to their own right to self-fulfillment. The combination of emotional detachment with the attempts to convince a
child of his favored position in the family is a good prescription
for a narcissistic personality structure. (Lasch 1991, 50)

Why is this a danger for the church? The church advocates for people to be caring, and caring takes empathy. If you can put yourself in the
shoes of others it is hard to treat them as objects and inflict pain. A lack of
empathy can be seen in a range from lesser to greater in three steps as one
moves from the narcissists, to obsessively manipulative people, and finally
to psychopaths. Goleman notes that everyone in this group shares in vary-
ing degrees the traits of "malevolence and duplicity, self-centeredness
and aggression, and emotional coldness." He then goes on to argue that
"glorifying me-first motives and worshiping celebrity demigods of greed
unleashed and vanity idealized, may be inadvertently inviting these types
to flourish" (Goleman 2007, 118). When this cultural tendency saturates
the church and its leaders, the church's ability to prophetically confront
narcissism and its more dangerous manipulative and psychopathic cousins
is seriously impaired.

The cultural tendency toward accepting anxious-avoidant relationships as normal is joined by the tendency in the post modern lifestyle to
normalize anxious-ambivalent relationships. Kenneth J. Gergan's *The
Saturated Self: Dilemmas of Identity in Contemporary Life* describes postmodernism as a kind of "multiphrenia" that goes beyond the pathology
of the split personality to the saturation of the self with multiple voices.
Today, however, living with multiple selves is not considered a pathology.
It is considered normal (Gergan 1991, 73–74). This raises ambivalence,
and the dark triad of avoidance—narcissism, obsessive manipulation, and
psychopathic behavior—almost to the status of the reigning ideology for
our society, which in turn undermines the church's ability to function prophetically at the very time when a prophetic stance is desperately needed
and a modeling by the church of secure, generous love and respect for other
people is so important.

Gergan concludes his analysis of postmodernism by saying, "Thus, as
social saturation adds incrementally to the population of self, each impulse

toward well-formed identity is cast into increasing doubt; each is found absurd, shallow, limited, or flawed by the onlooking audience of the interior" (Gergan 1991, 73). This personal ambivalence is supported by the way we arrange ourselves in communities.

Today we no longer enjoy face-to-face relationships but instead have become communities of "collage" (unshared) "cardboard" (unpopulated for most of the day) and "symbolic" (electronic) relationships (Gergan 1991, 211–116). These many factors conspire to make us a nation of anxious-avoidant and anxious-ambivalent people in need of a church to sponsor and advocate for secure attachment, but which is unable to lead the way because it is co-opted by society. Instead of clearly standing for and being a place where love, like that expressed by St. Paul's classical view (1 Corinthians 13), is shared, it teaches anxious relationships by what it does and sometimes even by what it says about the so-called "gospel" of personal, self-centered success preached from large and small pulpits.

It is interesting in this context to take another look at the title of Robert Karen's book *Becoming Attached: First Relationships and How They Shape Our Capacity To Love.* This book is usually read to understand attachment theory and the research on which it is based, but it can also be read as a primer for church health. Church *health* needs to be distinguished from church growth, because the need for growth has ironically made the church so anxious about acquiring new members that it often becomes unhealthy. It loses the ability to foster the kind of secure and attuned love among its members that is the hallmark of the Christian tradition.

If churches were places of consistent warmth and attunement for children then children could become more securely attached to God, the church, and primary others in the community. If secure attachment were made the priority for ministry then church growth would take care of itself because the children would return to mother church, not because of skillful marketing, but because it is their nature to seek healthy attachment and flee from situations that promote the dysfunctional communities of insecure attachment.

The playing of the third level of the game then is about the existential coherence that attachment theory brings to the four themes that emerged from the history of theology. It is this coherence that brings personal meaning in terms of secure attachment to how children are nourished in their Christian identity by the way people in the church relate to each other. This kind of meaning is almost all nonverbal. It is created by how people live with each other, not by what they say.

The Fourth Level of the Game: Action

We turn now to the fourth level of the Gateway Game. It is time to take action based on what has been learned from the other three levels. The unconscious shaping of our views about children in the church can now be consciously coped with by a better understanding, so that grace within can cooperate with the grace in the world around us to work for children in truly creative ways for the long run. To take action is to use the game to challenge the informal doctrine and begin to guide and learn from children in new ways. This is roughly what happened to Joseph Knecht in Hermann Hesse's novel *The Glass Bead Game*.

Theodore Ziolkowski succinctly sums up how this took place: "Knecht's life represents typologically the radicalization of the intellectual, who moves from the *vita contemplativa* not to the opposite extreme of the *vita activa*, but to an intermediate position of responsible action controlled by dispassionate reflection. It is essential to understand that Knecht's defection from Castalia, far from implying any repudiation of the spiritual ideal, simply calls for a new consciousness of the social responsibility of the intellectual" (Hesse 1969, xvi-xvii). One becomes fluent in the game not to flee the game but to take "responsible action controlled by dispassionate reflection." The point is to not only change the way we think but the way we act.

The hero of Hesse's novel, it seems to me, is really the game itself, its promise and limitations. Joseph Knecht, whose name means "servant" in German shows its promise and limitations by what he does. The former *Magister Ludi* dies in the service of a single student at the end of the novel. His death warns those who continue to play the game about its limited reality and to witness to how the game can (in our terms) clear the way for grace. It does this by connecting the grace within us to the grace in the world, which makes one a co-creator with God, an intimacy that Hesse sought in all his novels and in his life, although he never put it quite this way.

The game's fourth level takes place when individuals put down this book and work for children in their own families, parishes, hospitals, schools, homes and other arenas in which they play a part. The fourth level also operates in a limited way within in the pages of this book when in the next chapter a proposal is presented for a formal doctrine of children to replace the *de facto* one. The related spiritual practice that is sketched in the next chapter will help guide further action for children and openness to what they have to teach adults. With all this in mind it is now time to sum up and then look ahead to the final chapter.

Conclusion

The game we have been playing in this chapter is in fact the explication of the informal doctrine of children that has been adopted unconsciously by the church. It is now time to confront this *de facto* doctrine to see how it might be changed to become more adequate.

In 1984 George A. Lindbeck published his classic *The Nature of Doctrine*. He was looking for a way to frame ecumenical discussions of doctrine so that theologians could do more than merely disagree, so he looked at the nature of doctrine itself and how it functions in the church. He identified four approaches to doctrine—the "propositionalist," the "experiential-expressive," the "two-dimensional model," and the "cultural-linguistic"—and he discussed them along with such features of doctrines as their accidental, conditional, irreformable, irreversible, official, operational, permanent, practical, reversible, temporary, and unconditional characteristics. This is all very interesting, but we will focus on chapter 4 in which he discussed "Theories of Doctrine" (Lindbeck 1984, 73–88) and pointed out that doctrine might be unstated as well as stated.

First, he defined stated doctrine as "communally authoritative teaching regarding beliefs and practices that are considered essential to the identity or welfare of the group in question." He then noted that doctrines may be "formally stated or informally operative." He sharpened this point by saying, "To disagree with Methodist, Quaker, or Roman Catholic doctrine indicates that one is not a 'good' Methodist, Quaker, or Roman Catholic" (Lindbeck 1984, 74). The problem with the doctrine of children is that it is not part of any particular denomination's conscious identity. The informal doctrine works mostly at the unconscious and peripheral level, which makes it resistant to change.

Secondly, he noted that there are some features of common belief that are not officially stated and, indeed, in some denominations there is advocacy for a "creedless approach," although that definition functions as part of a *de facto* creed. An example of a doctrine that is not officially stated but is operative is that "God is love." This is so implicit and pervasive in Christian life and practice that it has not been reduced to a formal doctrinal statement but operates all thorough Christian thought and practice. This informal doctrine has been unchanging since the beginning of Christianity.

Sometimes, however, informal doctrines change. An example is that for most of Christianity's history slavery was accepted by the church. How one ought to manage slaves was discussed but the assumption was that slavery was included in Christian thought and practice. This informal doctrine prevailed until the nineteenth century when the Christian church began to speak out explicitly against slavery.

The doctrine of children is also an informal doctrine and, like the slavery assumption, it also needs to be changed. The operative doctrine about children in the church is primarily one of ambivalence, ambiguity, and indifference. There have been suggestions that the high view of children is important, as we have noted, but our informal, operative doctrine tells us that children are to be approached with ambivalence, ambiguity, and indifference although with some acknowledgement that children are a biological means of grace. They bridge the generations and bring the potential of grace with each new generation, but that is a very limited view of children's positive contribution to the church.

Lindbeck has also argued that the way implicit doctrines become explicit or operational as official ones is by controversy (Lindbeck 1984, 75). This is how the community makes up its collective mind and formally makes a doctrinal decision. What will be proposed in the next chapter then is suggested to promote such controversy.

Today we have the understanding and ability to shift from the informal doctrine of children to one that is more adequate. It is time to take action now. A formal doctrine of children may be a long time coming, but individuals can act immediately to change the informal one by the way we speak about and treat children in the church. The informal doctrine can be reformed by a new spiritual practice while awaiting the formation of a formal doctrine.

The formal doctrine can resolve many of the problems of the informal one. The mixture of the high and low views about children that produce the church's ambivalence, which is so destructive, can be replaced by an explicitly high view. The ambiguity that involves such rich and deep inconsistencies can be acknowledged as the reality of the situation and the church can be more careful as well as caring when children are considered. Indifference can be set aside, stepped over, or gone around, like any stumbling block, with full intention. The peripheral role of children as a means of grace can be moved to the center of theology and spiritual practice. In the next chapter we will consider how this can be done and why it should be done.

CHAPTER

9

CHILDREN AS A MEANS OF GRACE:
A Proposal for a formal Doctrine of Children

This painting was done during one of the research classes, which laid the foundations for Godly Play from about 1974–1994. Lindsay made this painting in Houston on September 12, 1985, at age seven and on the same day she painted a picture of The Mustard Seed. She said, referring to Joseph, "I forgot the nose but he is happy. Jesus is happy. Mary is real happy. They found a place to stay."

Her comments about *The Parable of the Mustard Seed* focused on the birds. She said that the bird in the upper right was not sure he wanted to live in the tree because he didn't have a nest. The bird over the head of the person who "put the tiny seed in the ground," who seems to be covered with seeds or bursts of light, is far away. The one on the ground by the planter of the mustard seed is eating. On the left a bird

is coming down to rest on the ground. (She appears to be assuming that the many birds nested in the tree are comfortable and need no further comment.)

Today Lindsay and her husband live with their young son in the Washington, DC, area. She left Houston to attend Hampshire College where she studied ethics and developed a special interest in the work of Paul Roceur. She then went on to Vanderbilt to complete her MTS but gave up her idea of a joint degree in law and instead went to work in religious outreach for the Democratic National Committee and also did fundraising for the national Catholic Social Justice Lobby.

Thea (1941–2009) and I kept the originals of this painting because Lindsay gave it to the Children's Center. We made slides of most children's paintings with their

▲ *The Parable of the Mustard Seed,*
Lindsay Gerber Gonzales
(seven years old), 1985
Center for the Theology of Childhood,
Denver, Colorado, USA

permission and also recorded what they said about them as part of the foundational research for Godly Play, but sometimes such gifts were made and we kept them. This painting with its companion Holy Family are now hanging in Denver at the Center for the Theology of Childhood, which is the research and development part of the Godly Play Foundation.

◀ *The Holy Family,* Lindsay Gerber Gonzales (seven years old), 1985
Center for the Theology of Childhood, Denver, Colorado, USA

T his chapter proposes that children are a means of grace. A more elaborate doctrinal statement may come in time from the church, but for now this simple proposal is enough to get the conversation started. This chapter will also discuss why children are especially suited to be a focus for and to communicate grace. This is because of the intensity with which the biological, psychological, social and spiritual dimensions of grace are unified in them through the creative process. Finally, a spiritual practice will be suggested, based on the classical seven sacraments, or kinds of ministry, to help make the proposed doctrine more than mere words.

Considering Children as a Means of Grace

It is startling to think of children as sacraments. This is in part because of the power that the unexamined *de facto* doctrine has on us. What is even more startling, however, is to realize that at some level we already know this to be true, despite not being accustomed to thinking about children in this way. Still, this proposal sounds wildly extravagant and even naïve. It calls to mind the romantic view of children in the nineteenth-century portrayed by T.C. Gotch's painting *The Child Enthroned*, which was placed at the beginning of chapter 6. This proposal, however, is not naïve.

The sacramental view of children proposed stands solidly in the mix of the *de facto* doctrine's reality, as was discussed in the last chapter. The ambivalence, ambiguity, indifference, and grace by which the church has considered children is realistic. What this proposal does is merely shift the emphasis toward grace and away from the church's emphasis on ambivalence, ambiguity, and indifference. This should also come as no surprise. Jesus' sayings about adults knowing God by welcoming children and needing to be like children to be mature act like words of institution for this proposed sacrament.

The drama of suggesting children are a means of grace can be seen in Emil Nolde's painting *Christ and the Children* (*Christus und die Kinder*) at the beginning of chapter 7. The energy of the children as a means of grace and the resistance to recognizing this are expressed in terms of light and dark by Nolde's visual logic. At first one is tempted to think of the light radiating out from the children to the onlooker, as the children reflecting Christ's light, as if they were mirrors, but there is something much more active and powerful going on. It is embodiment. The children absorb Christ's presence and make it manifest rather than only superficially and passively reflecting it.

The children's faces embody Christ's presence at least as much as bread and wine do. The raw, undifferentiated energy of grace can be felt as it flows out from God as light in the painting through the children to the viewer. The children are the means by which we can receive God's light without being overwhelmed by Christ's presence. The children, according to this logic, are at ease with being a means of grace. The women know this as they push the children forward, but the closed, darkened faces of the disciples show that they don't yet understand either Christ's presence or how it is being embodied in the children. It is understandable that they are muttering among themselves! Besides, the light is so bright that it is painful to the eyes, but they are also very shortsighted and fearful to turn away and defensively discuss which one will be the most important in Jesus' misunderstood kingdom.

Part of the strangeness of thinking about *children* as sacraments is that we are accustomed to thinking about sacraments as being something we can control better than children, like a touch, oil, water, bread, or wine. The profound meaning of Jesus' breaking bread and sharing wine in the first century must have seemed as strange and out of control to those people as thinking of children as sacraments is to us, especially when compared to what the priests did exclusively in the temple. But isn't that the point? A means of grace is not meant to be able to be controlled by people because the grace is God's.

Not everything Jesus did or said, as reported in the gospels, establishes a sacrament. The special case of children, however , is a kind of communication of God's overflowing exuberance that is unified and intensified in them. The unity of this energy is experienced in three ways all at once and all the time, although we might emphasize one way more than the others at various times. The "overflowing" quality of this energy comes from the inner workings of the Holy Trinity as Catherine Mowry LaCugna has argued:

> ↩ The images of "begetting" and "spirating" express the fruit-
> fulness or fecundity of God who is alive from all eternity as
> a dynamic interchange of persons united in love . . . The

> centrifugal movement of divine love does not terminate
> "within" God but explodes outward . . . To be the Creator,
> that is, to be in relation to creation as the Creator is not a rela-
> tion added on to the divine essence, ancillary to God's being.
> To be God is to be the Creator of the world . . . . The reason
> lies entirely in the unfathomable mystery of God. (LaCugna
> 1991, 354–55) ᴸᵒ

God is known in this continuously overflowing energy, which means that God's power is not experienced as a zero sum game. One does not have to subtract creativity from God when it is added to God's creatures. As creating creatures (with limitations, of course, when compared to God's unlimited energy), made in the image of the "Creator" we multiply rather than restrict God's creative power when we create with the grace that God has given us. In fact children are necessarily creative. If they cannot intuitively create they will fail to thrive.

Still, why is it so important to set *children* aside as sacraments? What is so unique about them? They are special because of the intensity and the unity of the grace that is so powerfully embodied in them as their deep identity. What does that really mean? We turn to that discussion now.

Grace, the Creative Process and Human Identity

The theological doctrine of the *Imago Dei* and evolutionary psychology agree that the fundamental identity of humankind involves the creative process. Evolutionary psychology uses *ethology*, the study of animals in their natural environments, *sociobiology*, the study of the evolution of behavior, and *cognitive science*, the study of brain and mental processes, to reach its conclusions. Theology integrates the revelation of *scripture, reason, tradition,* and *experience* to make its discoveries. There is no larger paradigm that includes these two approaches to knowledge, so we must move forward using both theology and science in parallel, like two voices singing the same note but an octave apart, to make suggestions rather than draw conclusions. Still, the agreement about the fundamental importance of the creative process across the paradigm boundaries is suggestive and rings true.

The theological concept of the *Imago Dei* argues that we are creatures made in the image of the Creator and are, therefore, creators as well. God also gave us the gift of language to name God's creatures (Genesis 2:19) and to use in our creating. In the letter to the Hebrews the author begins by talking about the many ways "God spoke to our ancestors" and that now "in these last days he has spoken to us by a Son" (Hebrews 1:1–2). This Son is called the "the Word" in John's gospel (John 1:1–5). These few references illustrate how both the Hebrew Scriptures and the Christian Scriptures have closely aligned God, creation and speech.

These theological observations fit with what evolutionary psychology tells us about the purpose of the long period of dependence that human infants experience. It provides our unique creativity and language ability. As Terrence Deacon has said, we are a "symbolic species" in which the co-evolution of language and the brain has taken place (Deacon 1997) to give us our language-related creativity that is unique among the species and has greatly helped our survival.

The Life-Giving Circle

The creative process feels like it flows in a circle. In theological terms it opens to God's energy and, when all goes well, the circling around results in something new, redemptive, and constructive. In scientific terms the creative process is a positive feedback loop. A negative feedback loop regulates, like when a thermostat shuts off a heat source when the temperature goes too high. A creative or positive loop does not establish conditions of predictability and stability. It enhances change and instability. Positive loops referencing themselves at different levels of the brain, as a kind of feedback of loops on loops, may be the way the human sense of self is created (Harth 1995, 67–73). The creative loop keeps spinning, like the spinning top of Nicholas of Cusa, to give us stability as long as we live by its motion. There is also a closing phase in the process, which gives temporary stability to discoveries, but when closed the process is always ready to be opened again.

Let us take a brief tour around this life-giving circle. The process begins in a variety of ways. Sometimes the process is opened by wonder. At other times a tragedy shatters the meaning that had been assumed to hold the world together. This causes us to pick up the pieces to fashion a new world view. It can also begin when something is experienced that is so sublime it cannot be incorporated within ones assumptions, so the loop goes into action to discover what kind of world is necessary for such beauty to be possible. The process can also be opened by play and its way of thinking "as-if."

In theological terms the raw energy of God's overflowing grace pushes and pulls the movement in the circle. Grace pushes the movement to find a more adequate answer or pattern for reality. Grace pulls the movement by the lure of God that promises a more adequate life when one cooperates with grace and the creativity within works together with God's creativity in the world around us.

The event in the world that pushes and pulls the movement in the creative loop can be mundane—such as "What shall we have for supper?" or "Where did I leave my keys?"—or it can be monumental like "What shall I do with my life?" Many sleepless nights and days of reverie can result as this powerful process begins to move relentlessly toward a new and more adequate pattern of meaning and then closes around its discovery to make one's world more realistic.

As the raw energy of grace moves one around the loop, the sense of time is altered, becoming faster or slower than ordinary, clock time. The circling might last for a few moments or many years by clock time before the new insight is felt. When the discovery is made the energy shifts the opening to the closing phase of the process. This can often be felt, sometimes even before the discovery is known in language. As the insight is articulated it becomes shaped by the language of the world one lives in. This might be the language of a homemaker or anywhere along a spectrum of language that extends to that of the mathematician and others.

The moment of insight has been a puzzle to people in the West because it has been considered both dangerous and beneficial. The history of the imagination tends to be divided into its safe or rational aspects, which are considered constructive, and its destructive and dangerous uses (Brann 1991, Kearney 1988, Warnock 1978). This double vision has been paralleled in the history of play, as Spariosu's study has shown (Spariosu 1982). In his terms he found themes of pre-rational and rational play reoccurring in the West. Pre-rational play is a manifestation of power that is sheer emotion and arbitrary violence. Rational play tames this to be more logical and consistently constructive.

To continue around the circle of the creative process, the insight may become conscious in creatively charged bits and pieces. Eva T.H. Brann gave priority to how seeing and hearing reveal the discovery in her *The World of the Imagination: Sum and Substance* (Brann 1991). Smell, taste, and touch are not as imagistic but they stimulate auditory and optical responses. Other senses such as heat, gravity, and posture don't seem to carry the insight into consciousness since they are more over-all senses without a focused object (Brann 1991, 13–17).

The coming to consciousness of the insight can also be described in a more comprehensive way by drawing on Gardner's seven ways of knowing. People frame the new idea in intra-psychic terms like Freud's, in mathematical terms like Einstein's, in visual art like Picasso's, in music like Stravinsky's, in words like T. S. Eliot's, in dance like Martha Graham's, or in social terms like Gandhi's (Gardner 1993). Whatever sense or organizational preference carries the insight into consciousness, it is felt to be significant, so the process shifts into its closing phase to develop the insight more completely.

As we said, the first step is the scanning process. The second step is the insight. The third step is the development of the insight. The fourth and last step is closure. Closure is usually achieved by making a compromise between an idealized goal and an adequate realization of it.

People seem to prefer different parts of this cycle (Berryman 1991, 93–102). Those who love the freedom of the opening phase are reluctant to shift to the closing phase of the creative process. They love scanning and don't really want to make a discovery that might commit them to a particular point of view. Others who find the scanning part of the creative process painful will sometimes endure its discomfort to enjoy the pleasure of resolving its openness with a discovery. A third type of personality cannot stand either the freedom of unlimited scanning or its instrumental use for discovery. These people prefer to begin with someone else's idea and develop it. They like to conserve what is best of the past, but not create anything new themselves. Finally, there are people who do not like any of the preceding three steps. They prefer to stay in control of the process by deciding which ideas developed by others to keep and which to discard. Their only risk is the success of the idea they have decided to sponsor. It is not that people of this fourth type are not creative. They deal with a secondary kind of creativity about the usefulness of the creativity of others.

The securely attached person, it seems to me, is interested in the whole cycle—the exploration, the discovery, the refinement of the discovery, and finally the closure that provides a new place of meaningful safety. The pleasure of completing the whole cycle is self-motivating, so the securely attached person is always ready to venture out to explore once again.

Anxiously attached people, however, have difficulty carrying the process all the way through to completion, so they miss the pleasure and safety of the completed cycle. Their anxious attachments diminish their enjoyment of life and dim the *Imago Dei* within. The fracturing of the creative process by their anxious relationships can also frustrate the creativity of the people around them. This can result in blocking any community's openness to grace, including the church's.

When the raw grace in God's creation flows through the creative process it becomes available to humankind to help us cooperate with God as co-creators. Children usually participate in the flow of this process naturally, which makes them uniquely gifted to reveal the fundamental identity of humankind described by both science and theology.

There is a second reason why children are especially suited to reveal grace. This is because the creative process works in them in an intense and unified way, moving at first around the circle like a single tone. This tone often develops unevenly over time as children grow into adulthood it can become a discord. If people continue to develop, however, this discord can resolve into a single harmonious chord for the child-like adult. What was merged in the child and differentiated in the adult becomes re-integrated in the graceful person.

This is akin to what Hermann Hesse was talking about in his "A Bit of Theology," mentioned in chapter 1. As he put it, "we find the same typical experiences always in the same progression and succession: loss of innocence, striving for justice under the law, the consequent despair in the futile struggle to overcome guilt by deeds or by knowledge, and finally the emergence from hell into a transformed world and into a new kind of innocence" (quoted in Ziolkowski 1965, 55–56). In our terms this "new kind of innocence" is the harmonious integration of the four dimensions of the creative process which we will expand on in a moment.

There is a third reason why children are especially suited to be a means of grace. This was briefly mentioned in the last chapter but not followed by any further explanation. It was observed that both the high and the low views and each of the eight kinds of ambiguity have some reality to them. Indifference also points to the necessary reality that there are times when one must pay attention to matters other than children. What this suggests is that while these differences can be distinguished by logical categories, during the flow of life they are all relevant, related and part of the reality of children. What appear to be opposing realities become integrated in fact and coherent in thought when they are considered as part of the creative process.

The reality of children and their meaning is expansive when the creative process opens. The wonder of the whole period of childhood, the sinless aspect of their nature, their involvement in change, the teaching they do, the maturity they show, the blessings they give, the uniqueness of each actual child and the pervasive deep meaning of children are all appreciated. As the circle begins to close children are more associated with specific cognitive developmental and social stages, are considered involved in the limitations of sin, need permanence, need to learn, are immature, are trouble, are generalized as a concept, and are shot through with the logical complexity of all eight ambiguities.

When children are considered from the standpoint of the opening phase of the creative process with wonder they stimulate adults to be more childlike. On the other hand, when children are considered in terms of the closing phase of the creative process they are understood in terms of control and power.

The full meaning of children is known when the approaches characteristic of the opening phase and the set of assumptions characteristic of the closing phase are joined by the whole circle of the creative process. This is one reason why it is difficult for people who are not securely attached to understand that children are sacraments. Those insecurely attached see this proposal as being either too open and silly or too closed and rigid. Either alternative is wrong. Both alternatives are right when joined together. The idea of children as sacraments needs the whole circle of the creative process to be experienced for adequate understanding.

We turn now to the four characteristics of the graceful person to discuss how the creative process works biologically, psychologically, socially, and spiritually to provide the traits of love, flow, play, and contemplation in the graceful person. These dimensions of the creative process share similar structures, as we shall see, which suggests their common origin in the child's unified revelation of grace.

The Biological Dimension of the Creative Process

At the biological level of the creative process, people are drawn together to create offspring by a "limbic resonance" that attracts them to each other. This connection is named and described by Lewis, Amini, and Lannon in *A General Theory of Love* (Lewis, Amini, and Lannon 2000). This book begins with Pascal's aphorism that the heart has reasons of its own and then describes how after an attachment with another person is created by the limbic system, the neocortex makes up reasons why the attachment has been made. The limbic system is that part of the brain where our "emotional intelligence" resides. It developed before the neocortex and at times overrides it (Goleman 1995), which is why limbic resonance is so important for understanding the biological roots of love.

The kind of language most appropriate for connecting the neocortex and the limbic system—as Lewis, Amini, and Lannon agree—is poetry. Robert Frost wrote that a poem "begins as a lump in the throat, a sense of wrong, a homesickness, a love sickness. It is never a thought to begin with" (quoted in Lewis et al. 2000, 34). This explains why poetry is so important for the creative process to function and for the whole structure of the Christian language system to include poetry to communicate, as much as possible, the nonverbal. emotional aspect of love. When Christian communication is conceived of as only propositions and admonitions then the energy of grace is drained out of it.

Lewis, Amini, and Lannon published their book in 2000. They noted that discussions about love had to that point seldom included its biology. The study of love's biological dimension has continued to progress, so that by 2006 Daniel Goleman could write that "To untangle love's mysteries, neuroscience distinguishes between neural networks for attachment, for care giving, and for sex." Love is an "elegant balance, an interplay that, when all goes well, furthers Nature's design for continuing the species." He went on to say that "This underlying neural wiring interacts in differing combinations in love's many varieties—romantic, familial, and parental—as well as in our capacities for connecting, whether in friendship, with compassion, or just doting on a cat. By extension, the same circuits may be at work to one extent or another in larger realms, like spiritual longing or an affinity for open skies and empty beaches" (Goleman 2007, 189–190). He too echoed Pascal's observation but without its poetry by saying that "Love's reasons have always been subcortical, though love's execution may require careful plotting" (Goleman 2007, 190).

The creative process at the biological level not only aids in connecting people to create offspring and care for children but also has long-term implications for aging adults. Erik Erikson noted the importance of caring for the next generation as one grows older and coined the term "generativity" to emphasize this. People are sometimes drawn into stagnation by self-absorption as they grow older and their energy declines. This presents a developmental crisis with one of two outcomes—generativity or stagnation. The path of generativity, which includes the stimulation of creativity in the next generation, leads to ego integrity and wisdom while stagnation leads to an old age of despair and disgust.

Erikson's generativity resonates with Jesus' observations that to become spiritually mature we need to welcome and become like children. The child helps stimulate creativity in the adult, and when adults mentor children it helps children be more secure, which makes them more able to help adults be child-like, which in turn stimulates the adult to be more mature, which establishes another loop of creativity as a kind of mutual blessing. Much of this mutual blessing is felt at the biological level, even if it remains mostly unconscious.

Love's roots may be in biology, but it also has psychological, social, and spiritual dimensions. For example, it takes creativity in all of these dimensions to maintain the warmth of a loving relationship. It is surprising sometimes to realize just how creative people need to be in their day-to-day lives to remain "in love," as the changes of each decade are coped with. Finally, as couples get older and their energy declines or they become involved in serious health difficulties (or both), their creative resources are tested just to help each other stay alive each day with dignity and grace and hopefully a touch of wry humor.

The Psychological Dimension of the Creative Process

New ideas and ways of doing things involve the psychological dimension of the creative process. This level of the process is merged with the other three in children and slowly becomes more differentiated as one grows older. The understanding of the psychological dimension of the creative process took a leap in 1965 when one of the modern pioneers in this field, Mihaly Csikszentmihalyi, finished his doctoral thesis.

"Dr. C," as he is sometimes called, had studied a group of male artists who worked intensively with great concentration and enjoyed their work immensely. What he found curious was that they seemed to lack interest in the resulting product of their efforts for which they got little affirmation from the culture. The common explanation in those days for such drive, as the artists exhibited, was primarily Freudian. The painters' behavior was thought to result from sublimating repressed instinctual cravings. Csikszentmihalyi, however, thought that there was too much genuine excitement and involvement with the emerging forms and colors to explain what was happening in terms of a substitution for something else, such as sex or power. These people really loved what they were doing.

First, Csikszentmihalyi looked for an explanation by studying play. Then he focused on something very close to play, the creative process. The painters, he thought, were enjoying the way the creative process felt as they used it, which made it self-motivating. In 1975 he published *Beyond Boredom and Anxiety* (Csikszentmihalyi 1975), which argued that creativity appears in a middle range of activity between the extremes of tedious rigidity and anxiety-producing chaos. This was true not only of painting but also of mountain climbing and other activities he investigated. When one is neither over-whelmed by chaos nor under-whelmed by boredom, a kind of "flow" can be felt, which he described more fully fifteen years later in a book by that name (Csikszentmihalyi 1990).

Flow takes place when the goals are clear and there are stimulating challenges that match one's skills without overwhelming them. Accurate feedback is also involved, which shows how improvement can take place. Concentration becomes deeply focused. Since all of one's energy is invested in the task, self-consciousness disappears. The result is that energy seems to be created rather than dissipated, and this is pleasurable. Csikszentmihalyi's description of how the creative process flows, what it involves, and why it is self-reinforcing has been accepted today as a major contribution to the field of psychology.

In 1988 Csikszentmihalyi first published *Optimal Experience: Psychological Studies of Flow in Consciousness* (Csikszentmihalyi 1992). The argument of this book, which involved thirteen authors and twenty-two chapters, was that flow is the key to optimal experience in humankind. In contrast to studying what goes wrong with people, this book studied what is optimal. This scientific description of optimal experience is a companion to what might be called the graceful person by the theological paradigm.

The Evolving Self gives a concise description of what happens when flow is missing from people's lives (Csikszentmihalyi 1993, 197–199). People attempt to artificially produce it by activities that are "wasteful or destructive, and in such cases, the result of seeking enjoyment is entropy, rather than harmony." Artificially induced flow, such as by drugs, is dangerous because it lacks real and constructive challenges, so it does not stretch skills that lead to complexity and health. The same could be said for grace.

The Social Dimension of the Creative Process

The social dimension of the creative process has interested philosophers and scientists for centuries. Two recent books, however, are of special interest. They are Howard Gardner's *Creating Minds* (Gardner 1993) and Mihaly Csikszentmihalyi's *Creativity* (Csikszentmihalyi 1996). Gardner noted in his book that when Csikszentmihalyi asked, "Where is creativity?" instead of the more usual, "What is creativity?" the study of creativity made a huge leap forward (Gardner 1993, 37).

Csikszentmihalyi's answer to his question is that creativity is located in three major centers of activity. One center is "the domain," where "a set of symbolic rules and procedures" apply. A second center is "the field," which includes "all the individuals who act as gatekeepers to the domain." The third center of activity is "the person," who works in a particular domain (or sets up a new domain) and moves beyond personal creativity into being creative socially when the field accepts the new idea (Csikszentmihalyi 1996, 27–28).

Gardner's book also defined the creative person in social terms. A creative person "solves problems, fashions products, or defines new questions in a domain in a way that is initially considered novel but that ultimately becomes accepted in a particular cultural setting" (Gardner 1993, 35). The triangle of relationships Gardner used to guide his studies included the "individual," both as a child and as a master. A second focus of interest is "the work," which includes the relevant symbol system of the domain or discipline in which the creative individual is working. The third center of interest is "other persons." They are family and peers in the early years, which later expand to rivals, judges, and supporters (Gardner 1993, 9). An idea that is personally novel becomes socially new and significant through the interaction among individuals, domains, and fields (Gardner 1993, 36).

When creativity becomes social it becomes a game to be played with others. This creates energy unless the play disappears from the system; then what was open and creative becomes rigid or chaotic and the game, as playful, self-destructs. It is not always easy to notice when play disappears from a system of relationships. One might still pretend to play by "going through the motions," but you and those watching can tell. It is obvious when professional athletes are working at the game and when play takes over.

We have now looked at three dimensions of the creative process—the biology of love, the flow of personal creativity, and the play of its social nature. Love, creativity, and play have often been intermingled and confused since they are all dimensions of the creative process. What has been less noticed is that contemplation also overlaps with love, creativity, and play. We turn to that discussion now.

The Spiritual Dimension of the Creative Process

Abelard had been dead about thirty years when Richard (d. 1173) arrived at the Abbey of St. Victor just outside the walls of Paris in the early 1150s (Richard of St. Victor 1979, 3). He may have come from the area we now call Scotland to study with Hugh of St. Victor, a monk with a capacious mind who was cloistered at the abbey but also active in the schools of Paris. He had fully integrated his intellectual life with the life of contemplation.

The abbey had been founded by William of Champeaux in 1108. This was the same William who was Abelard's teacher in Paris about 1100. William lived at the abbey as an Augustinian canon regular until he became bishop of Chalons in 1113. Martin Luther entered this same order, but in Erfurt, some four centuries later.

Richard became the primary spiritual writer in the West during the twelfth century. His influence spread into the next century to Bonaventure (1221–1274), a contemporary of Thomas Aquinas in Paris, and in the fourteenth century Richard's writing also impressed Dante (1265–1321), who referred to him in his *Commedia* as one "who in contemplation was more than man" (Dante 1975, 115). ("e di Riccardo,/ che a considerar fu piu che viro," *Paradiso* 10:131.). When Richard wrote during the twelfth century he shared with others a lively awareness of and respect for the different kinds of knowing.

Richard distinguished the knowing of the spirit by contemplation from the knowing of the body by the senses and the knowing of the mind by reason. He wrote that "Contemplation is the free more penetrating gaze of a mind suspended with wonder concerning the manifestations of wisdom" (Richard of St. Victor 1979, 157). This definition will now be compared to definitions of the other dimensions of the creative process to show the similarity of their structures.

A Convergence of Creating Structures

Love, flow, play, and contemplation have similar structures. This is why they have been called dimensions of the creative process. To show this similarity we shall begin with love, as defined in 1 Corinthians 13:1–13. Paul was expansive and poetic in his definition. Still the overlap with contemplation, flow, and play is clear.

Love is a gift, freely given and received. In Paul's terms it is patient, kind, not jealous, not boastful, not arrogant, and not rude. The experience of love is also deeply engaging. Paul writes that it bears, believes, hopes, and endures all things. It is so engaging that it lasts forever. Loving is done for itself. There is no extrinsic goal. That is why jealously, arrogance, and boasting are not part of its reality. It has links to other kinds of activities, much like play does. The way Paul speaks about this is to connect love with both the spiritual gifts, which are nothing without love (1 Corinthians 12:27–13:2) and to ethics when he calls loving one's neighbor as fulfilling the law (Romans 13:10). Love is also pleasurable, but not in any superficial way. The pleasure has the depths of the crucifixion and the heights of the resurrection in it. It manifests the Easter joy that Paul experienced when he became "in Christ." This is why he included joy in his understanding of the kingdom of God. It involves righteousness, peace, and joy in the Holy Spirit (Romans 14:17).

Love has been interpreted in many ways, from Plato's *Symposium* to the Last Supper. It has been discussed briefly in the economy of poetry and at length as in works like Irving Singer's three-volume work on *The Nature of Love* (Singer, 1984, 1984, 1987). It was Singer who noted that "When the amorous imagination ricochets back and forth, each person seeing himself as both lover and beloved—a new totality results, an interacting oneness" (Singer 1984, 22). Even in a brief history like Carter Lindberg's *Love: A Brief History through Western Christianity* (Lindberg 2008) the complexity of love is undeniable and, it seems to me, that its complexity shares a similar structure with contemplation, flow, and play. These similar structures in schematic form are as follow:

Contemplation (Spiritual) Richard of St. Victor	Flow (Psychological) Csikszentmihalyi	Play (Social) Garvey
1. Contemplation is the free	(1. Free choice implied)	1. Voluntary
2. More penetrating gaze of a mind	2. Concentration is deep	2. Active engagement
	Self-consciousness disappears The sense of time is altered	
3. Suspended with wonder	3. No experience is "autotelic" (worth having for itself)	3. No extrinsic goal
4. Concerning manifestations of wisdom	4. Feedback is immediate	4. Links to creativity, learning languages, and social roles
	Goals are clear Skills match challenges Control is possible Problems are forgotten	
(5. Is pleasurable implied)	(5. Is pleasurable implied)	5. Is pleasurable

All four dimensions of the creative process are pleasurable and self-reinforcing. Loving invites love like flow, play, and contemplation invite their counterparts. The descriptions of contemplation and flow do not explicitly include pleasure but it can be inferred, as is indicated by the parentheses. For example, Csikszentmihalyi's artists continued to paint even when there were no extrinsic rewards. They remained engaged because they loved doing it. When it comes to contemplation the mystics have often spoken of the pleasure they experience in the extravagant terms of "ecstasy."

All four experiences are voluntary. You cannot force someone to love, enjoy flow, play, or contemplate. The additional details about flow fill in rather than conflict with the descriptions of love, play, and contemplation.

For example, they add helpful information to Richard's "more penetrating gaze of a mind," his "suspension with wonder," and the involvement he described with "manifestations of wisdom." At the same time the description of flow also amplifies Garvey's "active engagement," while her suggestion that play is related to the creative process, language learning, and the learning of social roles, which provides the rudiments of ethics, makes the other structures richer.

These four dimensions of the creative process are all present potentially in children but are not yet distinguished. This makes their creative energy intense. In addition, children can stimulate all four dimensions of the creative process in adults because they are all potentially present in them. This stimulus is unconscious and natural. For all these reasons it seems rather unremarkable to consider children to be a means of grace. In addition, both the scientific and the theological paradigms operating in parallel but in agreement, support this.

The next step then is to say how the sacramental quality of children is part of the life of the church. What is surprising is that this means of grace is already at work in the classical sacramental system or traditional kinds of ministry but in ways that are seldom noticed. This is why the discussion moves now to how children are involved in the seven classical rites to provide the basis for a spiritual practice that can make the proposed formal doctrine of children more than merely words.

Seven Ways Children Are Graceful

Thinking about children as a means of grace needs to include not only a formal doctrinal statement, but also a way to incorporate children into people's lives as sacraments. This can be done by adding an awareness of children to each of the seven classical sacraments, which might also be thought about as acts of ministry in some parts of the Christian family.

Reframing the present classical sacraments to include children has the advantage of not needing special approval by any church judicatory. Indeed, such approval may be a long time coming if it ever comes about and will need much more preliminary study than this volume can provide. Still, much good can come from drawing attention by sermons, workshops and other means to how children can act in a sacramental way in the church's present ministry and worship.

This proposal is made to the whole church—East and West, Catholic and Protestant—so it runs the risk of satisfying no one on matters of detail, but, again, the goal is only to make the proposal and expect that the details of a formal doctrine and sacramental practice will be worked out by each part of the Christian family in an appropriate way.

Each of the seven kinds of ministry, associated with the seven classical sacraments will now be discussed to suggest in a preliminary way what can be done to re-frame each rite to bring children more into the foreground as a means of grace.

Holy Baptism

Baptism has been practiced by Christians since the first century and shows by immersion, pouring, or sprinkling with water that God adopts us as his children and includes us in Christ's body, the church. It is a symbol of salvation and marks an entry into the mystery of that process as well as into the community committed to making that process known and available to all.

During the baptism of children the congregation participates at least by watching in the holding, the touching, the pouring or entering of the water, and the words of the sacramental act itself. The baptized children concentrate and communicate grace as they are baptized into the promise of new life.

After the baptism in many parishes the worship leaders carry the infant or accompany older children around the congregation to introduce the newly baptized person to the community and affirm the baptismal promises made. What needs new or additional emphasis is that the children also bless the congregation as they move through the community. You can see this in the people's faces as the child comes close to them. The sermon of the day and classes about baptism need to speak more directly about this so the congregation can be more sensitive to the nonverbal communication of grace that the child embodies and communicates to the congregation.

There is another dimension to the welcoming of the newly baptized that is not often spoken about. Jesus said that if we welcome these little ones, then we also welcome him and the One who sent him. This saying, attested to in all three Synoptic Gospels (Matthew 18:5, Mark 9:37, Luke 9:48), makes it explicit that welcoming children identifies them as a means of grace for knowing God. They not only bless the congregation as they move through it but they reveal God as they are welcomed.

Holy Communion

Over the centuries there has been a great deal of discussion about when it is appropriate for children to receive communion. This discussion has distracted adults from something much more fundamental. Holy Communion is a mystery, so reaching the age of reason "to understand it" is at least of questionable value. A mystery is known by participating in it and children are much better at that than adults. For example, when babies are brought to the rail for communion (or when the elements are brought to them with the rest of the congregation) they are often being held. For a time they watch what happens from the safety of the person holding them. They participate vicariously. A moment will come, however, when they will reach out. To refuse them at this critical time is to say nonverbally that they are not part of the family, even if they are baptized. Their bodies will remember what our actions deny.

To deny children Holy Communion when they reach out for it goes against everything that Christ stood for when he invited the little ones to come to him to be blessed, despite the disciples' objections. The story of inviting the little ones to come to him is told in all three Synoptic Gospels and brings children into the foreground in this rite (Matthew 19:13–15, Mark 10:13–16, Luke 18:15–17). This story also signals that children are a means of grace for the adults to learn from, as the disciples needed to learn from Jesus' parable of action.

Many in the Christian family consider baptism and communion to be the only sacraments. There is, however, a long tradition of five additional rites. Some denominations continue this tradition and others have moved away from it. An Anglican compromise calls these five acts "sacramental rites" rather than sacraments. These five kinds of spiritual practice have to do with confirmation, ordination, holy matrimony, reconciliation of a penitent, and healing. Most Christians can agree that these actions are important and perhaps fundamental to the church's identity and ministry in whatever language they are referred to or form they take. Each of these rites will now be considered in turn.

Confirmation

Confirmation did not exist before the third century as a sacramental practice separate from baptism and it did not become a regular practice until after the fifth century. The apostles and then bishops in patristic times practiced the laying on of hands and meant by this something about the descent of the Holy Spirit, such as happened to the apostles at Pentecost. This "descent" continues to this day, but Joseph Martos has observed that there are no parallels in other world religions to this rite. There are rituals of initiation, transition, and intensification in other religious, however, and the present rite has something of all of these elements in it (Martos 1982, 207).

The laying on of hands to confirm infant baptism or to receive a person from another part of the Christian family is practiced in various forms throughout the church, but what is revealed by children in this symbolic act? This rite does not seem to refer to or involve them at all!

Children are present in the congregation during this rite and act as challenges to those confirmed and those looking on in three ways. First, the young people being confirmed are no longer children, so they are challenged by what it means to be spiritually mature. Jesus spoke of spiritual maturity as becoming like a child. Is becoming child-like one of their conscious goals? How will they do that? Will they move toward the children in the congregation now that they are no longer children? They will need to be conscious of this challenge and go out of their way to be near children. This is especially true during adolescence when children are likely to be considered distractions to most of what young people want to do and in addition they remind them of the developmental period they have just left behind and hold somewhat in contempt.

Second, children also challenge the adults looking on at confirmation to ask themselves whether or not they have properly prepared the young people involved for a mature life in the church. Have they helped these young people develop an inner working model of the classical Christian language system before they entered adolescence? Can the confirmands think in Christian terms about the new identity they are struggling to develop as young people? Can they discuss the meaning of life and death with their friends in an intelligent and informed Christian way? Do they know how to think about and make wise ethical decisions to lead a Christian life? Proper preparation for confirmation and the continuing support and education during adolescence is especially important today because our culture does not support the learning and creative use of the Christian language system. Many in our society do not understand how Christian language works or even consider it important to know. What is most important, however, is whether the young people being confirmed are able to identify the movement of grace within them and in the world around them so they can be co-creators with God. Much was promised at baptism. Have the promises been kept?

Third, now that the confirmed young people are no longer children, they need to be challenged to help prepare the children of the congregation for their confirmation and engage in the other tasks that support the congregation. Will they become teachers in the church school? Will they become mentors to the children who are in the communicants' class? Will they help with worship? What will they do that is real to help the general life of the congregation? These three challenges are made by children merely by being present in the congregation. It is, therefore, a good idea to have all the children stand at some point when the young people are being confirmed and to preach about the challenges they make by their presence at this time.

Ordination

All religions have leaders who perform rituals and are sometimes thought of as symbols and bearers of symbols. In the early years of the Christian religion the only priests recognized were the Jewish temple priests. As time passed, Christians began to think of Jesus' death as a sacrifice, like the sacrifices of animals that had taken place in the temple in Jerusalem. By about the middle of the third century those who presided at the communion table began to be thought of as ordained. Today Christian clergy are often thought of in a broad way as those who share in a life of service. In a sense all Christians are set apart to be symbols and bearers of symbols, but it is still helpful to have those who act formally as leaders identified by some kind of liturgical act.

The rite of ordination sets people apart and designates them as leaders in the community. The rite intensifies the sense of being servant leaders and asks for God's help to carry out this vocation through Christ and by the grace of the Holy Spirit. The laying on of hands is the gesture that focuses all of this meaning in one act and places the leader in a historical line of leaders going back to Jesus and the disciples.

The relationship between leaders and children needs to be radically revised when children are considered to be sacraments. The rite of ordination needs to be broadened to include a spiritual practice that involves the sacrament of children on an equal basis with the other sacraments.

Observing the sacrament of children by church leaders is as important each week as providing leadership during the weekly worship celebrated in the church, baptizing and offering holy communion. Each priest, deacon, or bishop—all the ordained clergy by whatever name they are called and from whatever tradition they come—need to find a way to be with a child or a few children from the congregation and their families each week. This is when the leader listens to children, moves toward them with openness, and feels not only a connection with them but learns from them verbally and nonverbally.

This spiritual practice is not primarily to support and honor the children and their families, although it will do that. It is to benefit the spiritual leader. The practice of this rite will, no doubt, be avoided and discounted by some leaders for all sorts of reasons but those who depreciate it are the very ones who need it most. The greater the resistance to this larger interpretation of the responsibilities of ordination, the greater the need is for the one ordained to practice its wisdom.

Leaders need to welcome children to know God and they need to be like them to enter the kingdom. How can they lead without knowing God and the kingdom? The weekly practice of participating in the sacrament of children will bring the leader closer to children so that welcoming them and becoming like them will be more likely. The threat to the leader is that he or she cannot control what will happen in the meetings with children, so this will be called a "waste of time," or "unimportant" and be allowed to be scheduled out of the day to avoid it. This is understandable. In these meetings the sacramental children act like parables, which are always disturbing, but those who have the ears to hear will hear God speak in them. Perhaps, the most threatening part of meeting on a weekly basis with children for ordained clergy is that coming close to children can disrupt career plans and take one down paths unthinkable for the ambitious. Clearing the way for grace is not always comfortable. When the grace within connects with the grace in the world around one, life is full of God's surprises.

Holy Matrimony

There have been marriages in one form or another since prehistoric times. In the history of Christianity, marriage was always considered sacred in a broad way, but before the eleventh century there was no such formality as a Christian marriage. Even when Peter Lombard treated marriage as one of the seven sacraments in his *Sentences*, written some time between 1147 and 1150, there were still many theologians who had difficulty accepting this idea. The Lombard himself thought there was something different about this sacrament and wondered if it were really a means of grace like the others. After all, it involved financial arrangements and existed before the coming of Christ. Perhaps the most troubling aspect of it was that it involved sex. In the sixteenth century the Council of Trent re-affirmed the ritual for marriage and attempted to curb abuses, while the Protestants argued that marriage could not be a sacrament because it was not scriptural.

When the celebration and blessing of a marriage is reframed so that children move to the center of interest we find that they are already mentioned more in the rite than may have been noticed. The Episcopal Book of

Common Prayer, for example, is realistic about their presence in a marriage and treats them as a gift. In the opening paragraphs of The Celebration and Blessing of a Marriage the prayer book says that marriage is for "the procreation of children and their nurture in the knowledge and love of the Lord." This is re-affirmed in one of the prayers for the couple, which says "Bestow on them, if it is your will, the gift and heritage of children, and the grace to bring them up to know you, to love you, and to serve you. *Amen.*" This prayer is marked as optional. Perhaps this is because of sensitivity to those previously married or those who are too old to have children, but shouldn't it be prayed anyway? Perhaps, it should be prayed with even more awareness during the weddings of those who have been married before and those who marry later in life and may not expect children to be part of their life together. All marriages blessed and celebrated in the church need to be aware of the "gift and heritage of children" that is involved, even if it might be complicated. Why?

It has been noted many, many times in this book that Jesus said that welcoming children helps one welcome God and that one needs to become like a child to enter the kingdom. How can you do either if there are no children around to welcome or to show you how to be childlike? It has also been mentioned that Erik Erikson coined the term "generativity" to emphasize the need for people to mentor the next generation as one grows older. This helps move elders toward integrity and wisdom rather than self-absorption and despair. Both theology and developmental psychology, then, call for children to be moved into a more central role in the blessing and celebration of marriages for the good of all involved, including those who are older and/or previously married. The fact that this may take creativity to find an appropriate way to be accomplished is assumed.

The union of same-sex couples by whatever name it is called includes all the same issues about children mentioned above. How is the couple going to welcome children to know God or become like them to enter the kingdom if there are no children around? Like anyone else, gay couples need to face how they will avoid self-absorption and despair in old age and find ways to turn toward the next generation as mentors. Even if a committed relationship is honored and supported by a house blessing, which may be less than desired but still recognizes their love and the home in which it is nurtured, the question of children needs to be raised.

I realize that there are legal questions involved in the term "marriage" that need to be solved for committed gay couples. Much creativity and care is being applied to finding fair solutions in the legal realm. What is within the province of this book is to keep firmly focused on the centering of marriage around children. Many heterosexual *and* homosexual people will find this uncomfortable and a challenge, but all can see that this is important. We need not be distracted, then, by these challenges from acknowledging the important role of children in marriage.

How then can children as a means of grace be moved toward the middle of concern in the rite? Again, the homily can refer to this, but the most important time to bring this up is in the privacy of the counseling that takes place before the wedding, the house blessing, or some other liturgical practice. The main question is how children as a spiritual practice will be included in the life of the couple over the long term. The rite then is enlarged to include the counseling before the marriage and during the days that come after the wedding day. It is an important act of ministry to see that the involvement with the sacrament of children is discussed, planned for and incorporated into the richness of committed relationships.

Reconciliation

The rite called "The Reconciliation of a Penitent" in the Episcopal Book of Common Prayer is an example of the ministry of reconciliation that is exercised by Christian people for each other throughout the Christian family. People joke sometimes that "confession is good for the soul," but they are right. Still, this is only part of the classical Roman Catholic rite from which this tradition comes. The whole act of ministry includes confession, absolution from guilt, and the assignment of works of penitence. This is not far from what modern psychological therapy aspires to when it treats people and gives them assignments for short-term therapy to help free them from the demons that bind them.

In parts of the Christian family it is the priest who employs this rite and counsels people to be honest about their actions and motives. Absolution is pronounced on behalf of Christ and the church when people seriously try to make sense out of what has tied them in knots and look for ways to amend their lives in the future. This pattern of listening, forgiveness, and support for an amended life, however, is an act of ministry that all Christians can and should provide for one another.

Reconciliation breaks the cycle of revenge as an unworkable way to deal with the destructive acts among us. It provides a way for people to become creative in constructive ways. Reconciliation is practiced informally among all Christians, but when it is practiced formally in the confessional setting or in public worship, where do the children fit in?

When people listen to children with care they hear that they are greatly concerned about what is fair. "That's not fair," is a shout often heard on playgrounds and in homes. This cry becomes sacramental when children achieve reconciliation without guile. "I'm sorry," is not heard as much as "That's not fair," because children need to be taught how to say, "I'm sorry," *and mean it* when they have wronged someone. They also need to learn to decide if they can forgive when they are the one who has been wronged to complete the process of reconciliation. One of the most important things that children can learn during early, middle, and late childhood is how to pause when relationships have been broken and problem-solve.

Wise teachers spend a lot of time showing children the rite of reconciliation, although they may never have heard of it. Teachers say things like: "Use words. Don't hit." "Say you're sorry." "No, stand there and look at each other." "When someone says she's sorry it's not over. The other person needs to say, 'That's okay.'" "You have to say 'okay' and mean it. Then it is over." "Now let's problem-solve so this won't happen again."

The rite of reconciliation needs to be enlarged to include what the children can teach as well as teaching them what they need to know about reconciliation. Seeing children become reconciled teaches adults that this is possible and miraculous. To see that, however, the congregation needs to be reminded to do everything in their power to foster the teaching of this process to children. Teaching this and seeing this take place among children, both communicate grace and children are in the middle of it.

For children (and probably adults as well) the action concerning reconciliation needs to be as close to the breakdown as possible to make the teaching meaningful. Children need mentors who do more than talk about this. Of course, sermons concerning this critical human interaction need to be preached and workshops need to be held but spiritual leaders and congregations need to become directly involved in schools and other settings where there are children so this can be taught directly and strongly supported by the action of the Christian community.

Reconciliation is the only way forward for graceful living, but many congregations and denominations that should be leading the way are involved in endless recriminations. When church people are not at peace with their neighbors they cannot show the way to an aching world. The sacrament of children is desecrated when congregations and their leaders, who should know better, work for division instead of reconciliation. Mother church needs to be a safe place that is consistently warm, supportive, and attuned with children so they and adults can move forward together toward a better life. This takes a kind of toughness and tenderness that results in speaking the truth in love, and that matters.

Anointing

The rite of anointing involves oil, at least in some traditions, and touching to communicate God's grace. The gestures and words compress all that science and theology can provide into a simple but intense act. It does not dismiss either. It intensifies, supports, and gives them focus. When children are moved more to the center of this rite, their ability to touch, to hug, to love, and to feel honest sorrow can be better acknowledged as they join with the adults at the edge of existence to do what cannot be said. Children can be a means of grace when there is sickness and when there is death by their very presence and touching.

The presence of children when people are sick or dying is sometimes acknowledged by adults as being "good medicine." This is true but it needs more formal acknowledgment by inviting children to visit the sick with their parents, so they can become experienced with and more equal partners in such situations. This is not exploiting them. Their presence both receives and gives energy in manifold ways.

The ultimate limits to life are absolutely tangible when people are sick or dying. Children receive by being there because they need to know that the limits to life are real, but they are also a means of grace because they are not overwhelmed by death. They are curious, need support and are able to care about the sick and dying in an uncomplicated way that is good for sad and weary adults to see. A child may go out and pick flowers and bring them to the bedside, as our daughter did when her grandmother was dying, or help to make a favorite food and bring small portions to the sick and dying and help them enjoy it by their company and love, as three generations did when the beautiful Thea, my wife, was dying.

Children also receive from being in these boundary situations because they learn what the ultimate boundaries are so they can take them into consideration as they plan their lives and make ethical decisions, which also deepens their ability to be a means of grace. Too often ethics is practiced within the limits of one's culture instead of the ultimate environment. Children need to know better and keep the existential limits of all people in mind, but to know this takes experience. This is why they need to know sickness and death and be supported by wise adults as they touch the edges of existence. What we all need to know is that at the edge of life we are all children, dependent on each other and God.

The actual experience of the ultimate environment is very important in our culture because television teaches children that sickness and death ought to be responded to with flip, sarcastic, or overly sentimental and contrived responses. Both television and video games also imply that death does not involve suffering or finality, despite the continuous and graphic portrayals of violence on the flat screen. This is because pressing a button starts the game over again or changing the channel relieves the anxiety. Illness is hard and death is final. This is why we are called to love and help one another. Children intuit this and know what to do when they encounter reality instead of "virtual reality." What they need is to be completely recognized as one of those who cares and can help care.

When children show that they care and are sad, they sometimes help adults to grieve. In an opposite way they help adults who are anxious and confused about the sickness or dying of a loved one. When they are present the adults need to bear up and be leaders for the children (and for each other). This empowerment by the children's weakness is unexpected, perhaps, but it is powerful.

When the church's rituals decay, their structure is lost, so we do not know what to do or say when science can no longer help us. Children and adults can't live without rituals in such situations, so children ask, "What are we supposed to do now?" This question challenges adults to provide the leadership and structure for the pastoral support that is so desperately needed at such times. Again, weakness can give strength if we know what to do together as we make our way along life's boundaries.

Looking back over these seven significant turning points in the life and death of human beings, it is clear that children need to be more centrally involved in these ministries, even if there is no agreement about their sacramental nature. They need to be part of these significant times to show as much as they are shown. This does not mean that children should be exploited but that the generations need to walk to the edge of life together for everyone's benefit.

Conclusion

This book shows that, once again, the "loyal and uncritical repetition of formulae," is always "inadequate," as Rowan Williams has observed. Jesus' parabolic and high view of children needs to be made "strange" once more, so it can be read "freshly and truthfully from one generation to another" (Williams 2001, 236). What Jesus said about children is more nuanced than a single view can capture and more helpful to meet the needs of the church today than has been previously realized.

This book has only pointed in the direction of a formal doctrine of children. It has not provided the details nor a program for reform. It is in a hurry, so it can only *propose* a formal doctrine and its related spiritual practice. Even that, however, is complicated, so the question still needs to be asked, "Where shall we begin?" The answer is really quite simple. I suggest that you try an experiment to see if this book is on the right track. You can then draw your own conclusions.

To perform this experiment you will not need to waste any energy getting permission from leading persons or committees in your denomination or local church. This experiment needs no money to perform. No schedule needs to be set up or coordinated. It does not involve any of the so-called "great" or "hot-button" issues being debated in the church today. What does it involve? Let me tell you a story about that and then the rest is up to you.

A mother came up to me after church. She was determined to get my attention. As the other people drifted away, she remained and finally said firmly that there was something I needed to know.

"Yes?"

"Our daughter saw you going by before church. You didn't notice us. You were on your way to the sacristy."

"That *is* a busy time."

"Here is what you need to know. Our daughter said, "There goes the man who is always glad to see me.""

There was a lot packed into the child's comment and, like in the story that began this book, a prior relationship was involved. I had invited the children to come with their parents to sit on the floor at the foot of the chancel steps each Sunday after the nine o'clock family service at Christ Church Cathedral in downtown Houston. We gathered for at most ten minutes while I told them a story. The stories were about such things as the book on the eagle's back (the open Bible on the lectern), why there are three steps to climb when you go into the chancel, or why the place they were sitting in was called "the crossing." These stories helped the children learn how "to read" the symbolic nature of the church where they worshipped. This was also important because it showed the parents how to talk to their children about the church and what to look at and talk about when they showed them around, which was also encouraged and supported.

The mother's urgent message made me realize that I began each Sunday at the crossing by looking slowly around the group gathered, as a smile formed, and I said, "I'm glad to see you." It was true. I was glad to see them and they knew it.

What if *you* were remembered by the children of your church as the person who is always glad to see them? What if each time you saw a child, you stopped, focused on the child (while infinity forms around you), and said "I'm glad to see you"?

It may no longer be possible for you to get down to the child's eye level to say this, but you can always make a profound bow or offer to shake hands. This will take a minute at most. Stop, focus, speak. You may not even mean what you say at first, but if you do this, one day you will mean it, because the children will help you, and when you do mean these words the children will know it.

As your custom spreads throughout the congregation and people become warm, consistent, and attuned to children—I predict that your church will change and, as Jesus said, you will slowly over time discover that when you welcome a child you welcome him and the One who sent him. Such a fundamental discovery will enrich everything you do and show the way into the kingdom for you and the congregation. The congregation will become a healthy place, where unhealthy people can come to heal and all will thrive. The church will no longer be a place of ambivalence, ambiguity, or indifference toward anyone. It will be a place of grace.

REFERENCES

Abelard and Heloise. 2003 (Revised Edition). *The Letters of Abelard and Heloise,* Translated and Introduction by Betty Radice. London: Penguin Books.

Angelus Silesius. 1986. *The Cherubinic Wanderer.* The Classics of Western Spirituality. New York: Paulist Press.

Aquinas, Thomas. 2003. *On Evil.* Translated by Richard Regan and edited with an Introduction and Notes by Brian Davies. Oxford University Press.

Anderson, Joan. 2004. *A Walk on the Beach.* New York: Broadway Books.

Aries, Philippe. 1962. (French 1950) *Centuries of Childhood.*

Artz, Frederick B. 1958, Third Edition. *The Mind of the Middle Ages: An Historical Survey: A.D. 200–1500.* New York: Alfred A. Knopf.

Atkinson, Clarissa W. 2001. "'Wonderful Affection': Seventeenth-Century Missionaries to New France on Children and Childhood" in *The Child in Christian Thought.* Minneapolis, Minnesota: William B. Eerdmans.

Augustine. 1984. *Augustine of Hippo: Selected Writings* trans. and intro. by Mary T. Clark. New York: Paulist Press.

_____. 1991. *Confessions.* Translated by Henry Chadwick. Oxford: Oxford University Press.

Bakke, O. M. 2005. *When Children Became People: The Birth of Childhood in Early Christianity.* Minneapolis, Minnesota: Fortress Press.

Barth, Karl. 1959. German 1957. *Christmas.* Edinburgh: Oliver and Boyd.

_____. 1960. *Anselm: Fides Quaerens Intellectum.* Richmond, Virginia: John Knox Press.

Bendroth, Margaret. 2001. "Horace Bushnell's Christian Nurture" in *The Child in Christian Thought.* Minneapolis, Minnesota: William B. Eerdmans.

Berryman, Jerome W. ed., Fowler, James W., and Keen, Sam. 1978, 1985 second edition. *Life Maps: Conversations on the Journey of Faith.* Waco, Texas: Word Press.

_____. 1991. *Godly Play: A Way of Religious Education.* San Francisco: HarperSanFrancisco.

_____. 2002. *The Complete Guide to Godly Play,* Volume 1 of 8 Volumes, 2002–2009. Denver, Colorado: Morehouse.

_____. 2004. "Children and Mature Spirituality" in *Sewanee Theological Review,* Christmas 2004, Volume 48:1, pp. 17–36.

_____. 2005. "Playful Orthodoxy: Reconnecting Religion and Creativity by Education" in *Sewanee Theological Review,* Volume 48:4, pp. 437–454.

_____. 2007. "Children and Christian Theology: A New/Old Genre." *Religious Studies Review,* Vol. 33, No. 2 (April 2007), pp. 103–111.

_____. 2009. *Teaching Godly Play: How To Mentor the Spiritual Development of Children.* Second Edition, Revised and Expanded. Denver, Colorado: Morehouse.

Boehme, Jacob. 1978. *The Way of Christ.* New York: Paulist Press. The Classics of Western Spirituality.

Boethius. 1999. *The Consolation of Philosophy.* London: Penguin Books.

Bouwsma, William J. 1988. *John Calvin: A Sixteenth Century Portrait.* Oxford: Oxford University Press.

Bradt, Kevin M., SJ. 1997. *Story As a Way of Knowing.* Kansas City: Sheed & Ward.

Brann, Eva T. H. 1991. *The World of the Imagination: Sum and Substance.* Lanham, Maryland: Rowman and Littlefield Publishers

Brekus, Catherine A, 2001. "Children of Wrath, Children of Grace" in *The Child in Christian Thought.* Edited by Marcia J. Bunge. Minneapolis, Minnesota: William B. Eerdmans.

Brown, Peter. 1969. *Augustine of Hippo.* Berkeley, California: University of California Press.

Bunge, Marcia J, Ed. 2001. *The Child in Christian Thought.* Grand Rapids, Michigan: Wm. B. Eerdmans Publishing Co.

_____. General Editor. 2008. *The Child in the Bible.* Grand Rapids, Michigan: William B. Eerdmans Publishing Company.

Bunyan, John. 2003. *The Pilgrim's Progress.* Oxford: Oxford University Press, World Classics New Edition.

Burge, James. 2003. *Heloise and Abelard: A New Biography.* New York: HarperCollins.

Burns, J. Patout. 1981. *Theological Anthropology.* Philadelphia: Fortress.

Bushnell, Horace. 1979. *Christian Nurture.* Grand Rapids, Michigan: Baker Book House.

Calvin, John. 1958. Calvin: Commentaries. Edited by Joseph Harooutunian. Library of Christian Classics. Philadelphia: Westminster Press.

_____. 1960. By John Calvin: The Heart of Calvin's Enduring Ideas...from his own Writings. Selected by Hugh T. Kerr. New York: Association Press.

_____. 2006. Institute of the Christian Religion. Edited by John T. McNeill and Translated and indexied by Ford Lewis Battles.. Library of Christian Classics. Louisville: WestminsterJohnKnox Press.

Caplan, Frank and Theresa. 1973. *The Power of Play.* New York: Anchor Press/Doubleday.

Capps, Donald. 1995. *The Child's Song: The Religious Abuse of Children.* Louisville, Kentucky: Westminster John Knox Press.

Caputo, John D. 1986. *The Mystical Element in Heidegger's Thought.* New York: Fordam University Press.

Crain, William. 2005. *Theories of Development: Concepts and Applications.* (Fifth Edition). Upper Saddle River, New Jersey: Pearson/Prentice Hall.

Carroll, John T. 2008. "What Then Will This Child Become," in *The Child in the Bible.* General Editor, Marcia J. Bunge. Grand Rapids, Michigan: William B. Eerdmans Publishing Co.

Casalis, Georges. 1964, French 1959. *Portrait of Karl Barth.* New

Chadwick, Henry. 1967. *The Early Church.* New York: Penguin.

_____. 1986. *Augustine.* Oxford: Oxford University Press.

Cheney, Mary A. 1880. *Life and Letters of Horace Bushnell.* New York: Harper and Brothers.

Chesterton, G.K. 1959. *Orthodoxy.* Garden City, New York: Image Books, A Division of Doubleday & Co.

Clark, Elizabeth A. 1991. "From Origenism to Pelagianism: Elusive Issues in an Ancient Debate." Princeton Seminary Bulletin. Vol. XII, No. 3. New Series, 1991.

Connor, James A. 2006. *Pascal's Wager: The Man Who Played Dice with God*. New York: HarperCollins.

Crossan, John Dominic. 1975. *The Dark Interval: Toward a Theology of Story*. Niles, Illinois: Argus Communications.

Crossan, John Dominic and Reed, Jonathan L. 2004. *In Search of Paul: How Jesus's Apostle Opposed Rome's Empire with God's Kingdom*. New York: HarperCollins.

Crouzel, Henri. 1989. *Origen: The Life and Thought of the First Great Theologian*. San Francisco: Harper and Row.

Csikszentmihalyi, Mihaly. 1975. *Beyond Boredom and Anxiety*. San Francisco: Jossey-Bass.

_____ and Isabella Selega Csikszentmihalyi, eds. 1992. *Optimal Experience: Psychological Studies of Flow in Consciousness*. Cambridge: Cambridge University Press. Paperback Edition.

_____. 1990. *Flow: The Psychology of Optimal Experience*. New York: HarperCollins.

_____. 1993. *The Evolving Self*. New York: HarperCollins.

_____. 1996. *Creativity: Flow and the Psychology of Discovery and Invention*. New York: HarperCollins.

Cunningham, Hugh. 1995. *Children and Childhood in Western Society Since 1500*. London: Longman.

Danielou, Jean. 1955. *Origen*. New York: Sheed and Ward.

Dante, Alighieri. 1975. *Dante Alighieri: The Divine Comedy, Paradiso*. Translated with a Commentary by Charles S. Singleton. Princeton: Princeton University Press. Bollingen Series LXXX.

Davies, Brian. 2003. "Introduction." In *On Evil*. Oxford: Oxford University Press.

Deacon, Terrence. *The Symbolic Species: The Co-Evolution of Language and the Brain*. New York: W.W. Norton, 1997.

DeVries, Dawn. 2001. "Be converted and become as little children" in *The Child in Christian Thought*. Edited by Marcia J. Bunge. Minneapolis, Minnesota: William B. Eerdmans.

Dowley, Tim. Editor. 2002. *Introduction to the History of Christianity*. Minneapolis, Minnesota: Fortress Press.

Edmonds, David and Eidinow, John. 2006. *Rousseau's Dog: Two Great Thinkers at War in the Age of Enlightenment*. New York: HarperCollins.

Edwards, Robert L. 1992. *Of Singular Genius of Singular Grace: A Biography of Horace Bushnell*. Cleveland, Ohio: The Pilgrim Press.

Egan, Harvey D. 1998. *Karl Rahner: Mystic of Everyday Life*. New York: The Crossroad Publishing Company.

Engelstein, Laura. 1999. *Castration and the Heavenly Kingdom*. Ithaca, New York: Cornell University Press.

Elkind, David. 2007. *The Power of Play: How Spontaneous, Imaginative Activities Lead To Happier, Healthier Children*. Cambridge, Massachusetts: Da Capo Press.

Erikson, Erik H. with Joan M. Erikson. 1997. *The Life Cycle Completed: Extended Version with New Chapters on the Ninth Stage of Development*. New York: W.W. Norton & Co.

Evans, G.R. 1989. *Saint Anselm of Canterbury*. New York: Continuum.

_____. 2001. "Anselm of Canterbury." In *The Medieval Theologians*. Edited by G.R. Evans. Oxford: Blackwell Publishing.

_____. 2007. Introduction in *The First Christian Theologians: An Introduction to Theology in the Early Church*. Edited by G.R. Evans. Oxford: Blackwell Publishing.

Freud, Sigmund. 1913. *The Basic Writings of Sigmund Freud*. Trans. and Intro. by A.A. Brill. New York: The Modern Library, Random House.

Gardner, Howard. 1993. *Creating Minds*. New York: HarperCollins.

Garvey, Catherine. 1977. *Play*. Cambridge, Massachusetts: Harvard University Press.

Gergen, Kenneth J. 1991. *The Saturated Self: Dilemmas of Identity in Contemporary Life*. New York: HarperCollins.

Gilson, Etienne. 1960, French 1948. *Heloise and Abelard*. Ann Arbor, Michigan: The University of Michigan Press.

Graham, W. Fred. 1978. *The Constructive Revolutionary John Calvin: His Socio-Economic Impact*. Atlanta: John Knox Press.

Greaves, Richard L. 1969. *John Bunyan*. Abingdon, Berkshire: Burgess and Son.

Gritsch, Eric W. 1982. *Born Againism: Perspectives on a Movement*. Philadelphia: Fortress Press.

Goleman, Daniel. 2006. *Emotional Intelligence*. New York: Bantam Books. Tenth Anniversary Edition.

_____. 2007. *Social Intelligence: The Revolutionary New Science of Human Relationships*. New York: Bantam Books. Paperback Edition.

Gundry, Judith M. 2008. "Children in the Gospel of Mark, with Special Attention to Jesus' Blessing of the Children (Mark 10:13–16) and the Purpose of Mark" in *The Child in the Bible*. Edited by Marcia J. Bunge. Grand Rapids, Michigan: William B. Eerdmans Publishing Company.

Harth, Erich. 1995. *The Creative Loop: How the Brain Makes a Mind*. New York: Addison-Wesley, Helix Books.

Hastings, Adrian; Mason, Alistair; and Pyper, Hugh, editors. 2000. *The Oxford Companion To Christian Thought*. Oxford: Oxford University Press.

Hattersley, Roy. 2003. *The Life of John Wesley: A Brand from the Burning*. New York: Random House.

Heitzenrater, Richard P. 2001. "John Wesley and Children" in *The Child in Christian Thought*. Grand Rapids, Michigan: William B. Eerdmans.

_____. 2003. *The Elusive Mr. Wesley* (Second Revised Edition). Nashville, Tennessee: Abingdon Press.

Herzog, Kristin. 2005. *Children and Our Global Future: Theological and Social Challenges*. Cleveland, Ohio: The Pilgrim Press.

Hesse, Hermann. 1956. *The Journey To The East*. New York: Picador.

_____. 1969. *The Glass Bead Game*. New York: Holt, Rinehart and Winston.

Heywood, Colin. 2001. *A History of Childhood*. Cambridge, UK: Polity Press in association with Blackwell Publishing Lit.

Higton, Mike. 2004. *Difficult Gospel: The Theology of Rowan Williams*. New York: Church Publishing Incorporated.

Hindley, Geoffrey. 2003. *The Crusades: A History of Armed Pilgrimage and Holy War*. New York: Carroll & Graf Publishers.

Hinsdale, Mary Ann. 2001. "Infinite Openness to the Infinite: Karl Rahner's Contribution to Modern Catholic Thought on the Child." in *The Child in Christian Thought*, ed. Marcia J. Bunge. Grand Rapids, Michigan: William B. Eerdmans.

Hodge, Charles. 1847. "Bushnell on Christian Nurture," in *Biblical Repertory and Princeton Review*. Princeton, New Jersey: Princeton Theological Seminary.

Hooker, Richard. 1888. *Laws of Ecclesiastical Polity*. London: George Routledge and Sons.

Huizinga, Johan. 1955. *Homo Ludens: A Study of the Play Element in Culture*. Boston: Beacon Press.

Hymans, Diane J. 1992. *The Role of Play in a Cultural-Linguistic Approach to Religion: Theoretical Implications for Education in the Faith Community*. DEd Dissertation. Richmond, Virginia: The Presbyterian School of Christian Education.

_____. 1996. "Let's Play: The Contribution of the Pretend Play of Children to Religious Education in a Pluralistic Context" in *Religious Education*. Vol. 91, No. 3. (Summer), pp. 368–381.

Jensen, David H. 2005. *Graced Vulnerability: A Theology of Childhood*. Cleveland, Ohio: The Pilgrim Press.

Jones, Ernest. 1963. *The Life and Work of Sigmund Freud*. Edited and abridged by Lionel Trilling and Steven Markus. New York: Basic Books, Anchor Books edition.

Karen, Robert. 1998. *Becoming Attached: First Relationships and How They Shape Our Capacity to Love*. Oxford: Oxford University Press, 1998.

Kearney, Richard. 1988. *The Wake of Imagination*. Minneapolis: University of Minnesota Press.

Keen, Sam. 1969. *Apology for Wonder*. New York: Harper and Row.

Kelber, Werner. 1983. *The Oral and the Written Gospel*. Philadelphia: Fortress Press.

Kelly, J.N.D. 1975. *Jerome: His Life, Writings, and Controversies*. New York: Harper and Row.

_____. 1995. *Goldenmouth: The Story of John Chrysostrom: Ascetic, Preacher, Bishop. Ithaca*, New York: Cornell University Press.

Kirkpatrick, Lee A. 2005. *Attachment, Evolution, and the Psychology of Religion*. London: The Guilford Press.

Kress, Robert. 1982. *A Rahner Handbook*. Atlanta, Georgia: John Knox Press.

Kung, Hans. 2002. *Great Christian Thinkers: Paul, Origen, Augustine, Aquinas, Luther, Schleiermacher, Barth*. New York: Continuum.

LaCugna, Catherine Mowry. *God for Us: The Trinity and Christian Life*. San Francisco: HarperCollins, 1993.

Lasch, Christopher. 1991. *The Culture of Narcissism: American Life in An Age of Diminishing Expectations.* New York: W.W. Norton.

Lewis, Amini and Lannon. 2000. *A General Theory of Love.* New York: Random House.

Lindbeck, George A. 1984. *The Nature of Doctrine: Religion and Theology in a Postliberal Age.* Philadelphia: The Westminster Press.

Lindberg, Carter. 2008. *Love: A Brief History Through Western Christianity.* Oxford: Blackwell Publishing.

Lohse, Bernard. 1985. *A Short History of Christian Doctrine from the First Century to the Present*, Revised American Edition. Philadelphia: Fortress Press.

Luther, Martin. 1948. *The Martin Luther Christmas Book.* Translated and arranged by Roland H. Bainton. Philadelphia: Muhlenberg Press.

Marris, Peter. 1991. "The Social Construction of Uncertainty: in *Attachment Across the Life Cycle*, Ed. Parkes, C.M., Hinde, J.S., and Marris P. London: Routledge.

Marsden, George M. 2003. *Jonathan Edwards: A Life.* New Haven: Yale University Press.

Martos, Joseph. 1982. *Doors to the Sacred: A Historical Introduction to Sacraments in the Catholic Church.* New York: Image Books.

Marty, Martin E. 2007. *The Mystery of the Child.* Grand Rapids, Michigan: Wm. B. Eerdman's.

Mayer, Wendy and Allen, Pauline. 2000. *John Chrysostom.* London and New York: Routledge.

Menzies, Allan. 1965. Editor. *The Ante-Nicene Fathers*, Volume X. Grand Rapids, Michigan: Wm. B. Eerdmans Publishing Company.

Mercer, Joyce Ann. 2005. *Welcoming Children: A Practical Theology of Childhood.* St. Louis, Missouri: Chalice Press.

Miles, Margaret R. 1985. *Image as Insight: Visual Understanding in Western Christianity and Secular Culture.* Boston: Beacon Press.

Miller, David L. 1973. *Gods and Games: Toward a Theology of Play.* New York: Harper and Row, Harper Colophon Books.

Miller-McLemore, Bonnie J. 2003. *Let the Children Come: Reimagining Childhood from a Christian Perspective.* San Francisco: Jossey-Bass.

_____. 2007. *In the Midst of Chaos: Caring for Children as Spiritual Practice.* San Francisco: Jossey-Bass.

Moltmann, Jurgen. 1972. *Theology of Play.* New York: Harper and Row.

Muller, Peter. 1992. *In der Mitte der Gemeinde: Kinder Im Neuen Testament.* Neukirchenr.

Mullin, Robert Bruce. 2002. *The Puritan as Yankee: A Life of Horace Bushnell.* Grand Rapids, Michigan: William B. Eerdmans Publishing Co.

Nicholl, Charles. 2004. *Leonardo da Vinci: Flights of the Mind.* New York: Viking.

Nicholas of Cusa. 1997. *Nicholas of Cusa: Selected Spiritual Writings.* The Classics of Western Spirituality. New York: Paulist Press.

Nicolson, Adam. 2003. *God's Secretaries: The Making of the King James Bible.* New York: HarperCollins.

Oberman, Heiko A. 1992. *Luther: Man Between God and the Devil.* New York: Image Books, Doubleday.

O'Donnell, James J. 2006. *Augustine.* New York: Harper Perennial.

O'Connell, Marvin R. 1997. *Blaise Pascal: Reasons of the Heart.* Grand Rapids, Michigan: Eerdmans.

Origen. 1979. *An Ehortation to Martyrdom, Prayer, and Selected Works.* New York: Paulist Press. The Classics of Western Spirituality.

Osborn, Eric. 2005. *Irenaeus of Lyons.* Cambridge: Cambridge University Press. First Paperback Version.

Osiek, Carolyn, Balch, David L. 1997. *Families in the New Testament World.* Louisville, Kentucky: Westminister John Knox Press.

Ozment, Steven. 2001. *Ancestors: The Loving Family in Old Europe.* Cambridge, Massachusetts.: Harvard University Press.

Panksepp, Jaak. 1998. *Affective Neuroscience: The Foundations of Human and Animal Emotions.* Oxford: Oxford University Press.

Perdue, Leo G., Blenkinsopp, Joseph, Collins, John J., Meyers, Carol. 1997. *Families in Ancient Israel.* Lousisville, Kentucky: John Knox Press.

Pascal, Blaise. 1995. *Pensees.* (revised edition) London: Penguin Books.

Pitkin, Barbara. 2001. "The Heritage of the Lord" in *The Child in Christian Thought.* Editor Marcia J. Bunge. Minneapolis, Minnesota: William B. Eerdmans.

Rack, H. 2002. *Reasonable Enthusiast: John Wesley and the Rise of Methodism* (revised edition.) Nashville, Tennessee: Abingdon.

Rahner, Hugo SJ. 1965. *Man at Play or Did You Ever Practise Eutrapelia?* London: Burns and Oates.

Rahner, Karl SJ. 1971. "Ideas for a Theology of Childhood" in *Theological Investigations,* Volume VIII:33–50. New York: Herder and Herder.

_____. 1985. *I Remember*: An Autobiographical Interview. New York: Crossroad.

Redondi, Pietro. 1987. *Galileo Heretic.* Princeton: Princeton University Press.

Reed, Bruce. 1978. *The Dynamics of Religion: Process and Movement in Christian Churches.* London: Darton, Longman and Todd.

Rees, B. R. 1988. *Pelagius: A Reluctant Heretic.* Woodbridge, Suffolk, England: Boydell Press.

Richard of St. Victor. 1979. *Richard of St. Victor: The Twelve Patriarchs, The Mystical Art, Book Three of the Trinity.* The Classics of Western Spirituality. New York: Paulist Press.

Riley-Smith, Jonathan. 1987. *The Crusades: A Short History.* New Haven: Yale University Press.

Rist, John. 2001. "Augustine of Hippo." In *The Medieval Theologians,* Ed. G. R. Evans. Oxford: Blackwell Publishing.

Robb, Peter. 1998. *M the Man who Became Caravaggio.* New York: Hanry Holt and Company, Picador.

Rorem, Paul. 2001. "Augustine, the Medieval Theologians, and the Reformation." In *The Medieval Theologians,* Ed. G.R. Evans. Oxford: Blackwell Publishing.

Rousseau, Jean-Jacques. 1979. *Emile on Education.* Translated by Allan Bloom. New York: Basic Books.

Schleiermacher, Friedrich. 1990. *Christmas Eve: Dialogue on the Incarnation.* Translated with Introduction and Notes by Terrence N. Tice. Lewiston, New York: The Edwin Mellen Press, San Francisco: EM Texts. This is a reprint of the John Knox 1967 translation.

_____. 1991. *Friedrich Schleiermacher: Pioneer of Modern Theology.* Ed. Keith W. Clements. Minneapolis: Fortress Press.

Secor, Philip B. 1999. *Richard Hooker: Prophet of Anglicanism.* Tunbridge Wells, Kent: Burns and Oats.

Secor, Philip B. and Gibbs, Lee W. 2005. *The Wisdom of Richard Hooker: Selections from Hooker's Writings with Topical Index.* Bloomington, Indiana: Authorhouse.

Selinger, Suzanne. 1998. *Charlotte von Kirschbaum and Karl Barth: A Study in Biography and the History of Theology.* University Park, Pennsylvania: Pennsylvania State University Press.

Serrano, Miguel. 1968. *C.G. Jung & Hermann Hesse: A Record of Two Friendships.* New York: Schocken Books. Paperback Edition.

Shortt, Rupert. 2003. *Rowan Williams: An Introduction.* Harrisburg, Pennsylvania: Morehouse Publishing, A Continuum Imprint.

Singer, Irving. 1984. *The Nature of Love: Plato to Luther* (Second Edition). Chicago: The University of Chicago Press.

_____. 1984. *The Nature of Love: Courtly and Romantic.* Chicago: The University of Chicago Press.

_____. 1987. *The Nature of Love: The Modern World.* Chicago: The University of Chicago Press.

Snow, Edward. 1997. *Inside Bruegel: The Play of Images in Children's Games.* New York: North Point Press, Farrar, Straus and Giroux.

Southern, R.W. 1990. *Saint Anselm: A Portrait in a Landscape.* Cambridge: Cambridge University Press.

Spariosu, M. 1989. *Dionysus Reborn: Play and the Aesthetic Dimension in Modern Philosophical and Scientific Discourse.* Ithaca, New York: Cornell University Press.

Stern, Fritz, Ed. 1956. *The Varieties of History.* New York: Meridian Books.

Stiegman, Emero. 2001. "Bernard of Clairvaux, William of St. Thierry, the Victorines." In *The Medieval Theologians* edited by G.R. Evans. Oxford: Blackwell Publishing.

Stortz, Martha Ellen. 2001. "Where or When was your Servant Innocent?" in *The Child in Christian Thought.* Marcia J. Bunge, Editor. Minneapolis, Minnesota: William B. Eerdmans.

Strohl, Jane E. 2001. "The Child in Luther's Theology: "For What Purpose Do We Older Folks Exist, Other Than to Care for . . . the Young" in *The Child in Christian Thought.* Minneapolis, Minnesota: William B. Eerdmans.

Sutton-Smith, Brian. 1997. *The Ambiguity of Play.* Cambridge, Massachusetts: Harvard University Press.

Thompson, Marianne Meye. 2008. "Children in the Gospel of John" in *The Child in the Bible.* General Editor, Marcia J. Bunge. Grand Rapids, Michigan: William B. Eerdmans Publishing Co.

Tilley, Terrence W. 1990. *Story Theology.* Collegeville, Minnesota: The Liturgical Press.

Tomkins, Stephen. 2003. *John Wesley: A Bbiography*. Grand Rapids, Michigan: William B. Eerdmans Publishing Co.

Traina, Cristina L.H. 2001. "A Person in the Making: Thomas Aquinas on Children and Childhood" in *The Child in Christian Thought*. Minneapolis, Minnesota: William B. Eerdmans.

Untermeyer, Louis (editor). 1960. *The Britannica Library of Great American Writing*. Chicago: Britannica Press

Walker, Williston. 1959. *A History of the Christian Church (Revised Edition)*. New York: Charles Scribner's Sons.

Warnock, Mary. 1978. *Imagination*. Berkeley: University of California Press. Paperback Edition.

Weber, Hans-Ruedi. 1944. *Jesus and the Children*. Loveland, Ohio: Treehaus Communications.

Weisheipl, James A. 1974. *Friar Thomas D'Aquino: His Life, Thought, and Work*. Garden City, New York: Doubleday.

Werpehowski, William. 2001. "Reading Karl Barth on Children" in *The Child in Christian Thought*, Marcia J. Bunge (ed). Grand Rapids, Michigan: William B. Eerdmans Publishing Co.

Williams, Rowan. 2000. *Lost Icons: Reflections on Cultural Bereavement*. New York: Morehouse Publishing.

_____. 2001. *Arius: Heresy and Tradition*. Grand Rapids/ Cambridge: Wm. B. Eerdmans Publishing Co.

_____. 2002. *Writing in the Dust: After September 11th*. Grand Rapids, Michigan: William B. Eerdmans Publishing Company.

_____. 2004. "Origin." In *The First Christian Theologians*. G.R. Evans Editor. Oxford: Blackwell Publishing.

_____. 2005. *Why Study the Past?: The Quest for the Historical Church*. Grand Rapids, Michigan: William B. Eerdmans Publishing Company.

Wood, Diana, ed. 1994. *The Church and Childhood*. Volume 31, Studies in Church History. Oxford: Blackwell Publishers.

Zeller, Bernhard. 1971. *Portrait of Hesse*. New York: Herder and Herder.

Ziolkowski, Theodore. 1965. *The Novels of Hermann Hesse: A Study in Theme and Structure*. Princeton: Princeton University Press.

_____. 1969. "Forward" in *The Glass Bead Game*. New York: Holt, Rinehart, and Winston.

_____. 1972. *Fictional Trans-figurations of Jesus*. Princeton New Jersey: Princeton University Press.

INDEX

A

Abelard, Peter, 64, 73–76, 98, 105, 202, 210
    Origen and, 74–75
    Yes and No (Sic et Non), 75

Acts
    2:1-4   27
    4:33   213

Address to the Christian Nobility of the German Nation (Luther), 94

Against the Enemies of Monasticism (Chrysostom), 49

Ainsworth, Mary, 216, 218

Also a Mother: Work and Family as Theological Dilemma (Miller-McLemore), 174

ambiguity, 24–25, 197–226

The Ambiguity of Play (Sutton-Smith), 191

ambivalence, 24–25, 197–226

Amini, Fari, *A General Theory of Love*, 237

Anderson, Joan, *A Walk on the Beach*, 186

Angelus Silesius. *See* Scheffler, Johann

anointing, 253–54

Anselm, 64, 70–73, 202
    Anselm: Fides Quarens Intellectum (Barth), 155, 157
    Cur Deus Homo (Why the God-Man?), 71
    Monologion, 71
    Proslogion, 72

Anselm: Fides Quarens Intellectum (Barth), 155, 157

"Aphorisms on Pedagogy" (Schleiermacher), 147

Apology (Justin Martyr), 36

Apology for Wonder (Keen), 187

Aristotle, 77–78, 118, 130, 148

Arius: Heresy and Tradition (Williams), 164

attachment, 213, 215–21, 223, 237–38

Augustine (saint), 28, 38–39, 54–60, 77–78, 100, 110–11, 202–3, 208
    Augustinus (Jansen), 128
    Calvin and, 181
    Christian Teaching, 58
    Confessions, 32, 55–57, 60
    Free Choice of the Will, 58
    Luther and, 93–94
    On the Trinity, 58
    Pelagius and, 51–54
    The Teacher, 58–59

Augustinus (Jansen), 128

Averroes, 77

B

The Babylonian Captivity of the Church (Luther), 94

Bakke, O. M., 36
    When Children Become People, 206–7

baptism, 51, 109, 131, 182, 245
    On the Merits and Remission of Sin and the Baptism of Infants (Pelagius), 53

Barmen Declaration, 7, 155

Barth, Karl, 147, 153–58, 180, 203
    Anselm: Fides Quarens Intellectum, 155, 157
    Christmas, 156
    Church Dogmatics, 7, 155–56, 158, 178

Becoming Attached: First Relationships and How They Shape Our Capacity to Love (Karen), 216, 223

Bendroth, Margaret, 152

Bernanos, Georges, *The Diary of a Country Priest*, 186

Berryman, Jerome W,
    The Complete Guide to Godly Play, 171

Godly Play, 171, 220
   Life Maps, 187
   Teaching Godly Play, 171

Beyond Boredom and Anxiety
   (Csikszentmihalyi), 239

biology
   creative process and, 237–39, 241
   grace and, 226
   mystical experience and, 79
   sociobiology, 219–20, 232

"A Bit of Theology" (Hesse), 6–7, 236

Bleuler, Eugen, 25

Boehme, Jacob, 119–22, 129, 140, 202
   The Way to Christ, 120

bonding, 217

"born again" experience, 21–22, 120–21,
   139–40

Bowlby, John, 216–17, 220

Brann, Eva T. H., *The World of the
   Imagination: Sum and Substance,* 234

Bruegal, Peter, *Children's Games,* 88–89,
   115

Bunge, Martha J., 172–74
   The Child in Christian Thought, 173
   The Child in the Bible, 20
   Families in Ancient Israel, 174
   Families in the New Testament World,
     174

Bunyan, John, 119, 122–24, 140, 202
   *Grace Abounding to the Chief of
     Sinners,* 123
   The Pilgrim's Progress, 9–10, 32,
     122–24, 210

Bushnell, Horace, 142, 150–53, 203
   Christ in Theology, 152
   Christian Nurture, 152–53
   Life and Letters of Horace Bushnell
     (Cheney), 151
   The Puritan as Yankee (Mullin), 150

C

Callistus (pope), 37

Calvin, John, 98–104, 147, 180, 202
   Augustine and, 181
   The Institutes of the Christian

   Religion, 99–100, 102

Caravaggio, *Madonna di Loreto,* 114–15

Carroll, John T., 20

*The Celebration of Christmas: A
   Conversation* (Schleiermacher), 149, 156

Charismatic Movement, 22

Cheney, Mary Bushnell, *Life and Letters
   of Horace Bushnell,* 151

The Cherubinic Wanderer (Scheffler), 122

Chesterton, G. K., Orthodoxy, 189

The Child Enthroned (Gotch), 144–45,
   230

The Child in Christian Thought (Bunge),
   173

The Child in the Bible (Bunge), 20

children
   Children and our Global Future
     (Herzog, K.), 183, 206
   Children in Congregations Project,
     177
   "Children in the Gospel of John"
     (Thompson), 20–21
   Children's Games (Bruegal), 88–89,
     115
   consumer identity and, 177
   controlling, 132–33
   converting, 132–33
   feminist view of, 174–76, 178
   formal doctrine of, 228–56
   in gospels, 8–9
   grace and, 24, 172, 179–82, 197–226,
     230–56
   high view of, 12–20
   identity issues of, 177, 179, 188, 223,
     232, 247
   indifference toward, 5, 9, 20–27,
     84–86, 212–13
   *Jesus and the Children: Biblical
     Resources for Study and Preaching*
     (Weber), 173
   Jesus traditions and, 2–28
   Let the Children Come (Miller-
     McLemore), 95, 171, 175, 192
   Let the Children Come Unto Me
     (Cranach), 95, 168–69, 171
   low view of, 9–12, 19

in nineteenth century, 146–47
On Vain Glory and How Parents Should Bring up Children (Chrysostom), 50
in twentieth century, 154–66
Welcoming Children (Mercer), 176
When Children Become People (Bakke), 206–7

Children and our Global Future (Herzog, K.), 183, 206

Children in Congregations Project, 177

"Children in the Gospel of John" (Thompson), 20–21

Children's Games (Bruegal), 88–89, 115

Christ in Theology (Bushnell), 152

The Christian Faith (Schleiermacher), 148–49

Christian Nurture (Bushnell), 152–53

Christian Teaching (Augustine), 58

Christmas (Barth), 156

Christus und die Kinder (Nolde), 168, 171, 230–31

Chrysostom, John, 48–53, 59–60, 202
Against the Enemies of Monasticism, 49
Concerning Priesthood, 50
On Vain Glory and How Parents Should Bring up Children, 50

church
The Babylonian Captivity of the Church (Luther), 94
The Church and Childhood (Wood), 173
Church Dogmatics (Barth), 7, 155–56, 158, 178
crossing of, 255–56
history of, 65–67, 90–93, 116–19
identity issues of, 67, 164, 225, 246
schools of, 69–70
Why Study the Past: The Quest for the Historical Church (Williams), 164

The Church and Childhood (Wood), 173

Church Dogmatics (Barth), 7, 155–56, 158, 178

Cimaue, *Madonna Enthroned with Child, St. Francis, St. Domenic and two Angels,* 62–63

communion, 166, 245–46, 248

Communist Manifesto (Marx and Engels), 146

The Complete Guide to Godly Play (Berryman), 171

Concerning Priesthood (Chrysostom), 50

confirmation, 246–48

consumer identity, and children, 177

contemplation, 242–43

contingency ambiguity, 206–7

Contra Celsum (Origen), 34

controlling children, 132–33

converting children, 132–33

1 Corinthians
12:27-13:2   242
13   223
13:1-13   242
13:4-7   42
14:20   42, 103

corporal punishment, 130

Council of Trent, 92, 115, 118, 249

Cranach, Lucas (the Elder), 95
Let the Children Come Unto Me, 95, 168–69, 171

Creating Minds (Gardner), 240–41

creative process, 232–44
biology and, 237–39, 241
Creativity (Csikszentmihalyi), 240
psychology and, 239–40, 243
social dimension of, 240–41, 243
spiritual dimension of, 241–42

Creativity (Csikszentmihalyi), 240

Crossan, John Dominic, *The Dark Interval: Towards a Theology of Story,* 193–94

crossing, of a church, 255–56

crusades, 67–69

Csikszentmihalyi, Mihaly
  Beyond Boredom and Anxiety, 239
  Creativity, 240
  The Evolving Self, 240
  *Optimal Experience: Psychological
    Studies of Flow in Consciousness*,
    240

cultural identity issues, 222–23

The Culture of Narcissism (Lasch), 190,
  221–22

Cur Deus Homo (Why the God-Man?)
  (Anselm), 71

Cyprian, 204

D

da Vinci, Leonardo, *Last Supper*, 2–3, 12

*The Dark Interval: Towards a Theology of
  Story* (Crossan), 193–94

Darwin, Charles, 146–47, 215
  The Descent of Man, 146–47
  *On the Origin of Species by Means of
    Natural Selection*, 146

*De apice theoriae (On the Summit of
  Contemplation)* (Nicholas of Cusa),
  82–83

*De concordia liberi arbitrii cum donis
  divinae gratiae (On the Harmony of Free
  Will with the Gifts of Divine Grace)*
  (Molina), 128

*De docta ignorantia (On Learned
  Ignorance)* (Nicholas of Cusa), 82

De ludo globi (On the Ball Game)
  (Nicholas of Cusa), 81

De malo (Concerning Evil) (Thomas
  Aquinas), 78

De possest (Nicholas of Cusa), 91, 93

Deacon, Terrence, 233

Demian (Hesse), 6

The Descent of Man (Darwin), 146–47

developmental ambiguity, 206

The Diary of a Country Priest (Bernanos),
  186

Dickinson, Emily, 5

doctrine of children, formal, 228–56

Doctrine of Original Sin Defended
  (Edwards), 140

Dolbin, Nina, 6

The Dynamics of Religion (Reed), 220

E

Edwards, Jonathan, 132–33, 137–42, 147,
  151, 202, 204
  Doctrine of Original Sin Defended,
    140
  *A Faithful Narrative of the Surprising
    Work of God*, 138
  Freedom of the Will, 140
  The Nature of True Virtue, 140
  "The Wrath of God," 138

Eliot, George, *Silas Marner*, 145

Eliot, T. S., 200, 235

Elkind, David, *The Power of Play*, 192

Emile (Rousseau), 135–36, 150

Engels, Friedrich, *Communist Manifesto*,
  146

Ephesians, 4:13-14   43

Erikson, Erik, 238, 250
  The Life Cycle Completed, 186

Erikson, Joan M., 186

The Evolving Self (Csikszentmihalyi), 240

F

*A Faithful Narrative of the Surprising
  Work of God* (Edwards), 138

Families in Ancient Israel (Bunge), 174

Families in the New Testament World
  (Bunge), 174

feminist view of children, 174–76, 178

Fideus, 204

formal doctrine, of children, 228–56

Fowler, James W., 22

Free Choice of the Will (Augustine), 58

Freedom of the Will (Edwards), 140

French Canada, 129–32

Freud, Sigmund, *Totem and Taboo,* 25
Frisch, Karl von, 217
Froebel, Friedrich, 148–49
Frost, Robert, 237
Fundamentalist Movement, 22

G

Galatians, 3:28   41
Galileo, 73, 118
games
    Children's Games (Bruegal), 88–89,
      115
    De ludo globi (On the Ball Game)
      (Nicholas of Cusa), 81
    Gateway Game, 200–201, 224
    The Glass Bead Game (Hesse), 6–7,
      28, 201, 224
    Gods and Games: Towards a Theology
      of Play (Miller), 191
Gardner, Howard, *Creating Minds,*
    240–41
Gateway Game, 200–201, 224
A General Theory of Love (Lewis, Amini,
    and Lannon), 237
Genesis
    2:18   96
    2:19   232
Gergan, Kenneth J., 221
    The Saturated Self: Dilemmas of
      Identity in Contemporary Life, 222
The Glass Bead Game (Hesse), 6–7, 28,
    201, 224
Godly Play™, 5
Godly Play (Berryman), 171, 220
Gods and Games: Towards a Theology of
    Play (Miller), 191
Golden Rule, 21
Golelmon, Larry, 176
Goleman, Daniel, 218–19, 222, 238
    Social Intelligence: The Revolutionary
      New Science of Human
      Relationships, 216

Gonzales, Lindsay Gerber
    The Holy Family, 228–29
    The Parable of the Mustard Seed,
      228–29
gospels
    children in, 8–9
    "Children in the Gospel of John"
      (Thompson), 20–21
Gotch, Thomas C., *The Child Enthroned,*
    144–45, 230
grace
    biology and, 226
    children and, 24, 172, 179–82,
      197–226, 230–56
    De concordia liberi arbitrii cum donis
      divinae gratiae (On the Harmony of
      Free Will with the Gifts of Divine
      Grace) (Molina), 128
    Grace Abounding to the Chief of
      Sinners (Bunyan), 123
    Graced Vulnerability: A Theology of
      Childhood (Jensen), 179
    Paul and, 17, 24, 26
Grace Abounding to the Chief of Sinners
    (Bunyan), 123
Graced Vulnerability: A Theology of
    Childhood (Jensen), 179
Gritsch, Eric W., 22

H

Harlow, Harry, 217
Harris, John, 26
    Richard Hooker and the Snow Ball
      Fight, 198–99, 213
Hebrews, 1:1-2   233
Heidegger, Martin, 159
    The Principle of Ground, 122
Heloise, 73–76, 98
Herzog, Frederick, 183
Herzog, Kirstin, 183–85
    Children and our Global Future, 183,
      206
Hesse, Hermann, 5–7
    "A Bit of Theology," 6–7, 236
    Demian, 6

The Glass Bead Game, 6–7, 28, 201, 224
"Hours in the Garden," 6, 200
Journey to the East, 6
Narcissus and Goldmund, 6
Siddhartha, 6
The Steppenwolf, 6
high view, of children, 12–20
Higton, Mike, 163
Hinsdale, Mary Ann, 160–61
Hippocrates, 85, 207
history
    of church, 65–67, 90–93, 116–19
    Love: A Brief History through Western Christianity (Lindberg), 243
    Why Study the Past: The Quest for the Historical Church (Williams), 164
Hitler, Adolf, 7, 155
Hodge, Charles, 153
Holy Communion, 27
The Holy Family (Gonzales), 228–29
Homo Ludens (Huizinga), 191
homosexual marriage, 250–51
Honegger, Martin, 159
Hooker, Richard, 26, 104–9, 202
    The Laws of Ecclesiastical Polity, 106
    Richard Hooker and the Snow Ball Fight (Harris), 198–99, 213
"Hours in the Garden" (Hesse), 6, 200
Huizinga, Johan, *Homo Ludens*, 191
Hume, David, 136, 140, 150
Hutcheson, Frances, 140

I

I Remember: An Autobiographical Interview (Rahner, K.), 159
"Ideas for a Theology of Childhood" (Rahner, K.), 160, 188
identity issues
    children and, 177, 179, 188, 223, 232, 247
    church and, 67, 164, 225, 246

consumer identity, 177
cultural, 222–23
The Saturated Self: Dilemmas of Identity in Contemporary Life (Gergan), 222
Ignatius of Antioch, 36, 46
Imago Dei, 48, 232, 235
In der Mitte der Gemeinde: Kinder im Neuen Testament (Müller), 173
In the Midst of Chaos (Miller-McLemore), 193
indifference, toward children, 5, 9, 20–27, 84–86, 212–13
The Institutes of the Christian Religion (Calvin), 99–100, 102
Irenaeus, 37, 44–46, 59, 181, 202, 208
Irish School of Ecumenics, 3
Isaiah, 11:6   214

J

Jansen, Cornelius, *Augustinus*, 128
Jansenism, 126, 128
Jensen, David H., 179–82
    Graced Vulnerability: A Theology of Childhood, 179
Jesuit missionaries, 129–32
Jesus and the Children: Biblical Resources for Study and Preaching (Weber), 173
Jesus traditions, and children, 2–28
John
    1:1-5   63, 233
    1:1-14   6, 213
    2:4   22–23
    2:13-17   20
    3:3-8   21
    19:26-27   23
John the Baptist, 13–14, 20
Journey to the East (Hesse), 6
Julian of Norwich, 110
Justin Martyr, 36, 39
    Apology, 36

K

Karen, Robert, *Becoming Attached: First Relationships and How They Shape Our Capacity to Love*, 216, 223

Keen, Sam, 191
  Apology for Wonder, 187

Kirkpatrick, Lee A., 219–20

Kirschbaum, Charlotte von, 154, 158

Kung, Hans, 155

L

LaCugna, Catherine Mowry, 231–32

Lannon, Richard, *A General Theory of Love*, 237

Lasch, Christopher, *The Culture of Narcissism*, 190, 221–22

Last Supper (da Vinci), 2–3, 12

Last Supper (Piasecki), 2–3, 12, 27

Laval, François de, 129

Laws (Plato), 215

The Laws of Ecclesiastical Polity (Hooker), 106

Lectionary A, 4

Let the Children Come (Miller-McLemore), 95, 171, 175, 192

Let the Children Come Unto Me (Cranach), 95, 168–69, 171

Lewis, Thomas, *A General Theory of Love*, 237

Life and Letters of Horace Bushnell (Cheney), 151

The Life Cycle Completed (Erikson, E.), 186

Life Maps (Berryman), 187

Lindbeck, George A., *The Nature of Doctrine*, 225–26

Lindberg, Carter, *Love: A Brief History through Western Christianity*, 243

Locke, John, 140

Lohse, Bernard, 180

Lorenz, Konrad, 217

Lost Icons: Reflections on Cultural Bereavement (Williams), 162, 165, 208

love
  Becoming Attached: First Relationships and How They Shape Our Capacity to Love (Karen), 216, 223
  A General Theory of Love (Lewis, Amini, and Lannon), 237
  Love: A Brief History through Western Christianity (Lindberg), 243
  The Nature of Love (Singer), 243
  Paul (saint) and, 242

Love: A Brief History through Western Christianity (Lindberg), 243

low view, of children, 9–12, 19

Loyola, Ignatius, 99, 104

Luke
7:31-35	13
9:46-48	15
9:48	245
9:59-62	10
10:21	20
12:51-53	11
14:26	11
17:1-2	18
18:15-17	17, 246
18:17	19
18:29-30	10
19:45-48	20

Luther, Martin, 93–98, 111, 137, 202
  Address to the Christian Nobility of the German Nation, 94
  Augustine and, 93–94
  The Babylonian Captivity of the Church, 94

M

Madonna di Loreto (Caravaggio), 114–15

Madonna Enthroned with Child, St. Francis, St. Domenic and two Angels (Cimaue), 62–63

Maimonides, 77

Man at Play (Rahner, H.), 26, 166, 191

Marcel, Gabriel, 187

Mark

3:21	23
3:35	23
9:33-37	15
9:37	245
9:42	18
10:13-16	16–17, 246
10:15	19
10:29-30	10
11:15-19	20
13:12-13	10

Marris, Peter, 220

Martos, Joseph, 246–47

Marty, Martin E., 185–89
  Modern American Religion, 185
  The Mystery of the Child, 185
  Righteous Empire, 185

Marx, Karl, *Communist Manifesto,* 146

Mather, Cotton, 139–40

matrimony, 249–51

Matthew

5-7	21
10:34-36	11
10:37-38	11
11:16-19	12–13
11:25-26	20
18:1-5	14–15
18:3	19
18:5	245
18:6-7	18
19:10-12	11
19:12	46
19:13-15	16, 246
19:29	10
21:15-16	19–20

Mazarin (cardinal), 128

Mechthild of Magdeburg, 110

Mercer, Joyce Ann, 176–79, 192–93
  Welcoming Children, 176

meta-ambiguity, 206, 211

Miller, David, *Gods and Games: Towards a Theology of Play,* 191

Miller-McLemore, Bonnie J., 174–76
  Also a Mother: Work and Family as Theological Dilemma, 174
  In the Midst of Chaos, 193

Let the Children Come, 95, 171, 175, 192

missionaries, 129–32

Modern American Religion (Marty), 185

Molina, Luis de, *De concordia liberi arbitrii cum donis divinae gratiae (On the Harmony of Free Will with the Gifts of Divine Grace),* 128

Moller, Martin, 120

Moltmann, Jurgen, *Theology of Play,* 191

Monologion (Anselm), 71

Moravian Pietists, 147

Müller, Peter, *In der Mitte der Gemeinde: Kinder im Neuen Testament,* 173

Mullin, Robert Bruce, 152
  The Puritan as Yankee, 150

Museo Pio Cristiano, 31

The Mystery of the Child (Marty), 185

mystical experience, and biology, 79

N

Napoleon, 146, 149

Narcissus and Goldmund (Hesse), 6

The Nature of Doctrine (Lindbeck), 225–26

The Nature of Love (Singer), 243

The Nature of True Virtue (Edwards), 140

Neale, Robert E., 191

Newton, Isaac, 118

Nicholas of Cusa, 64, 81–84, 202, 214, 233
  De apice theoriae (On the Summit of Contemplation), 82–83
  De docta ignorantia (On Learned Ignorance), 82
  De ludo globi (On the Ball Game), 81
  De possest, 91, 93

Nicodemus, 21, 24

Nobel Prize
  Hesse and, 5–6
  Lorenz and, 217

Nolde, Emil, *Christus und die Kinder,* 168, 171, 230–31

O

On Religion: Speeches Addressed to its Cultured Despisers (Schleiermacher), 148

On the Merits and Remission of Sin and the Baptism of Infants (Pelagius), 53

On the Origin of Species by Means of Natural Selection (Darwin), 146

On the Spirit and the Letter (Pelagius), 53

On the Trinity (Augustine), 58

On Vain Glory and How Parents Should Bring up Children (Chrysostom), 50

ontology, 15–17, 26

Optimal Experience: Psychological Studies of Flow in Consciousness (Csikszentmihalyi), 240

ordination, 248–49

Origen, 34, 37, 46–49, 53, 55, 59, 202, 211
    Abelard and, 74–75
    Contra Celsum, 34

Orthodoxy (Chesterton), 189

P

The Parable of the Mustard Seed (Gonzales), 228–29

parables, 4–5, 15, 17–18, 21
    The Parable of the Mustard Seed (Gonzales), 228–29

Pascal, Blaise, 71, 119, 124–29, 140–41, 202, 237–38
    Pensees, 125–28
    Provincial Letters, 125, 128

Passover seder, 3, 12

Paul (saint), 5, 27–28, 40–44, 202
    grace and, 17, 24, 26
    love and, 242

Pax Romana, 24

pedagogical ambiguity, 204, 208

Pelagius, 39, 51–55, 58–60, 202
    Augustine and, 51–54
    On the Merits and Remission of Sin and the Baptism of Infants, 53
    On the Spirit and the Letter, 53

Pensees (Pascal), 125–28

Peter Lombard, *Sentences,* 249

Piasecki, Bohdan, *Last Supper,* 2–3, 12, 27

Pietists, Moravian, 147

The Pilgrim's Progress (Bunyan), 9–10, 32, 122–24, 210

Plain Account of Kingswood School (Wesley), 136

Plato, 148
    Laws, 215
    Republic, 215
    Symposium, 242

play, 12–14, 16, 242–43
    The Ambiguity of Play (Sutton-Smith), 191
    The Complete Guide to Godly Play (Berryman), 171
    Godly Play™, 5
    Godly Play (Berryman), 171, 220
    Gods and Games: Towards a Theology of Play (Miller), 191
    Man at Play (Rahner, H.), 26, 166, 191
    The Power of Play (Elkind), 192
    Teaching Godly Play (Berryman), 171
    Theology of Play (Moltmann), 191

political-religious conflict, 116–17

Polycarp, 37–38, 44

The Power of Play (Elkind), 192

The Principle of Ground (Heidegger), 122

Proslogion (Anselm), 72

Provincial Letters (Pascal), 125, 128

Psalms
    8:2   20, 101
    23   101
    127:3   103

psychology, and creative process, 239–40, 243

punishment, corporal, 130

The Puritan as Yankee (Mullin), 150

R

Rahner, Hugo, *Man at Play*, 26, 166, 191

Rahner, Karl, 158–61, 178, 203
  I Remember: An Autobiographical Interview, 159
  "Ideas for a Theology of Childhood," 160, 188
  Spirit in the World, 159

reconciliation, 251–52

Reed, Bruce, *The Dynamics of Religion*, 220

reference ambiguity, 206, 210–11

relationship ambiguity, 206, 210

religious-political conflict, 116–17

Republic (Plato), 215

Richard Hooker and the Snow Ball Fight (Harris), 198–99, 213

Richard of St. Victor, 241–44

Richter, Gregory, 120

Ricoeur, Paul, 22

Righteous Empire (Marty), 185

Romans
  1:7   24
  13:10   242
  14:17   242

Rousseau, Jean-Jacques, *Emile*, 135–36, 150

Rowan Williams: An Introduction (Shortt), 163

S

Santa Maria delle Grazie, 2

The Saturated Self: Dilemmas of Identity in Contemporary Life (Gergan), 222

Scheffler, Johann, 121, 159
  The Cherubinic Wanderer, 122

Schiller, Friedrich, 148

Schleiermacher, Friedrich, 133, 142, 147–50, 155–56, 166, 180, 203
  "Aphorisms on Pedagogy," 147
  The Celebration of Christmas: A Conversation, 149, 156
  The Christian Faith, 148–49

On Religion: Speeches Addressed to its Cultured Despisers, 148

Sentences (Peter Lombard), 249

Serrano, Miguel, 6

Shaftesbury (lord), 140

Shortt, Rupert, *Rowan Williams: An Introduction*, 163

Siddhartha (Hesse), 6

Silas Marner (Eliot, G.), 145

Simons, Menno, 175–76

sinfulness ambiguity, 206–7

Singer, Irving, *The Nature of Love*, 243

social dimension, of creative process, 240–41, 243

Social Intelligence: The Revolutionary New Science of Human Relationships (Goleman), 216

sociobiology, 219–20, 232

Socrates, 36

Spariosu, Mihail, 148

Spirit in the World (Rahner, K.), 159

spiritual ambiguity, 206, 209–10

spiritual dimension, of creative process, 241–42

The Steppenwolf (Hesse), 6

suicide bombers, 184

Summa theologiae (Thomas Aquinas), 77, 80

Sutton-Smith , Brian, *The Ambiguity of Play*, 191

Symposium (Plato), 242

T

The Teacher (Augustine), 58–59

Teaching Godly Play (Berryman), 171

Tertullian, 36

Theology of Play (Moltmann), 191

The Theology of Vladimir Nikolaevich Lossky: An Exposition and Critique (Williams), 162

1 Thessalonians, 2:7   42

Thomas Aquinas, 64, 76–81, 159, 202, 208
   De malo (Concerning Evil), 78
   Summa theologiae, 77, 80
Thompson, Marianne Meye, "Children in the Gospel of John," 20–21
1 Timothy, 3:4   43
Tinbergen, Nikko, 217
Totem and Taboo (Freud), 25
Trent, Council of, 92, 115, 118, 249
Trevelyan, George Macaulay, 190
Tyler, Bennet, 153

U

Ursuline missionaries, 129–32

W

A Walk on the Beach (Anderson), 186
The Way to Christ (Boehme), 120
Weber, Hans Ruedi, *Jesus and the Children: Biblical Resources for Study and Preaching*, 173
Welcoming Children (Mercer), 176
Werpehowski, William, 154, 156, 158
Wesley, John, 53, 133–37, 150, 192, 202
   Plain Account of Kingswood School, 136
When Children Become People (Bakke), 206–7
Why Study the Past: The Quest for the Historical Church (Williams), 164

Williams, Rowan, 8, 161–66, 203, 208, 254
   Arius: Heresy and Tradition, 164
   Lost Icons: Reflections on Cultural Bereavement, 162, 165, 208
   Rowan Williams: An Introduction (Shortt), 163
   The Theology of Vladimir Nikolaevich Lossky: An Exposition and Critique, 162
   Why Study the Past: The Quest for the Historical Church, 164
   Writing in the Dust, 163
Wood, Diana, The Church and Childhood, 173
The World of the Imagination: Sum and Substance (Brann), 234
"The Wrath of God" (Edwards), 138
Writing in the Dust (Williams), 163
Wyckoff, D. Campbell, 170

Y

Yes and No (Sic et Non) (Abelard), 75

Z

Zechariah, 12
Zeller, Bernhard, 6
Zinzendorf, Nikolaus Ludwig von, 133, 147
Ziolkowski, Theodore, 224